NEW DIRECTIONS IN CREATIVE AND INNOVATIVE MANAGEMENT

SERIES ON ECONOMETRICS AND MANAGEMENT SCIENCES

This is one of a series of books on econometrics and the management sciences sponsored by the IC^2 Institute of the University of Texas at Austin, under the general editorship of W.W. Cooper and Henri Theil. In this series, econometrics and management sciences are to be interpreted broadly, providing an opportunity to introduce new topics that can influence future activities in these fields as well as allow for new contributions to established lines of research in both disciplines. The books will be priced to make them available to a wide and diverse audience.

Volumes in the Series:

NEW DIRECTIONS IN CREATIVE AND INNOVATIVE MANAGEMENT
Bridging Theory and Practice

Volume 7 of Series on
Econometrics and Management Sciences

Edited by

YUJI IJIRI
ROBERT LAWRENCE KUHN

1988

BALLINGER PUBLISHING COMPANY
Cambridge, Massachusetts
A Subsidiary of Harper & Row, Publishers, Inc.

Excerpt on page 205 from "East Coker" in *Four Quartets*, copyright 1943 by T.S. Eliot, renewed 1971 by Esme Valerie Eliot, reprinted by permission of Harcourt Brace Jovanovich, Inc. and Faber & Faber Ltd.

International Standard Book Number: 0-88730-365-X

Library of Congress Catalog Card Number: 88-21998

Printed in the United States of America

Library of Congress Cataloging-in-Publication Data

New directions in creative and innovative management : bridging
    theory and practice / edited by Yuji Ijiri, Robert Lawrence Kuhn.
      p. cm. — (Series on econometrics and management sciences : v. 7)
      Papers presented at the Third International Conference on Creative
    and Innovative Management, held in Pittsburgh, Pa. June 2-3, 1987,
    sponsored by the IC^2 Institute of the University of Texas at Austin.
      Includes index.
      ISBN 0-88730-365-X
      1. Creative ability in business—Congresses. I. Ijiri, Yuji.
    II. Kuhn, Robert Lawrence. III. International Conference on
    Creative and Innovative Management (3rd : 1987 : Pittsburgh, Pa.)
    IV. IC^2 Institute. V. Series.
    HD53.N49 1988
    658.4—dc19   88-21998
                                                                 CIP

CONTENTS

v

LIST OF FIGURES

LIST OF TABLES

FOREWORD

Elizabeth E. Bailey

As dean of the Graduate School of Industrial Administration (GSIA), Carnegie-Mellon University, I am pleased that the conference on which this volume is based was held at our school. In 1949 *Fortune* did a survey of the graduating class of men (not women) who were going into business around the country. This is what they said:

> Looking to big business for security, a cautious generation turns its back on venture. If ever there was one, this will be a generation of managers—competent, certainly. The class of '49 will supply in abundant measure. Never has there been a class so absorbed with the technique and the desirability of making business more efficient.

> Yet the article expressed annoying concern about the class of 1949: Will this community-conscious group furnish any quota of free-swinging SOB's that we seem to need for leavening the economy? Or will it be so intent on achieving a super-lubricated, integrated private enterprise, a sort of socialization by big business instead of government, that it will prefer a static and thus a more manageable economy to a dynamic one? Will the class of '49, in short, be so tractable and harmonious to be incapable in 20 or 30 years hence of making provocative decisions?

Around that same time, a group of people in Pittsburgh were beginning to found the at what was then Carnegie Institute of Technology. It began with a gleam in the eye for a number of people. The same people have kept this gleam of provocativeness alive. Two members of that class were cosponsors of the conference on which

xiii

this book is based, George Kozmetsky from the IC^2 Institute in Austin, Texas, and my boss, Richard Cyert, president of Carnegie-Mellon. They have been very creative and innovative all of their lives.

Much of what we are trying to do in the 1980s is render a little more systematic our understanding of what it takes to have some oomph and freshness in an organization. For example, it is going to be remembered that, of all of the academic areas in which we are beginning to innovate right now, accounting may be the most fascinating. The field used to be very creative, went through a five-decade period of dormancy, and is only now becoming very innovative once again.

It is also interesting that a number of consulting firms are represented in this book. They use creative and innovative processes to enable firms to break through the barriers to generate imaginative new outputs in order to be responsive to the needs of their customers. The fresh insights that result from the interaction between academe, business, and consulting companies are the essence of our quest.

OVERVIEW

Yuji Ijiri
Robert Lawrence Kuhn

"Research methodology in creative and innovative management is about to take off," states George Kozmetsky in Chapter 2, which is derived from his keynote speech that opened the Third International Conference on Creative Innovative Management, the gathering on which this book is based. Building on the previous two conferences, this conference explored methodologies that are in the process of rapid development for better understanding of and fostering creative and innovative management. Held June 2-3, 1987 in Pittsburgh at the Graduate School of Industrial Administration, Carnegie-Mellon University, the conference was titled "New Directions for Research in Creative and Innovative Management."

The setting was most fitting for two reasons. First, George Kozmetsky, director of the IC² Institute of The University of Texas at Austin, which sponsored all three conferences, taught at this school thirty years ago. Second, over the past thirty years, Pittsburgh as a city of venture capitalists has focused on computers and high technologies. The spirit of creative and innovative management is abundant both at the school and in the city.

Our purpose here is nothing short of developing the field of creative and innovative management into a new discipline of academic business. The challenge is twofold: to conceive, catalyze, and effect rigorous research programs to build a firm intellectual foundation, and at the same time to encourage, establish, and enhance relevance

1

for applications in the real world of corporate competitiveness. We seek new ways to achieve comparative advantage for institutions contesting in a dynamic, global, hypercomplex, and ultracompetitive environment.

Two primary themes undergird this book, and we would like you to keep them in mind when reading each of the chapters.

1. What are the appropriate areas and proper methodologies to research creative and innovative management? How can we effectively and efficiently formulate and implement novel ideas into commercially viable products and services? The importance of research we recognize; it is the execution we seek. Look to target areas and define methods.

2. What are the optimal relationships between theory and practice in creative and innovative management? We have a special kind of "practice" represented in this book—a number of organizations and individuals with extraordinarily extensive experience in all aspects of stimulating and generating corporate creativity. These are the leading such organizations that work with major companies in stimulating all kinds of novelty, from original products to daring acquisitions. Here is the richest source of data, dense with creative and innovative experience. Their work spans decades and comprises hundreds of real-life examples. Here is the elusive quality of novelty generation almost quantifiable. Here is the real world. Think about research methodologies as you read these chapters.

Read closely and think together with us in this pioneering effort about the requisite methodology: How to make progress? This is not a canned set of formulas whereby we, the learned authors, teach you, the inquisitive readers, how to do it. Rather, this should be a more interactive work, with a pioneering spirit and open attitude.

How is optimal progress to be made? It can be catalyzed collectively. But it can only work in personal relationships, individually. We therefore encourage all readers to *interact*, to form relationships in creative and innovative management. Forge links between academic methodologists and corporate practitioners. Build bridges from the academic community to the world of business.

Form dyadic relationships. Get to know one another. Give to each other. This is a primary purpose of this book. There is more than synergy to be found here. It is true symbiosis, for neither can advance without the other. Practice without theory is neither controllable nor repeatable. Theory without practice is neither relevant nor viable. Each side has no choice but to cooperate.

Part I of this book is titled "Creative Management and Contemporary Society." The first chapter, by Richard Cyert, president of Carnegie-Mellon University, focuses on leadership and creativity, stating that a leader is a person who brings the subgoals and focuses of individual members of an organization in line with its central goal.

George Kozmetsky then examines the current state of development in creative and innovative management and reviews research activities in this area. He reports on the results of his own and his colleagues' teaching and research, using the construct and the model of creative and innovative process that have been developed in the process. Kozmetsky concludes, "By implementing creative and innovative management, we can develop links among key institutions to build a viable public-private infrastructure, a strong financial environment, a vibrant entrepreneurial spirit, and a commitment and dedication to risk taking and risk sharing."

Part II presents a fascinating historical perspective by Jean-Jacques Servan-Schreiber, chairman of the International Committee of Carnegie-Mellon University and a former cabinet minister of France. In "Creative Management and Public Policy," Servan-Schreiber reflects on a part of recent history, both in Europe and in the United States, with which he was personally involved. He describes diplomatic events where peace-makers were forced to invent innovative solutions. The author of *The American Challenge* (1968) and *The Knowledge Revolution* (1986), Servan-Schreiber concludes that "true security is higher knowledge," not military hardware.

At the end of each of the parts of this book, we include an edited transcript of the actual discussions that took place among the participants at the conference. We believe that such an interchange of ideas and viewpoints in an informal setting not only supplements the formal presentations but also greatly enhances our understanding of the key issues in research in creative and innovative management.

The conference was private, strictly for the speakers and invited guests. All attending were directly involved in creative and innovative management, whether from business or academe. We encouraged our speakers to be more catalyzers than instructors, more seminar leaders than teachers. Process, we declared, was as important as content. Active interaction occurred transcending the papers. New ideas were suggested.

Thus we decided to include a good part of the discussions in the book. Some editing was necessary, of course, but we did not touch the substance. We allowed the spontaneity and the brainstorming to remain. We did not demand linearity of thought in the book as we did not in the conference. How could we do otherwise when our point is creativity?

The third part of the book, "Quantitative Directions and Methodology," deals with quantitative and informational aspects as well as the impact of computers and communication technologies upon creative and innovative management. The moderator of the conference session, William W. Cooper of The University of Texas, Austin, introduces the four chapters of Part III.

Yuji Ijiri of Carnegie-Mellon University logically extends the existing double-entry bookkeeping framework to triple-entry bookkeeping. Methodologically, the proposal offers a new set of measurements, centered on the concept of income momentum, which will help creative and innovative managers to focus on the long-term impact of their activities rather than their short-term income effects. He argues that creativity and accountability are not in conflict if accountability is established at a higher point of the organizational hierarchy of goals.

George Geis of the University of California, Los Angeles, presents seven hypotheses of how the personal computer can stimulate creativity, namely by 1) encouraging playfulness, 2) relieving the routine, 3) providing rapid feedback, 4) containing risk, 5) incubating ideas, 6) presenting graphic imagery, and 7) fostering information flow and availability. In order to develop these antecedents of creativity, Geis emphasizes system variables such as ease of use, match with roles and tasks, user support, and connectivity as well as the organizational context that puts all these elements into an integrated framework.

Sara Kiesler of Carnegie-Mellon University discusses the impact of computer communication technologies upon individuals and organizations, especially upon their creativity and innovativeness. Such impact occurs because of technology's "deregulating effects" as a result of eliminating physical propinquity and reducing social context cues. The freer flow of ideas and viewpoints is evident when computer mail was compared with face-to-face meetings, Kiesler notes.

Robert Kaplan of Harvard University and Carnegie-Mellon University criticizes the lack of creative and innovative activities in management accounting during the past half century and attributes the phenomenon to several key factors. The changing business conditions now make it more conducive, Kaplan says, to develop creativity and innovative management. He emphasizes field studies as the basic research methodology and elaborates on the benefit of preparing and using teaching cases.

Implicit in the chapters of Part III is the viewpoint that management and its information systems are intricately tied together. This means two things. To understand creative and innovative management, researchers can often get valuable clues by studying its information systems. To promote creative and innovative management, the information systems must also become creative and innovative. The latter is a necessary condition, though not sufficient, for the development of creative and innovative management.

The five chapters of Part IV, "Behavioral Directions and Methodology," all deal with methodological issues relating to the behavioral directions for research. The part opens with an overview by the conference session moderator, Karl Weick of The University of Texas, Austin.

Chapter 10, by Arie Lewin, director of the Decision, Risk and Management Science Program, National Science Foundation, and a faculty member at Duke University's Fuqua School of Business, advocates contextual research strategies. Lewin examines, in particular, real-time longitudinal field studies, replicated research cases, and, most important, action research and intervention that are oriented toward engineering innovation events in an organization. He emphasizes that it is essential for the success of contextual research to have a fine team of managers and researchers.

Chapter 11 by Scott Isaksen of the State University College at Buffalo describes the creative problem-solving sessions in groups organized by the center for studies of creativity at the college. Following the theory that creative thinking and creative problem solving can be learned, Isaksen views this process as having alternating divergent and convergent phases for each of the six problem-solving steps, namely, mess finding, data finding, problem finding, idea finding, solution finding, and acceptance finding.

Robert Burnside, Teresa Amabile, and Stanley Gryskiewicz, all with Center for Creative Leadership, present their approach in assessing the organizational climate for creativity and innovation. Their chapter is based on "Critical Incident Interviews," in which subjects are asked to describe a case exemplifying high creativity and another exemplifying low creativity. Content analysis of the transcript identifies key environmental stimulants and obstacles to creativity, which are then used as a basis for preparing a "Work Environment Inventory," a detailed questionnaire dealing with the environment in which creative activities take place.

The next chapter, by Andrew Van de Ven of the University of Minnesota, lays out methodoligical preconditions for studying innovative processes, namely 1) a clear set of concepts about the object being studied, 2) systematic methods for observing change in the object over time, 3) methods for representing raw data to identify process patterns, and 4) a motor or theory to make sense of the process pattern. He then elaborates on each with an aim toward developing a theory of organizational innovation and change. Van de Ven's work is especially noteworthy because he is conducting what is considered to be the most in-depth study of innovation in industry.

Stephan Chorover of Massachusetts Institute of Technology criticizes the modern scientific paradigms. In his view they have promoted specialization at the expense of comprehensive perspectives on events that are taking place on the planet earth. He argues for the need to have a common base, or "home," from which we all view the issues at hand—and this common base should be the earth. Studies in creative and innovative management should therefore be carried out under this planet-oriented, ecological perspective, which establishes a new set of values and goals by which to evaluate creative and innovative management.

Methodological issues for behavioral directions for research in creative and innovative management are many, mainly because the behavioral aspects of creative and innovative management cut across many traditional disciplines that have their own established research methodology. The chapters in Part IV of the book highlight major issues involved in this respect.

Part V, "New Directions for Institutional Creativity," deals with institutional issues involved in fostering creative and innovative management in actual organizations. Elizabeth Bailey's introductory remarks are followed by five chapters.

The first, by Donald Gamache, chairman and chief executive officer of Innotech Corporation, talks about how to promote creativity and innovation in commercial organizations. Putting together a team of outside experts and client's personnel and using the "Briefing Document" as a tailored workbook, the process moves toward generation of information required for an investment decision and its implementation. A case study example of the methodology is presented.

In Chapter 17 Richard Harriman, president of Synectics, Inc., emphasizes the importance of analogy as the first idea-getting strategy and classifies it into direct analogy, personal analogy, and symbolic analogy. He elaborates on a way to overcome people's resistance to connecting seemingly unrelated matters, an ingredient of idea generation. Harriman reports on his firm's New Product Commitment Program, under which a sequence of sessions is held with the aim of developing new products.

The chapter by Robert Kuhn of the IC^2 Institute of The University of Texas, Austin, "Toward an Effective Methodology for Unifying Theory and Practice," was partially prepared from the transcript of a discussion session Kuhn conducted with the conference audience, focusing on how to promote interactions between academicians and practitioners.

The fourth chapter on the topic of institutional creativity is by William Miller, principal consultant, SAI Associates (formerly with SRI International). Miller reports on a research model called Strategic Innovation Management Assessment Profile (SI–MAP), which involves the linkage of 1) management practices that are the central determinant of the innovation climate, 2) innovation styles (innovators are divided into modifiers, vision-drivers, explorers, and experimenters), and 3) business performance measures relative to fostering innovation.

The final chapter, by Robert Kuhn of the IC^2 Institute and George Geis of UCLA, presents an argument that a study of personal commitment to organizational goals is essential for understanding creativity in an organization. They then introduce a novel approach in studying commitment stating that commitment can be better understood if it is studied in organizations where it takes its purest form—religious organizations. They develop a commitment model that is applicable to business organizations derived from this cross-organizational methodology.

It is our hope that this book will encourage interaction among academic researchers and commercial practitioners as well as help define new areas for rich research that will build a solid, knowledge-based foundation for managing innovation. We plan to continue our efforts with biennial conferences and subsequent proceedings. Our objective is nothing short of catalyzing the development of creative and innovative management into a new field of academic business.

Finally, we take great pleasure in thanking two extraordinary individuals for their roles in organizing the conference from which this book is derived: Ronya Kozmetsky, president of the RGK Foundation, and Raymond Smilor, executive director of the IC^2 Institute, The University of Texas, Austin.

CREATIVE MANAGEMENT
AND
CONTEMPORARY SOCIETY

1 LEADERSHIP AND CREATIVITY

Richard M. Cyert

Both Carnegie-Mellon University as a whole and its Graduate School of Industrial Administration (GSIA) take pride in trying to turn out graduates who are innovators. These people will not follow the beaten path but will cause an influx of ideas into American business, whether by starting new firms or by bringing new ideas to the ways managers of larger corporations develop outstanding firms. Fostering creative thought is our major objective at GSIA and at Carnegie-Mellon University as a whole.

Leadership, so critical in developing organizations that are to be innovative and creative, is a neglected subject in business schools in particular and academic departments in general. It is a topic that belongs to the social psychologists, who try to determine how leaders are selected. The notion of associating particular traits with leaders to the position that leadership was something that was somehow "God-given" and could not be taught. We tended to follow that unfortunately limiting idea. Therefore, we have not stressed the teaching of leadership, which in the long run is vital both for organizations that are already established and for new organizations. In developing a center for creative management at Carnegie-Mellon, starting with the Morgenthaler Chair in entrepreneurship, we have given a lot of thought to the various subjects that might be covered in such a center. Leadership is one of those vital subjects, and I believe that leadership can be taught. If we examine the nature of leadership and try to understand what leadership is and what it must do

11

in an organization, we can find many things to teach about it. In particular, trying to define leadership precisely can help us to understand the nature of leadership.

Two equally valid definitions of leadership both have many operational elements flowing from them that can be developed into a course and can generate material to be learned. One definition deals with subgoals of the participants of an organization, and the other deals with their attention focus.

One of the characteristic behaviors that everyone who has been in an organization will recognize (especially if he or she has tried to leave one) is that participants in an organization develop subgoals that are not necessarily consistent with the central goals of the organization. If you don't have the right incentive system, for example, you will find the sales forces trying to maximize sales dollars when they should emphasize those units that bring in the most profit, even if it means that sales dollars are less. In a university, there can be real tension between individual faculty members' personal goals of maximizing the amount of their research and the central desire of the university to do a good job in teaching. It is not an unresolvable conflict, but it does engender tension. Because research brings public recognition whereas teaching is basically private, there may be difficulty in getting faculty to put as much attention on teaching as on research.

The first definition of leadership is that the leader must bring about *conformity* between the subgoals within the organization and the central goals of the organization. There are many ways that we can show people how to bring about conformity between subgoals and central goals. In a real sense this is the fundamental difference between the leader and the politician. The leader attempts to bring about this conformity. The politician tends instead to cater to the subgoals and to make them stronger rather than to articulate and stress the central goals. Politicians are not found only in public life, but as managers in academia and in corporations. Since they do not try to bring about conformity, they do not exert leadership. And although they win popularity with the participants in their unit by strengthening their subgoals, they do not really make a contribution to the organization.

The second definition of leadership touches on one of the really vital variables in an organization: the *attention focus* of the participants. What are the people in the organization thinking about? What do they think is important? How do these matters relate to the matters the leader deems important? The leader must capture followers' attention and bring it to bear on the problems that he or she deems crucial for the organization. It is this process of bringing about conformity between the individual's focus and the focus the leader desires for the organization that is a real test and measure of leadership. Bringing about unanimity of focus is the crux of leadership.

The question of leadership is votal to creative management. It is through leadership that an organization develops into a creative entity. By having creativity and innovation as a goal, and by performing the leadership role in the proper way, an executive can drive an organization toward this kind of goal and make it much more effective. Leadership, then, is a vital ingredient deserving more time in university curricula. We must spend more time on looking at the ways in which leadership can contribute. Creative management is vital, not only in terms of what we want to do personally and organizationally, but in terms of what this country needs collectively and continually.

2 WHY NEW DIRECTIONS FOR RESEARCH IN CREATIVE AND INNOVATIVE MANAGEMENT?

George Kozmetsky

Research methodology in creative and innovative management is about to take off. A number of societal forces and internal institutional crises and problems are drivers for implementing creative and innovative management in practice and establishing the field as an academic discipline. New directions for research are now necessary to meet two critical needs of this evolving discipline:

1. To increase understanding in the field—that is, design, build, and expand the theoretical base

2. To increase understanding for use—that is, to find viable and timely solutions to current management's critical needs, problems, crises, and opportunities

The objective of this chapter is to explore three answers to the question posed by the title. Why new directions for research in creative and innovative management?

The first answer is a report on current IC^2 Institute-sponsored developments in creative and innovative management since 1982. The second answer is a brief review of selected research activities analyzed by type of methodology. The third answer is a report on the results of my own teaching and related research in creative and innovative management at the IC^2 Institute and the Graduate School of Business, The University of Texas at Austin.

15

CURRENT STATE OF DEVELOPMENTS
IN CREATIVE AND INNOVATIVE

Since 1982 the IC^2 Institute at the University of Texas at Austin has cosponsored three international conferences on creative and innovative management. Conference proceedings have been published and widely distributed. This section assesses how these conferences have facilitated the evolution of this discipline.

Preconditions for Development of Creative and Innovative Management

During the first conference on creative and innovative management, it was hoped that this unstructured field of inquiry could become a new and important academic discipline. The participants in that conference consisted of a very select group of researchers and practitioners in academia, government, and business. The nineteen presenters and discussants of invited papers at this conference had expertise and made contributions as follows: nine were predominantly in academe, one in business, one in government, three in academe and business, two in academe and government, and one in business and government. This conference was the start of our conscious effort to build the discipline of creative and innovative management.

The proceedings of the first conference provided background literature that could make an early contribution to identifying the foundations for continued systematic improvements in the present state of creative and innovative managerial abilities and practices. Clearly, there was a need to identify and structure the preconditions for molding the discipline of creative and innovative management. What, for example, were to be the necessary research, teaching, and management practices of this new area? Three classes of preconditions were identified as the result of this conference;

Begin to Drop a Number of Older Distinctions

1. Drop or blur the distinction between entrepreneur, manager, and administrator in the academic disciplines as well as between academia and the world of use and practice.

2. Distinguish between teaching small-scale creativity from that on a large scale.

3. Eliminate current distinctions between management practices and scientific research and development in all stages from conception to development to testing and successful commercialization.

4. Realize that in the governance of a democratic society a number of forces and problems are of such awesome proportions that they include changes that can themselves imperil the sometimes fragile consensus on which such societies rest.

Begin to Develop New Approaches

1. Improve the methodology for developing, implementing, and assessing comprehensive audits that form consensus on important issues in the public and private sectors.

2. Develop creative and innovative management for mature capital-intensive industries faced with declining demand for their products.

3. Extend strategic planning in the private sector to include production of jobs and the servicing of a large variety of constituencies.

4. Develop more innovative approaches to sharing of risk and uncertainty.

5. Formulate new planning models and approaches that emphasize flexibility and adaptability rather than only efficiency and effectiveness.

6. Evaluate the impact on the organization of accelerating innovations.

7. Determine the potential for success of using such methodologies as artificial intelligence and computerization to improve creativity and innovation in management.

Begin to Redesign and Design New Institutions

1. Redesign business and social institutions to deal with modern international competition.

2. Design new types of government, collaborations between industry, and academe accompanied by an expansion of accountability functions.

Prepare for Takeoff

The second international conference, Frontiers in Creative and Innovative Management, moved the discipline of creative and innovative management to the next stage of development. We were able to utilize the definition of creative and innovative management formulated by A. Charnes and W.W. Cooper during their editing of the book based on the first conference. Their definition of creative and innovative management had three dimensions. The first and second involve developing individual manager's abilities in two independent activities, creative management and innovative management. The third dimension, which couples the first two, is creative and innovative management. It involves acts of management collectively.

Creative management consists of new concepts, new ideas, new methods, new directions, and new modes of operation. The operative word is "new." Innovative management consists of the ability to implement creative ideas or to move successfully in new directions. The operative words are "to implement" and "to move successfully." Creative and innovative management focuses on coupling; that is, linking creative and innovative managements. The operative notion here is an "act of management" rather than the act of an individual.

Creative management generally is what managers of research and development organizations as well as technical entrepreneurs deal with—new things. Innovative management is what entrepreneurs must do, especially in the start-up phase, and what professional managers deal with, particularly in accounting, marketing, distribution, manufacturing, and finance. Creative and innovative management is the province of the leadership of organizations at all operational levels. It involves linking activities that concern allocating resources and their mechanisms with those that concern assessing their utilization.

The second conference was, therefore, an exploration. It was designed to identify problems and opportunities for creative and innovative management in private enterprise, government, not-for-profit institutions, universities, and other societal activities. The presenters, discussants, and moderators at this conference were a rich mixture representing diverse disciplines, sectors, and cultures. Six of the participants were university administrators involved with research, twelve were academic researchers, one was a government-based researcher, one was a business-based researcher, two were administrators of significant government laboratories or centers, and three were from large consulting firms. Each of these participants was considered to be on the leading edge of a particular field or expertise. They were thus in key positions to evaluate possibilities of and the necessity for creative and innovative management. The conference established that it was possible and, in many cases, necessary to develop the frontiers of this discipline. To extend the frontiers in creative and innovative management, we must do three things: 1) Successfully solve problems associated with society's crises, needs, and demands. 2) Improve our understanding of creative and innovative management. 3) Deal with challenges found in the public and nonprofit sectors. The specific findings under each category are as follows:

1. Successfully Solve Societal Problems

    a. Developing creative and innovative management can be a successful response to society's demands and needs within a hypercompetitive environment.

    b. There is a need to better understand the differences between incremental and revolutionary innovation.

    c. Uncertainty can be a driver to create the potential for innovation.

2. Improve Understanding of Creative and Innovative Management

    a. Extending cognitive structures for improving the problem-solving process can advance the understanding of creative and innovative management.

    b. Exploration of the transformation of creativity into innovation is possible by focusing on management style and approach.

    c. Differentiation of the psychodynamics of creativity and innovation is required in order to identify and extend creativity as acts of individuals and innovation as acts of a group.

    d. New organizational structures are critical for the basic exploitation of innovation through alliances.

    e. Attributes and characteristics of creative and innovative management are the same as those involved in the selection of top management and they appear and reappear in any theoretical or practical treatment of the subject.

    r. Linking individual creativity and corporate strategy is a critical force for corporate creativity.

3. Deal with Challenges

    a. Alternatives for creative approaches to the management and delivery of social services are necessary expectations of a modern, civilized society.

    b. The challenge to government research units is to create and create and maintain an environment where creative interdisciplinary collaborations can flourish, where new institutional ties for transference can be developed, and where anachronistic impediments to effective performance can be removed.

    c. The challenge to government social science institutions is to introduce new research styles in a larger institutional context while maintaining relevance and excellence.

    d. University management must increasingly stress the linkages among attention focus, reward systems, and improved communications for administration and faculty.

This conference served to reinforce the need to place more focus on the third dimension of creative and innovative management as acts of management. Creative and innovative management implies new managerial practices on the one hand and leadership to implement them on the other. Traditional management decision making has centered on efficiency and effectiveness. Creative and innovative management focuses on flexibility and adaptability to deal with the process of managing change, including the required public and private infrastructures. It is grounded in the belief that leadership makes a significant difference in the way organizations respond to and cope with change. It is deeply involved with creating real economic value and with adapting the personal aspirations of others to the evolving objectives of the firm and to the larger goals of American society. Creative and innovative management covers the nature of creative and innovative activities, organization design for improving creativity and innovation, organizational creativity and individual personality, creative and innovative management in public sector structures, joint public-private organizations and activities, strategies for academic research and curriculum, and implications for public policy.

REVIEW OF CREATIVE AND INNOVATIVE MANAGEMENT RESEARCH ACTIVITIES

Let us now turn to a review of the selected research efforts in the field of creative and innovative management. The analysis is restricted to work sponsored by IC^2 Institute. The published research sponsored by the IC^2 consisted of three major publications; the books based on proceedings of the first two international conferences and the *Handbook for Creative and Innovative Managers*, a major professional work, edited by Robert L. Kuhn, senior research fellow of the Institute (McGraw-Hill, 1988). These materials were what the program committee and board of editors deemed at the time were systematic themes that gave focus to significant research topics and important practical circumstances in order to advance the field.

Table 2–1 summarizes the research methodology found in the IC^2 Institute-sponsored materials. It compares four types of research methodologies with the published chapters in each of the three books on creative and innovative management. Table 2–2 defines the classes of research methodology: theory structuring, surveys, field studies, and reportage. The focus of research methodology has been

Table 2-1. Analysis of IC^2 Research Methodology.

Research Methodology	Volume 1	Volume 2	Handbook	Total
Theory structuring	5	17	39	61
Survey	1	0	2	3
Field studies	0	1	1	2
Reportage	1	6	28	35
Total	7	24	70	101

Table 2-2. Types of Research Methodologies.

1. Theory Structuring

    a. Fundamental understanding of broad concepts
    b. Ways to improve practice
    c. Hypothesis formulation
    d. Literature review and analysis

2. Surveys

    a. Data collection
    b. Questionnaires
    c. Interviews
    d. Development of databases

3. Field Studies

    a. In-depth review of one or more companies
    b. Direct observation of phenomena in natural settings
    c. Longitudinal in nature

4. Reportage

    a. "How it is done" in companies or other institutions (corporate names included)
    b. Company identification in support of statements
    c. Evidence of case study
    d. Commentaries on people and/or organizations

primarily theory structuring and reportage. As to be expected, less focus has been placed on surveys and field studies.

As a result of this body of knowledge, it is now possible and necessary to develop new directions for research in creative and innovative management. What is needed now is the theme of the conference on which the present book is based: state-of-the-art work, new directions for research, and leading-edge methodology in creative and innovative management. When this latest work are coupled with the previous work, we will be in a position to indicate more specifically the newer directions and priorities for improving the understanding of the field (substantive theory) and extending methodological improvement relevant to the field (methodological theory).

RESULTS OF TEACHING AND RESEARCH IN CREATIVE AND INNOVATIVE MANAGEMENT

Since 1985 I have taught a course examining the emerging theory and practice of creative and innovative management. A methodological approach used for this class is depicted in Figure 2-1, Framework for Teaching Creative and Innovative Management. The framework links theory for understanding and theory for use to measure not only efficiency and effectiveness but also flexibility and adaptability.

The core of the framework is the development and application of quantitative and bibliographic database systems. These systems utilize Project Quest, a university-industry cooperative project for new teaching and research applications. Project Quest provides the most advanced capabilities in personal computer hardware and software. The course permits the integration of knowledge bases and databases through interactive computer systems on the one hand and real-world applications on the other.

The knowledge bases and databases reflect how we have been learning about the scope and role of creative and innovative management. Six major databases and knowledge bases are kept up to date. They are designed for both understanding and use, and link theory with practice. The specific elements are as follows:

- *Bibliographies* on creative and innovative management and on supercomputers

- *Technology database* tracking eighty leading-edge technologies, with a particular focus on the supercomputer and biotechnology industries

- *Knowledge base on private capital developments* in venture capital, limited R&D partnerships, mergers, and acquisitions, and leveraged buy-outs

- *Case studies and company databases.* The case studies, gathered from articles in various professional journals and magazines, are kept up to date. Included is a specially prepared longitudinal macroconcentration database of giant U.S. companies, a longitudinal financial database on 1,600 Japanese companies, and the Datext CD–ROM database.

Figure 2-1. Framework for Tracking Creative and Innovative Management.

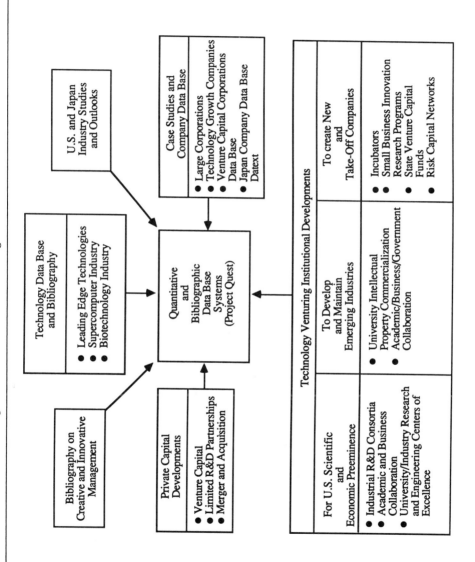

Table 2-3. Course Outline for Creative and Innovative Management.

Part I: Understanding Creative and Innovative Processes

            a. Overview
            b. Emerging theoretical perspectives
            c. Practical understanding–Overview

Part II: Structuring Creative and Innovative Management

            a. Organization
            b. Strategy
            c. Culture and environment
            d. Motivation and incentives
            e. Newer institutional relationships

Part III: Functional Elements for Creative and Innovative Management

            a. Measuring managerial effectiveness
            b. Finance
            c. Marketing
            d. Manufacturing
            e. Case studies

Part IV: Competition and Cooperation in Global Markets

- *Technology venturing institutional developments* knowledge base. The entrepreneurial process by which institutions and individuals share risks to commercialize technologies through new institutional arrangements is the subject.

Structured in four parts, as shown in Table 2-3, the course has had both theoretical and practical results. Results include the creative and innovative use of software packages, particularly in graphics, for analyzing information and making decisions, students' extension of bibliographic databases, analyses of new institutional developments for corporate or individual involvement, and the design and execution of innovative survey questionnaires for data acquisition. Students have developed case studies for quantitative measurement of the effectiveness of creative and innovative management in excellent companies and universities and colleges, and have provided policy inputs to federal and state legislatures and agencies.

New Directions for Advancing the Field of Creative and Innovative Management

A Working Construct. We are now able to develop a working construct of the key elements for creative and innovative management. This multidisciplinary construct (see Figure 2-2) and other related

Figure 2-2. Most Important Steps to Take to Improve Competitiveness, Reduce Excessive U.S. Trade Deficits, and Bolster U.S. Jobs and Incomes over the Next Five Years.

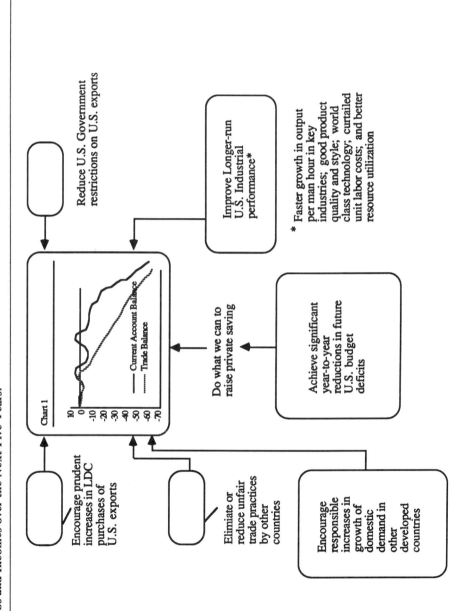

Reduce U.S. Government restrictions on U.S. exports

Improve Longer-run U.S. Industrial performance*

* Faster growth in output per man hour in key industries; good product quality and style; world class technology; curtailed unit labor costs; and better resource utilization

Do what we can to raise private saving

Achieve significant year-to-year reductions in future U.S. budget deficits

Encourage prudent increases in LDC purchases of U.S. exports

Eliminate or reduce unfair trade practices by other countries

Encourage responsible increases in growth of domestic demand in other developed countries

Chart 1

10
0
-10
-20
-30
-40
-50
-60
-70

—— Current Account Balance
.... Trade Balance

research raised important questions for research methodology. Some of these are as follows:

- Is it possible to develop creative leadership skills in the context of creative management so that managers do the right thing in contrast to doing things right?
- Is it possible that management of U.S. domestic basic industries and high-technology industries can overcome global competition without drastic changes to the American economic structure?
- How can the success of innovative management be judged before implementation?
- Are there rational models for quantitative evaluating excellence in companies?
- What organizational forms permit the effective linkages required for creative and innovative management?
- How can creative and innovative management accelerate the commercialization of technology and thus go beyond technology transfer?

A Model of the Creative and Innovative Process

Figure 2–3 is a model of the creative and innovative process that evolved from the course. The model shows that the creative and innovative process are part of a continuum. The input drivers are technology, problems, opportunities, and crises. The creative portion of the process requires talent, irrelevant generation of alternatives, criteria of appropriateness, recognition of appropriateness, and issue generation. The innovative portion of the process encompasses problem solving, generation of alternative solutions, selection of feasible initiatives, structuring the problem for successful solution, monitoring, and management style.

Currently organizations are short of management with the requisite know-how to manage both creatively and innovatively. U.S. business has yet to determine how to organize scientific advances or intellectual properties and a network of experts for timely development into new products that maintain a competitive cutting-edge industry. We need more educated and experienced facilitators in federal and industry research laboratories, universities, other research laboratories, and private firms to assist with this process.

Figure 2-3.   A Model for the Creative and Innovative Process.

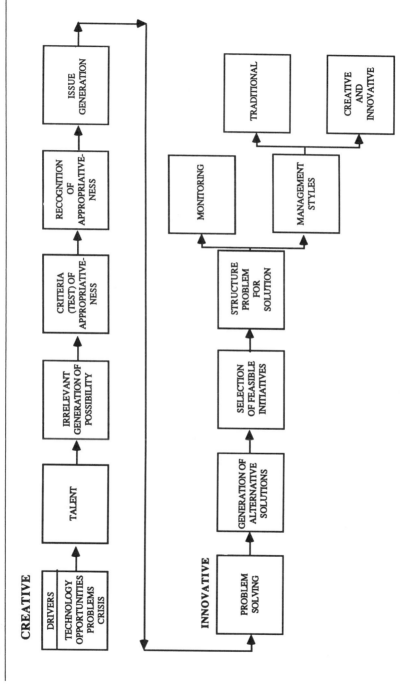

IC^2 work has shown that successful collaborative efforts among government laboratories, businesses, and universities are marked by three essential ingredients:

1. The problem requiring joint effort is real and not an empirical study. The pressure for a timely solution is so significant that it becomes a driver that focuses the collaborative efforts of all parties.

2. The problem has the attribute that it requires both creative and innovative solutions. The scientific members contribute the creative solution while the more practical members of the cooperative task force contribute the innovative solutions—that is, ways to implement successfully.

3. The person in charge of the collaborative effort must be responsible for practical implementation. He or she must have the confidence of their superiors. This person must keep the task force focused on the innovative aspects of the solution to the problem.

CONCLUSION

American management in government, universities, and businesses must change its style. Today's management has all too often shown the symptoms of bureaucratic or big business malaise. Inflexible organizations are committed to inflexible policies, avoidance of risk, and undue influence from existing successful organizations.

American management must rethink its scope and role. Those who manage creatively and innovatively will reap the benefits of sustained economic growth. They can play an important leadership role in dealing with newer strategies regarding global competition and cooperation.

The ability of the United States to compete successfully will require a newer order of cooperation among institutions and organizations that comprise our public-private infrastructures. By implementing creative and innovative management, we can develop links among key institutions to build a viable public-private infrastructure, a strong financial environment, a vibrant entrepreneurial spirit, and a commitment and dedication to risk taking and risk sharing.

PUBLIC POLICY APPLICATIONS

3 CREATIVE MANAGEMENT AND PUBLIC POLICY

Jean-Jacques Servan-Schreiber

Our common theme is "Creative Management"—a great art, touching all domains, in all ways. I shall address it strictly from my own limited, if precise, domain of expertise: applied history and public policy.

CREATING A GRAND VISION

A central lesson of applied history (and terrible management) that I have learned from my early youth is the central role played over a period of one hundred years—from the middle of the last century to the first half of this one—by the deep-rooted, passionate hostility between the two most powerful countries of Europe, at the heart of the modern world: France and Germany.

My own father's father was totally German, even Prussian. He became, in Berlin, the first political secretary to Chancellor Bismarck. Then in deep disagreement with the chancellor's policy of preparing war against France, he left his motherland, Prussia, and became an exile in Paris. And so it is that my father was born a French citizen.

Three wars in succession, each more devastating, exploded between my country and Germany: the first in 1870, the second in 1914, and the third in 1940.

After these three savage duels both nations were bled white, even amputated. Europe, the cradle of Western civilization, with all its various and powerful cultures (not only France and Germany, but Great Britain, Italy, Spain, Austria, Hungary—and more) had suffered

31

irreparable damage. And mostly from one poison: Franco-German hatred.

Such was the historical background for my first exceptional lesson in creativity, forty years ago, in Paris, in the field of public policy given to me by a modest man who was going to become the foremost European of our era. He was mobilized by his managerial passion to find a method and a structure to put an end, once and for all, to Franco-German hostility.

His name was Jean Monnet. He came from a bourgeois family in the city of Cognac, the birthplace of the famous liquor from which the Monnets had made a decent fortune.

But Jean Monnet had no inclination for selling cognac; that he left to his brothers. He was fascinated, from his student years, by the tragedy of the world, at the center of which was the folly of Europe, which he had seen firsthand during his own life. He was sixty when I met him; he was leading a regular, active, thoughtful life, starting each day with a two-hour walk to clarify his ideas around his passion for problem-solving.

He had been for a long time the first truly Franco-American citizen. He had served in World War I, at the age of 25, as a member of the Anglo-French delegation in the United States, in charge of negotiating a regular flow of arms and munitions to the bankrupt allied armies facing the formidable German military machine.

For three years (1914–17), spent mostly in the United States, Monnet's job was extremely difficult. America was neutral in the European war and American public opinion was dead set against any involvement. But the administration of President Wilson was resolved to provide all possible logistic help to both the heirs of William Pitt and the grandchildren of Lafayette, now comrades-in-arms, as long as it did not imply, but rather could prevent, sending a single American soldier across the ocean. So Jean Monnet's special mission.

He showed such an innovative mind, on the difficult grounds of neutral Washington, that twenty-five years later, in the legendary summer of 1940, when General De Gaulle had to flee from France with the flag, and Winston Churchill stood alone facing Hitler, against all odds, the man chosen by both to organize a permanent mission in the United States was again Jean Monnet.

Remembered as the perfect transatlantic manager, he started all over. He became a friend of Roosevelt and Marshall and was very successful, praised on both sides of the ocean.

No one else had been, in two successive world wars, such a managerial engine, across the vast Atlantic and the thick wall of neutralism, between the front line of battle and the Arsenal of Democracy.

Jean Monnet, after the second victory of the allies, had well earned honor and rest. He was sought after by the top corporate workd, because of his unique experience and exceptional network of decision makers. He only had to name his price. But he would not.

His deep passion, his total dedication for the third, and last chapter of his remarkable life was somewhere else—as I came to discover in his office where I now was his guest, alone, for lunch. It was the summer of 1948.

Jean Monnet, sitting at the small table, was, by then, the first "Planning Commissioner" of France, in charge of charting for the French government the most efficient course for rebuilding and modernizing the war-devastated country. He started by questioning me methodically on my two recent stays in West Germany from which I had published two series in the Paris daily, *Le Monde*.

I had chosen journalism by instinct, and by accident, although my training was very far from that. I was a graduate of France's Engineering college, Ecole Polytechnique, and a war veteran, as fighter pilot with De Gaulle's Free French, having been trained in Selma, Alabama, and in Detroit by the U.S. air force.

Both of these experiences, before the age of twenty, had left me with very little appetite for a so-called professional career. After Hitler, Pearl Harbor, Stalin, Hiroshima—the world, for a boy of twenty, was such an unprecedented field for economic reconstruction and political innovation that I was impatient to be part of the public policy debate, and decisions.

Back from the air force to civilian life, and after completing my university doctorate, I took an offer from the leading Paris newspaper, *Le Monde*, to become its editorial writer on foreign affairs. It came to me because of my two-year familiarity with the United States at war, and some juvenile, but passionate, essays as a postwar student on comparing U.S. flexible creativity with the centralized bureaucracy of Stalin. Thus I began publishing articles twice a week for *Le Monde*. And, now, here I was, facing the manager of the era: Jean Monnet.

After his long, meticulous questioning, he asked me to look at the wall on my left, where a very large map of Europe was displayed. He had circled, in one circle, France and Germany. And then he disclosed calmly the true object of his lunch:

You see, our problem is to avoid, this time, the pitfalls of all previous occasions. How can we create an ambitious, but realistic, pattern by which France and Germany would cease, once and for all, to be eternal enemies and made to be partners in a common venture.—A partnership so new and creative that both would have a built-in interest in its success, and never more the temptation, not even the means, to break away from its framework? Do you have any intuition about this central problem? If we solve this century-old fatal flaw, we should be able to advance on a whole new range of world problems. But this one, at the heart of Europe, has to come first. If not—Europe will remain divided, weak, and on the way to its final decadence.

Monnet was gazing fixedly at the map, that circle, these two eternal enemies, a torrent of blood, it seemed, between them: the River Rhine.

What he was looking for, this public policy manager, this transnational mind, was nothing less, it seemed, than the key to a miracle. I sat in silence, knowing how right he was. As a boy I had seen all the countries of Europe go under—in a matter of weeks, crushed by the superior power of Hitler's totally motorized legions and massive air cover. And then, as a soldier, I had seen the same invincible Nazi war machine stalled, and frozen, by the massive mobilization of the Soviet people armed with the superior weapons forged in the United States. So I gazed with Monnet at this map, this Europe of so many glorious cities—Rome, Venice, Athens, Barcelona, Paris, Strasbourg, Bruges, Antwerp, Rotterdam, London, the landmarks of civilization itself—now like ancient jewels on a crippled, sterile continent.

I had no prepared answer worth Monnet's attention. I made a few remarks, in a mood of approval and encouragement. And he went on until he started scribbling rapid notes on a pad in front of him.

Before I left he mentioned that he would probably draft a short memo, some three pages he said, on some intuition that had come to him during the discussion. He would call to show it to me to know the reaction of a man of my generation, forty years younger than his.

When that call came, some momentous events had happened in succession. In Asia, war, a dangerous war, had started in Korea between American and communist armies. In Europe, President Truman had to send forces, also, to fight against communist takeovers in Greece and Turkey. Across both oceans General Marshall, as Secretary of State, had begun to implement his famous plan to allow Western Europe and Japan to regain their own strength for survival and growth. And the Soviet Union, under Stalin, had exploded its first atomic weapons. The world was indeed changing fast.

I met again with Monnet. What struck me as central to his genius was that, obviously none of these events had for a moment distracted his attentions from his own single-minded obsession: to make France and Germany a one and only biological cell, the two parts being forever unable to separate and turn against each other.

The draft of a solution to this formidable public-management problem had indeed put in a memo of three short, handwritten pages. This was later to become quite famous, historical, and known as the Monnet Plan.

In simple language his innovative creation had the impact of the obvious.

Monnet said:

> The basic instruments of war between our two great countries have been made from the rich resources of both France and Germany, on the borders of the Rhine River, in coal and iron. The recurrent inevitability of war will not be reversed by nice feelings or good speeches. Let us go to the very root of things and propose that France and Germany put all their coal-mining and steel-making capacities in one common Pool, governed by one Authority, independent of the national sovereignties. This supra-national Agency will be controlled by a common board chosen by both parliaments, with its own executives.
>
> No part, whatsoever, of French or German coal mining or steel making capacities will remain outside the control of this new, and common, High authority.

Such was the core of the memo.

All sorts of other developments, commented Monnet, should then follow, over the years, making the two countries more and more interdependent and acting in concert. Then the future generations would take care of building the ultimate construction: A United Europe, probably a confederation somewhat on the model of Switzerland where three very different populations with three different languages and cultures (French, German, Italian) have merged into one solid country, united but diversified, with very strong regional and local powers. "But this," he said, "belongs to some still distant future. You will see it," he said, "I shall not. Let us start now, where we can act, and so with coal and steel."

His handwritten memo—now kept in the National Library of France—was adopted without change by France's Foreign Minister, the famous Robert Schuman, who was born in German-occupied Alsace on the Rhine, to become French only after World War II, and who still, as a patriotic and respected secretary of state, spoke with a thick German accent. Monnet could not have a better ally.

While Schuman convinced his colleagues of the French government, in a matter of two weeks, to approve the memo, Jean Monnet went to Bonn to meet the first postwar elected successor to Adolf Hitler as German Chancellor, Konrad Adenauer, also a native of the Rhineland, kept in seclusion throughout the twelve years of the Nazis' reign.

Adenauer became an instant convert and militant. He made his government ready to announce its approval two days after Paris would officially make the offer public. And at the agreed time it was done. Europe, in total surprise, was carried by a wave of emotion and hope.

To measure the audacity and the dimension of the event, I should briefly recall my first conversation with a president of France, which had taken place just two months before.

After one of my journeys to occupied Germany I felt very strongly that the German people I talked to, at all levels, were so embarrassed, troubled, by the revelation of what had happened to them under Hitler's spell, that they were truly prepared to accept, gratefully, any generous offer that could come from France to bring them out of their isolation.

So I asked my editor to organize for me an audience with the first president of postwar France, a respected veteran politician who had bravely fought in World War I, where he lost one eye. He belonged to the moderate wing of the Socialist party and his name was Vincent Auriol.

In the presidential office at the Elysée Palace, which I saw for the first time, with respect and timidity (my credentials were next to zero), I told President Auriol my impressions of Germany and suggested that France take the first step toward raising this great country from its knees by proposing a straight partnership, leading toward a European Union.

The elder statesman listened with care, approved the objective, and encouraged me to continue to explain these future prospects to the French opinion.

> But [he added] the official act you are asking for would be totally premature, and misunderstood. You are a very young man and I appreciate your idealistic impatience. But believe my experience: It will take at least a generation for the crimes of the Nazis to be forgotten and for the French to contemplate the idea of becoming partners with the Germans. You will learn, my young friend, that you cannot precipitate history. Maybe, when the few, in your generation, who have fought in this war are twenty years older, then you might take a public stand on some kind of partnership with Germany, but there is no way to attempt it in the near future. I like your vision but, for now it is only a dream.

I had to respect the wisdom of this statesman—until the meeting with Jean Monnet, who, as we have seen, although the same age as the president of the Republic, took the exact opposite view. The innovative manager versus the careful politician, and now Monnet was winning the day, with lighning speed.

The sequence of events that followed is well known. The Coal-Steel Pool, between France and Germany, was created and implemented. One by one, the other concerned European nations—Italy, Belgium, Holland, Luxembourg—joined this first, basic, pact. It became "the six-nation Community."

And then, year after year, they decided together, as a logical follow-up, to enlarge the concept and the authority, giving birth to the European Common Market, then the European Economic Commission, with two working-capitals: Luxembourg and Brussels, and then an elected European Parliament in the city of the Cathedral: Strasbourg.

The movement, reversing centuries of history, had become irreversible.

Even the great nationalistic passion of General De Gaulle, who later became president of France for eleven years (1958-69), could only slow down the construction of Europe, but never destroyed Monnet's brainchild.

De Gaulle was defeated in a referendum and left office. The European movement took fresh momentum.

I was, now at very close hand, since the mid seventies, working with two successive presidents—President Giscard d'Estaing and President Mitterrand—one from the right, one from the left, how Europe had become a ground for consensus and common action.

In the summer of 1987, despite all the devisive preparations for the 1988 presidential election in France, an agreement was discussed between these two honorable men and former opponents, Mitterrand and Giscard, for preparing the election of a confederate president of Europe, in the first years of the next decade.

Mitterrand, if reelected at the Elysée, as he well may be, would propose, with his European partners, Giscard, as former president and direct disciple of Jean Monnet, to serve as the first chief executive of Confederate Europe.

And then, with 1992 as a deadline, what is already called the "United Act of Europe" will create, with the twelve nations of the enlarged community (Great Britain, Spain, Portugal, and Greece havnow joined) a unified economic area with no tariffs, no passports, and a common basis for the various national currencies, called the ECU, already today accepted in international payments. The birth of a continent from the ashes of history.

Such is the remarkable case history, in creative management, of Jean Monnet and his three-page memorandum.

When he handed it to me in draft form to read, it was the year 1948. The final act of European unification, which I have just mentioned, is scheduled for 1992. Many in Europe and in the United States may have felt the progress, between concept and implementation, to have been very slow. Indeed, from Monnet's precise vision to the concrete emergence of a true European Union, it will have taken forty-five years!

But, in perspective, let us recall the many centuries—more than ten—of European rivalries, battles, crusades, to look with fresh eyes at the remarkable accomplishment of this less than half century that we have lived. Our children will look upon it as quite short and will read about it with gratitude having become citizens of Europe, and so able to start then, I feel confident, to build a larger, and soon needed, Atlantic Community, where Western Europe Union and the United States of America will pool their talents, resources, and creativity into one powerful engine of progress—to be able to compete with the phenomenal mobilization of educated minds and dedicated energies that already makes Asia look like the future leader of the twenty-first century.

I shall now, very briefly, add one or two examples—and then draw some suggestions for our common efforts to invent the future.

THE POWER OF A GREAT IDEA

This episode, the birth of a new Europe, shows the extent of the consequences due to the clarity of one mind, at the right moment. But, to tell the truth, the obsession of Frenchmen of my generation, although young disciples of Monnet, forty years ago, was not Europe. It was Vietnam. Yes, even then.

If difficult decisions were required for the complex construction of Europe, they were dwarfed by the one public policy problem of historical dimension: how for all of us to accept and manage the end of the Imperial Era for Western civilization, the end of our control of so many, and so large, Western-dominated countries in Asia and the Pacific, Africa and the Indian Ocean, Latin America and the South Atlantic.

Many populations, and diverse situations—cultural, economic, military—were involved in this unfolding drama of the West. And one single name became the symbol of it all, then and now: Vietnam.

My contribution to a momentous chapter of our common history, to the ongoing debate on this most sensitive public-management problem, will be limited to two short episodes in which I participated directly and the exceptional men who were, successively, in control of the decision-making process. One, French Prime Minister Mendés-France, the other U.S. President John Kennedy.

Pièrre Mendés-France, a World War II Free French pilot, already a veteran of prewar French politics, was essentially an economist. In fact he was chosen by General De Gaulle, in London, to be part of his wartime cabinet as economic minister. But he refused, and explained to De Gaulle that public men like himself, still in their prime (he was thirty-five) could not stay away from the raging military battles against Hitler; he had to return to his air squadron where he was a captain on British bombers, and flew combat-missions until the war's end.

Having returned to political life after the war, he refused to be part of any government again as long as clear priorities, which he had set in a brief document, were not adopted for the allocation of the scarce resources of France now facing three major problems in parallel: the reconstruction and modernization of the country; the building of Europe in an organized partnership with our neighbors; and, last but not least—certainly not in the mind of Mendés-France— the radical change in our relationship with our vast, prestigious, but ruinous, overseas possessions from the colonial era, and an end to our military presence.

I had the privilege to be the junior aide to Mendés-France, from the year 1949 for twenty years, until he retired. I learned so much from him on measuring events that, today I still recall almost every morning his insights and warnings.

His finest hour, quite unexpected to France as a whole, came with the need to conclude the drama in Vietnam from which Mendés-France, suddenly chosen by Parliament as prime minister, under the shock of defeat at Dien-Bien-Phu, had to extricate, with honor and a reasonable cease-fire, a large part of the French Army.

A peace conference on Vietnam was convened in Geneva in the summer of 1954, as it would again sixteen years later to put an end to the second Vietnam war, the American one. We had to deal from weakness, from a defeated, humiliated French expeditionary force.

At the conference table we were facing three men of no ordinary caliber. Foreign Minister Molotov, of the Soviet Union, closest associate of Joseph Stalin, still master in the Kremlin; Prime Minister Chou En Lai, of the People's Republic of China, representing Chairman Mao; and the future Prime Minister (then Foreign Minister) of Communist Vietnam, Pham Van Dong, representing Ho Chi Minh— together the whole Communist Empire, half of the universe.

Mendés-France, before going to that table, had to find a way to change radically the terms of the encounter, which were disastrous for us: one-fifth of the French military force in Vietnam had been crushed in the battle of Dien-Bien-Phu. We had to face defeat, pure and simple, and still try to negotiate, from there, a decent peace settlement.

This very situation would have to be faced, in various ways, by the Western powers in the coming decades. How to avoid, or abandon, a position of precarious military domination without creating a chain of disorders both in the far-distant countries involved and in the psyche of our own people, each of us, at home. Today the same delicate question is still with us. Forty years of struggling with it has not yet appeased the debate nor truly clarified the options for decision makers and executives.

Having followed closely what went on in the United States in the course of the past three decades, I have often wondered why knowledge and study of what happened to Europe, and very specifically to France, was not better used as warning and guidance to avoid the same traumatic experiences and the same proven errors.

It is not too late. With the exponential effects of ill-conceived, unprepared, punlic-management decisions by this great country, and in preparation for the most crucial presidential campaign in half a century, every relevant episode of the European experience should be examined and made useful to the great debate that is coming. The case of Mendés-France confronting both defeat, due to his predecessor's policy, and the massive front of a united communist world, is worthy of our attention.

One evening, before the peace meeting, the staff was working on a series of drafts for presentations and various diplomatic options. Taking me into another room, Mendés-France, refusing to be pressured either by the heavy machine of state, or by the infinite international rules of protocol, told me in very simple terms his essential intuition:

> We must find a completely different way. If, in the comfort of habits, we start negotiating in classical terms all the issues of such a complicated peace, one by one, two disasters will become inevitable. First; It will be endless. They can drag on for months and even more. Second: During this terrible cascade of protracted negotiations, full of inevitable suspicion, on both sides, the real misunderstandings due to the polarization of the world between East and West, we shall get into deeper and deeper military involvement. In the end there will be nothing to negotiate; only to abandon. So enemy No. 1, right now, is time. Time is against us. Is there a way to reverse this? Everything else is secondary. Think about this, and if you have a suggestion, make it as simple as possible, in a one-page memo, and we shall discuss it.

These strong instructions, and with no excessive respect for diplomatic precedents in history, forced me, by the sheer strength of Mendés-France's intuition, into innovation.

So I came to this simple suggestion: Refuse to be dragged into endless negotiations by giving the opponent, although victorious, an ultimatum. The peace agreement, on the essentials, must be signed in two weeks. Mendés-France should announce, in advance, that after the two weeks he would not continue, would resign as prime minister and send to Vietnam massive reinforcements and maximum air power to be at the disposal of the next prime minister.

I presented this memorandum to him the next day. This man, in a position of highest responsibility, facing immense pressure on the battlefront and at home, suddenly had to face my radical proposition. I was afraid I had gone too far. But in a matter of minutes the power of his intellect took control. He remained totally calm, showing no emotion—and he did not hesitate. He made, on the spot, two decisions and said:

> First, I think this is the idea. It can work, and I am prepared to take the risk. Second, you are not realistic in asking for two weeks, let us make it a month.

And that was all. Without further discussion he had his public speech prepared for the National Parliament where he explained, with eloquent sincerity and shrewd exploitation of such an announcement, that this time the army that had lost a battle was presenting those who had won with an ultimatum. One month . . .

Parliament could do nothing but approve; it did so without dissent. After all, if he failed he would be out in a month! The communist-world leaders in Geneva immediately felt the balance had changed. After all this was the only prime minister dedicated to a peaceful agreement. If he went, it would automatically lead to a larger war, with world consequences.

At the end of one month—not one more day, as Mendés-France made quite clear by making preparation for his departure, on the very eve of the deadline and calling the two official planes from Paris—peace was made. And never again, from that day, after more than a century of colonial rule, would any French force return to Vietnam.

The relief in France was extraordinary. Also, suddenly, was the feeling of admiration for this bold and successful act of statesmanship. Mendés-France, so isolated in all previous years, became an instant hero.

Then comes, I believe, the really interesting moment for our case study in creative management and public policy. What would he do with the capital of confidence and support earned brilliantly in a one-month battle of nerves? Normally, with the accumulated fatigue, and since it was now July and the famous French vacation-recess, he was fully expected to slow down and take time to prepare for other rounds starting in September, only six weeks away. He decided the opposite.

Having watched, first as a student, then as a member of parliament, the politics of the world since 1932, the era of Franklin Roosevelt and that of Hitler, then, as a pilot through the great battles, East and West, of the world war itself, and now the postwar events, Mendès-France explained to me the lesson he had learned: momentum, in the course of human affairs, must be exploited, or be lost.

So he decided to go, without delay, after other major unsolved problems.

One: To continue the movement of decolonization started in Vietnam and open the way to independence for our colonies in North Africa (Morocco, Tunisia, Algeria) before their people, frustrated for so long and getting desperate, also started armed rebellions against France, following the example of the Vietnamese.

Second: With the moral capital gained in breaking with a colonial past, France should try immediately to mobilize public opinions and governments, all over, toward a common decision to stop the madness of the nuclear arms race, still in its very beginning, and force a ban on all future tests. Since he was invited, after the peace-in-one-month of Geneva, to give the keynote speech at the United Nations Assembly, in September, he would use this public occasion to have both the United States and Soviet Russia face their responsibilities before a world dedicated to peace.

The two stories of what happened with these two decisions, in the management of public affairs, with the emergence of the powerful lobbies that we can see, today, in full light, I shall briefly summarize here.

In North Africa Mendès-France started his opening dialogue with Tunisia, with its still-imprisoned nationalist leader, Habib Bourgiba. Using his credit with a French public opinion massively hostile to the so-called abandoning of North Africa, Mendès-France negotiated without pause with Bourgiba, now free, the autonomy of Tunisia leading to independence.

He continued with Morocco. And then he was going to change peacefully, in a similar way, the relationship between France and Algeria. At that moment extremists on both sides, having watched his method, decided to shoot. In Algeria the nationalist armed groups, although still very small, started to kill French settlers. In Paris the very rich colonial lobby used its leverage in Parliament to full extent. The explosion and the corruption brought down the

Mendés-France government. Another sterile, poisonous war, like Vietnam—and again for eight years—started.

I was going to learn a lot more about its nature at close hand, being drafted as reserve officer into the French army fighting the Alegeian so-called rebels. But this is another story, for another day.

We now have to look rapidly at the result, no less relevant to us today, of the other campaign, on the other front—for a nuclear freeze at the United Nations. This was thirty years ago. One can imagine what a success would have added to the economic resources of the world taken away from the continuous nuclear race, with its high price in financial and, even more, human resources.

When the prime minister left Paris for New York, with his opening speech prepared and the proposals checked several times with our atomic specialists, he asked me not to come, because he had been informed that I was labeled in some Washington bureaus, since my role in the peace process in Vietnam, as a "pro-communist" militant. Mendés-France feared that this might add a problem to his extremely sensitive negotiation with the Americans on stopping the nuclear race.

I thought, with my U.S. wartime experience, and then two years as a Fulbright fellow, that, on the contrary, I might be of help, but I did not insist. This man was pursuing a heroic task, I should in no way even appear to make it more difficult. So I did not insist. I was wrong.

Three days later I received, in the very early morning, a call from New York. I knew the voice, but found it strangely strained. I listened, with care, as, Mendés-France, in a depressed mood, explained that he had spent ten hours in a row, at his hotel suite, encircled by Foster Dulles, the secretary of state, Admiral Radford, chairman of the joint chiefs of staff, two nuclear experts brought from Washington agencies, and on top of that the well-known, and quite popular with the U.S. establishment, French ambassador, Henri Bonnet, who had all taken part in the general assault.

Their objective was to stop Mendés-France, at all cost, from making his prepared appeal to a nuclear armistice. This, said the whole impressive group, would undermine the U.S. military program and could only serve the Soviets. America needed in a vital way, Mendés-France was told, two more years of testing before being able to consider a truce. The voice on the phone came to the conclusion:

> Believe me, it is impossible to go against such passionate opposition from our own friends. I have taken many risks, as you know, but this one I shall not. I do not want to be responsible for a weakening, or even worse, a breakdown

of the Franco-American friendship. I know that they are wrong. We may be missing a major opportunity to channel the resources of the industrial powers, and as you know, soon our own, toward a new development of the world, away from exponential military budgets; but I do not feel I can go further under the circumstances. This public appeal will have to be made at some later date.

It was not made and was never to be. The voice of reason, with the moral authority of the peacemaker, and with an Assembly at the UN, that would have massively muted any opposition to the nuclear armistice, had been effectively silenced. A great coup for the powers that President Eisenhower, watching in careful silence, not yet assured of his White House leverage in the Washington bureaucratic games, would finally and bravely denounce, six years later, as the greatest danger: "the military-industrial complex."

The Voice would never be heard again. The most daring French statesman of the postwar era, the innovator of the decolonization crusade, the passionate opponent of the arms race, was going to be stabbed by the powerful lobby of the rich Algerian settlers. He would never come back, until the sober, emotional speech of his friend and Prime Minister, François Mitterrand, now president of the Republic, paid him the homage of a nation in mourning, at his funeral service in 1982.

VIETNAM: AN OPPORTUNITY LOST

At some point, as always happens, the French military expedition in Algeria crossed the bridge between guerilla operations and real war. I was drafted, as a reserve officer, to lead commando operations in the southern mountains of Algeria called Djebels. I had refused to return in uniform as a pilot against an unarmed, ill-educated, and mostly defenseless (certainly in the air) Arab population.

It has been to this day a most valuable experience, living among the Algerian peasants, sleeping from village to village, seeing at firsthand how inefficient, almost ridiculous, our bombers, or more often helicopters, flying over our heads, were—and watching the revolt of a miserable population progressively developing into a shrewd, organized people's army. In many ways it was what had been two centuries ago, the French people's revolution and the Americans' against the colonial rule. The name of General de Lafayette, an aristocrat and a royalist, who understood in both our countries the surge to self-rule, is the true symbol, to this day, of the profound Franco-American community of mind.

In Algeria I could receive military-delivered mail once a week. There, in the autumn of 1957 a letter arrived from a young U.S. senator whom I knew only by name, John Kennedy. He was sending me a copy of his first major speech in the Senate on colonialism, taking Algeria and France as a case to be carefully studied and remembered. He wanted my reaction.

Kennedy's words were carefully tuned to the future. Taking the Algerian war as a tragic example of how Western civilization could misread the basic realities of the new era, he was specific and effective. I reread his text last week, the one he sent me at the time. What comes out is that Kennedy's criticism of the French blindness of thirty years ago, could be applied, almost word for word today to the vision of the Western powers looking at the Third World, that is also called "the South," and specifically for the United States itself looking south of its borders.

Little did I know that five years later I would have this letter in my pocket, and its message very much on my mind when I would sit with him, and that it would be in his office at the White House. I had also brought from Paris, preparing to answer his invitation, a thick, remarkable book published recently by French Colonel Jules Roy, who had served in Vietnam and after that war had spent two full years in that country to research, in detail, how a modern army equipped with tanks and covered by a full air force could have finally met with defeat at Dien-Bien-Phu, totally unprepared, both in Saigon and in Paris, for such a seemingly incomprehensible turn of events. The title of this thick, 800-page, well-documented, highly readable book was *Dien-Bien-Phu*. I placed a copy on the small, round table between President Kennedy's rocking chair and the visitor's sofa where I sat.

My host was extremely cordial and displayed his famous open-mindedness by mentioning a range of subjects he suggested we could discuss, today and tomorrow—and then asked me, kindly, in what order I preferred to discuss them.

I took a deep breath and gambled on the intelligence of the man. I told him that, on my way to Washington, I thought my duty would be to propose to talk about one topic, and one only. Then the deep breath: Vietnam.

He showed total surprise and disbelief. He mentioned the continuous tension with the Soviets since the Cuban crisis. He mentioned the expansionist potential of Communist China. He quoted my own testimony on the major national crisis in France due to the final upheaval in Algeria and now over so many other countries in Africa. He continued with the sensitive question of the balance of forces in

Europe, and specifically the rearming of Germany. He also knew quite well the number of voters casting their ballot for the various national Communist parties, not only in France and Italy, where they were over 25 percent, but across Western Europe. All these dangerous issues certainly had to be addressed promptly. But one was certainly not on the U.S. crisis watch, only a French nightmare—and that was Vietnam.

That was the end of 1962. And on the surface Vietnam, indeed, was nowhere a flashing red light in the war rooms of the world. But having gone through this agony, having seen how rapidly the lesson could be forgotten with France plunging blindly into another Vietnam called Algeria; having kept closely informed with what was going on in Saigon, capital of noncommunist South Vietnam, the regular arrival and growing number of U.S. so-called advisors to the local army, already under Eisenhower and accelerating in the past two years under Kennedy, because he was so preoccupied with other issues and other regions—my colleagues and I had decided, in our strategic sessions in Paris, that there lay the really explosive danger: a possible escalating of the American military expedition into the swamps of Vietnam.

We imagined with horror the profound consequences this new "march of folly," following France's path, leading also to final humiliation and defeat, only in much larger dimension both in the world and at home.

I reported exactly that to John Kennedy.

At first in total disbelief, then with decent interest, he listened. I thought, if I had attracted even a small part of his attention, this was enough for the day. The rest, the full documentation, for him and his defense aides, was there on his table: the convincing, exhaustive study by Colonel Jules Roy on Dien-Bien-Phu. I begged him to have his staff summarize carefully this French book into an explicit resumé for his own attention.

Before the end of the exchange John Kennedy, obviously not indifferent, called Defense Secretary Robert McNamara, and made an appointment for me the next day at breakfast. He asked to visit with him again after the discussion at the Pentagon.

The session with Secretary McNamara, to whose mastery of management I later devoted a chapter of a three-year study published as *The American Challenge*, to my surprise was quite disappointing. Alarmingly so.

After listening with care, the secretary of defense summarized his disagreement:

You see, it is not conceivable that an American force in Vietnam could meet, as you imagine, the sad fate of the French army. It is not a question of bravery but of technology. We have something your generals did not have and left them so vulnerable: thousands of helicopters. We can saturate the skies in Vietnam, if we happen to be so engaged, which I do not anticipate at all, with these helicopters. The guerillas would be overwhelmed, paralyzed. Your concern is not justified with divisions that can be airborne at will.

McNamara was obviously convinced by his own certitude. He had no idea of the creative capacities of General Giap and the well-rehearsed agility of his dedicated People's Army. We French knew how swiftly they could move under the cover of night and, if necessary, in continually renewed tunnels. And I had also seen personally, in Algeria, the French helicopters—they did exist, after all—make such long distant noise over our heads that they had missed, time after time, the nationalist guerrillas who were warned well in advance.

I did not argue. I simply reported this to the president at the White House as confirmation of my fears. He then asked the attorney general, his brother Robert, to converse with me. I found Bobby Kennedy extremely perceptive and sharing my concern. He would do what he could to keep the president informed, but he could not interfere with defense.

We left it at that.

I returned to Paris with no illusion of having achieved anything. The lessons we had learned in Vietnam, and then again in Algeria, and even the eloquent, convincing Senate speech by Kennedy himself—none of that would change the course of the war machine. It was strongly controlled, indeed, by the military-industrial complex. And, anyway, in a matter of months, Lyndon Johnson was the new guide from the Oval Office, with obvious appetite for a personal "victory" of his own, anywhere. The rest is history.

HOW CREATIVE MANAGEMENT CAN
CATALYZE PEACE AND PROSPERITY

I could go on with the description of many other personal experiences in the ambiguity (to say the least) of the management of our affairs in the recent past. I would like to, but I must stop. All the fairy tales left aside, I shall ask Carnegie-Mellon to consider my candidacy to run, together with the International Committee, a course in applied history and public-management. In the meantime where do we land?

From my exchanges of the recent months at Carnegie-Mellon, in Washington, at Stanford, at the Combined War College (or National Defense University) I have come to a rather simple conclusion that I bring to your attention for further thought, on the eve of an unprecedented presidential campaign, that will directly concern each of you, each of us. It is this: From the various experiences of our past—in good and bad public management—we can consider that, today and for 1988, three major questions must be put clearly to the public debate and will need effective answers.

First, can we accept continuation of the arms race with Soviet Union? What sense does it make, and who really believes a nuclear war would, under any conceivable circumstances, be the answer to anything? After forty years of this dreadful routine of nonthinking, and now on the verge of bankruptcy—East, West and South—can we find a way, inspired by Jean Monnet's successful audacity, to change the whole pattern? Can we afford not to do so?

Second, obsessed by the Soviet threat, are we not heading directly toward defeat, by putting all possible resources on that front while the second front is abandoned to neglect, to very little public-policy management, and inferior creativity? That second front, as we all know, is the economic, industrial, technological competition with Japan and Asia. It cannot be treated by wishful thinking, nor by insults. And, with the American and European economic landscapes already devastated, we cannot remain paralyzed.

All the talk about trade deficits and the Japan-bashing futility do very little to address this global reality: we have abdicated, one by one, almost every industrial sector to Asian superiority (in price, quality, and performance), and now we see a similar fate, for identical reasons, in the service sectors, the financial markets, and the like.

Must we continue to worry, routinely, endlessly, about a Soviet military assault that has been such a comfortable alibi for accumulating sterile hardware, at a huge price, and continue to abandon superior creativity to others? Time has come to wake up to the pressing challenge of Asian intellectual, cultural, creative superiority that could well seal the fate of our children and make us abandon the legitimate, I believe vital, ambition of being equal to the best in the twenty-first century. We, like others, would certainly not cherish the domination of distant owners and of a foreign culture.

These two pressing issues certainly deserve fresh thinking, and on top of them, nourished by them, is a third one, even more acute because it is inside ourselves. I have known it in my own country, under a similar set of circumstances, and it created havoc with the intelligence and coherence of France. In every modern country there is the risk of a divorce between the military establishment and the academic world, between army and university, between defense and culture, between Sparta and Athens. We must face it. It is our role.

This danger of civil disruption on the home front is greater in America today than anywhere else. Why?

Because, in this country, the armed forces are the most powerful of the world and the most sophisticated in technology. So their appetite for constantly fresh resources and trained minds is enormous. Their normal instinct is to colonize an ever larger part of the national budget and of the best universities.

The budget problem is well known and being debated all over. We can leave it aside, for today. The delicate, complex problem of universities versus the military establishment—that is truly at the heart of our responsibilities in problem-solving management.

I see the possibility, in this country, of a cultural civil war, with great potential for disruption. I can imagine a military America having in mind that the only real enemy is Soviet Russia, and so to prepare against it the only vital priority. The end result is an academic America concerned more and more with the threat of becoming second rate, dominated, in the economic, technological, then scientific and cultural, competition with Japan and Asia.

Two different Americas, alien to each other, with two different priorities, two different targets in mind, two opposite views for the future of the management of resources and the allocation of innovations. An internal schism that we certainly cannot afford if we are to meet the military and industrial challenges.

Twenty years ago, as I can testify, the minds, the debate, the passions, here and over the world, were circling around a dominant pole: "The American Challenge."

Today the challenge is to America. And the mood of the day, the elegant attitude is pessimism. That we are, America and the West, on the way to historical decadence.

The easiest thing for me would certainly be to pile evidence upon evidence that such is indeed the present course. Who among us could on the spot, name one industrial sector that is not today dominated by foreign, mostly Asian, competitors?

I have watched one American sector, in these same years, able to go against the mainstream of decadence and, on the contrary, increase its leading edge. That is higher education in universities of excellence of this country.

I have been direct witness to the coming of age of some great U.S. institutes into universities of the world. We see students from France and Japan, as well as Taiwan or mainland China, and students from

India and the Middle East—truly from the whole world—applying *en masse* to the unique departments of the best American institutes. There are, to take one example, seventeen different nationalities on the rather small campus of Carnegie-Mellon. It is fascinating to note the number of Japanese graduate students, sent and supported by their corporations, applying for the next semester to this Graduate School of Industrial Administration itself. It is many times more than was expected, twice as many as can be admitted, although all with top applications and fully supported by their corporations. Coming from the country most famous for superior management, what more eloquent proof could we expect?

As much as America has lost ground in manufacturing, agricultural, banking, service sectors, the fact remains that it has become, at the same time, the engine of superior learning for the world, the engine for creating knowledge and teaching knowledge.

Is this metamorphosis a positive, or a negative, trade-off?

I shall not pretend to forecast the future. I simply note these momentous facts. From these facts, good and bad, a completely different world environment has emerged around an America that is itself radically changed. The dogmas of yesterday belong to the past; it is time to recognize that they are gone, and to accept, without fear or prejudice, a new vision.

A vision is nothing, only a nice dream, unless it is supported by a precise prospect for implementing it.

Such was the radically innovative, but also very simple, plan by Jean Monnet that built Europe. Such was, as we shall always remember, the remarkable Marshall Plan. Such was, with Mendès-France, the making of peace in Vietnam in thirty days. Such was, in spite of some weaknesses in foreign policy at the beginning, John Kennedy's simplest and most effective plan—lighting the flame of the youth, giving it a real appetite, a joyful impetus, to create and master the future.

Taking the world as it is now, immensely more diverse and complicated than at any of these previous periods, we must clearly decide that the plan for the future will be conceived, most likely to be understood and made to work, if it is of utmost simplicity. Based on these past four decades of experience, it is my sincere belief.

So I shall not be shy with you in drafting conclusions that will probably look simplistic and unrealistic. Someone has to take the risk of being highly vulnerable to criticism. I shall do so from the lessons learned from all these great figures, as if they were still with us today.

Let me summarize three suggestions.

1. The hostile, if muted on the surface, relationship between the two Americas—the intellectual and the military—must cease, at all cost. And not with kindness, or good feelings, but from concrete, common action, leading to day-to-day partnership.

American defense is, first and last, American knowledge. No more, no less.

When the Soviets gave Syria their most modern surface-to-air (SAM) missiles to cancel the superiority of the Israeli air force, what did the Israelis do? They took two squadrons of U.S. fighter bombers and worked on them, amplifying their state-of-the-art computer technology, increasing manyfold the efficiency of the planes and their missiles. In parallel they retrained the pilots, day and night for months, in the air and in computerized simulation rooms.

On the screens of the flight-simulated rooms the pilots were reviewing, time after time, the whole Beka Valley, along the border of Syria, with each of its defense posts, from all angles, at all hours of light. It was, in its total sophistication a real innovation, and an act of faith in science and education.

On the day of the raid, much more than the Israeli squadron was at stake. Their target was nothing less than the full potential of the Warsaw Pact and Soviet missile capacity, facing the latest in Western computing art and excellence in human expertise. The stakes were high, not only for Israel and Suria but for the whole West and the whole East.

In thirty-five minutes all of the SAM batteries lay destroyed deep into the ground, all of the computerized fighter-bombers had returned to their base; the universe of the military, around the planet, had changed.

That was more than ten years ago. It remains true to this day, with consequences all around. True in the Middle east, where it paved the way for the historic peace conference that has been delayed by some last spasms of old ideological posturing but has become inevitable and logical. True in the Soviet Empire where it has, after deep and difficult soul searching and last-ditch conservative retrenchments, catapulted to power with Mikhail Gorbachev a new generation of scientifically educated minds, with apparently a new view of economic progress and the true substance of security. True in the U.S. Combined War College (now called National Defense University) where upcoming leaders of U.S. forces are now, of a new breed, with excellent degrees and continuous intellectual retraining. I had the privilege—and the relief—of taking part in the discussions to give birth to a new complex, of a very different nature: the university-defense complex, made of one and only common material: knowledge, new knowledge, more knowledge.

2. Since the worst mistake, on our part, would be to underestimate the fresh intelligence of the Soviets—we have to assume that they have come to the same conclusion: True security is higher knowledge, very far from the blind and ruinous accumulation of sterile hardware.

This also, of course, fits their urgent need to rebuild their obsolete economy by transferring a very large portion of resources and brains, monopolized by the military, to the creative part of the Soviet society and the massive, continuous, buildup of the educational system at all ages. This will necessitate the dissemination of the most advanced personal computers (or "work stations").

There would come the birth of the New Era. A partnership, in research, in laboratories, of East and West would be natural. Shared laboratories with the Soviets could do more than anything to transform the Soviet-American hostility into a far-reaching integration of efforts and minds in the common knowledge-revolution, where the old dogmas of the cold war could pale into insignificance.

This, at least, could create the necessary potential use the common, powerful tools of science, to attack the really deadly enemy of us all: the desperation of more than four billion struggling people, the Third World.

People who have ceased to believe (as I have seen at close hand, all through the 1980s, on their various sinking continents) in mendicancy or financial aid and clearly want to share creative knowledge. They want to have it to themselves. To make what they need, what they dream to conceive. They shall not, much longer, accept being our dumping place, at the impossible price of an exponential debt.

3. To implement this plan, which is a minimum, we must cease to treat the most creative (at this point) of all people—the Japanese and their neighbors—as the new enemies.

These people, from a culture admittedly foreign to ours (but also most refined), are going to choose, from the high position of their achievements, between a full opening to the world, if it is offered, and a renewed imperial temptation to dominate, if they feel our hostility to be deep-rooted and lasting. It is *our* choice, certainly difficult, but possibly the most far-reaching of all. Let us never forget that this choice will have to be made, much before the end of this century.

Partnership, real and intimate at home between university and defense should give the signal of a true renewal, of our own renaissance, leaving behind doctrines and ideologies of ancient times. From there we should be able to put an end, over the oceans, to the impossible "war on two fronts." And then, on the sheer strength of human intelligence, with a new coalition, profitable to each, of Western, Asiatic, and Russian creative cultures, we launch the first historical assault on global misery—Well into the next century and starting now.

Discussion

Moderator: Jean-Jacques Servan-Schreiber

Question: What is the greatest threat to freedom today?

Servan-Schreiber: Illiteracy. That such a great country as America, with such remarkable potential, neglects the kind of illiteracy that exists today in its youth is a tremendous threat.

Question: To freedom?

Servan-Schreiber: Of course—to the Country of freedom, to the Cause of freedom. We are not training the minds. What is our future? I told you of my respect for higher education in America. But what is done in the schools before that? What about the education of the younger people, before 16 or 18? What about the training of all the people who cannot go to college? America has essentially a small, well-trained elite. That can last only for some time.

Question: Do you sincerely believe that we can trust the communist leaders?

Servan-Schreiber: Not at all.

Question: If you can't trust them, how can you deal with them?

Servan-Schreiber: When did we decide we should try to trust the Germans, all former Nazis? With a century of bloody wars and 3 million French youth killed in those wars, how could we have confidence? This visionary man, Jean Monnet, made the gamble: to a deeper Franco-German common interest. It is time, today, to play the option of confidence. Ideologies are bankrupt. The first thing that we must establish is a new structure for peace. I see Gorbachev and others around him watching a little plane (with perhaps a bomb inside) land in Red Square, in front of Kremlin. Nobody had seen that plane arrive, nor had done anything about it. They don't treat that with indifference. In one week they have to remove the minister of defense and other top generals. The Russian bureaucracy is like the economy: bankrupt. The Soviets need a creative partnership with us; we also need it. I don't have confidence; I just see the facts. They need a revival of their economy. Let the Russian people have personal computers, very good ones. That should start to do away with centralized bureaucracies.

Question: What would be the equivalent of Monet's Coal-Steel Pool?

Servan-Shreiber: The true "steel" of today is knowledge. So I suggested: shared laboratories. If you show you are not afraid, and don't want others to be afraid either, so they can come and work with us in the best scientific labs and universities. Imagine the shock waves for building up of confidence. Let us not be afraid either of the Japanese and so create partnerships with them. If they are better at manufacturing, let them come. There are so many applicants from Japan to Carnegie-Mellon's Graduate School of Industrial Administration that it is a great homage. It is a great homage to GSIA, and also the intelligence of the Japanese. They are not afraid of becoming students in management in America's universities. We should accept this partnership. They can learn from us and we can learn from them. We can create new industries in partnership with them, as is being done already in many places in the United States. So there is a way to start with the USSR, and also with Japan. The global suggestion is that we aim at expanding markets—all of us together, not trying to sell to each other all that we are manufacturing. This becomes more impossible every day. Take the global market of the Third World, 4 billion people: It cannot buy because they still cannot create wealth. We can build it up as a market if we agree to share knowledge. Then creation, and wealth, will start. It would be a new cycle of development in the world economy.

Question: What you are suggesting is an exchange between the elites of the two societies that really will not affect the rest of those societies. How do you get down to the whole population?

Servan-Shreiber: It would be the same, hopefully, around shared laboratories. If you see on television American and Russian and other scientists working regularly, freely, together, imagine the interest and the debates. Imagine these American minds working on new assumptions, new projects—and, of course, with reciprocity in the East. Things will happen. The buildup of confidence will bear fruit. Everyone will feel concerned.

Question: What do you see as the future of the European economic community?

Servan-Schreiber: We also have to live with ambiguity. The unity of Europe is fragile. Sometimes, Europe is going backward. Sometimes, forward. At this moment, we have reason to hope that we are going to be making steps forward. In my country, France, I see one conservative leader of intelligence on one side and, on the other, one left-wing leader. And they are working together, for Europe, even though they have been direct opponents in domestic politics all through their lives. I even see Mitterrand, who might be reelected as president, preparing to help Giscard d'Estaing to become president of a Confederate Europe—it is not even a secret. I also see the new generation in Europe being interested in the European unity and wanting to go forward.

Question: What are the political and economic consequences of European Union in 1992?

Servan-Schreiber: A stronger Europe, able to deal with America and Japan to irrigate the masses of the Third World with knowledge—the great adventure of youth. We must let our youth have the means to build on a vast ambition: not only to renew their own industrial countries (America, France, Germany), but to free the people of the Third World from economic slavery. Not by aid and charity but by sharing the knowledge that they shall master as well as we. In the two years that I have been working closely with Carnegie-Mellon, I have been in public discussions, on continent after continent, about computers, computer science, and computer literacy in Latin America, Africa, and Asia. The fascination of the young people is even higher than in our own countries. They want the knowledge and they want to create; it is a profound instinct. They have their own ambitions, their own visions in their own cultures. They don't want a new high-technology colonial bond.

Cooper: Monnet introduced a concept that redefined independence and freedom, by creating a system or process of interdependence. What is freedom if the countries are going to go to war every generation? What is freedom if the economy is going to be devastated and if they are going to be marred by deficits? What freedom do they have in ideology with an economy full of injustices and ending up with a totalitarian society? All of these facts need to be redefined on the basis of the concept of interdependence so that we can create a universe that is worthy of our ideals. This is what Monnet did—he attacked those older definitions and introduced new concepts.

QUANTITATIVE DIRECTIONS AND METHODOLOGY

4 AREA INTRODUCTION AND OVERVIEW

William W. Cooper

This part of *New Directions for Research in Creative and Innovative Management* deals with quantitative directions and methodology in research on creative and innovative management. Two of the chapters treat the potential effects of some of the newer developments in microcomputer technology on management and the other two deal with accounting, which, next to arithmetic, is the oldest of the science-based disciplines used in management. The chapters by Geis and by Kiesler are built around the hypothesis-testing approaches that are standard in the social and behavioral sciences. These chapters conform closely to what was planned for this section. The other two, by Ijiri and by Kaplan, are built around possibilities for new responses to problems and opportunities in accounting and do *not* conform to what was planned.

As part of the group responsible for planning the conference on which this volume is based, I am fascinated by the fact that the more creative papers are the two that do *not* conform to what was planned. Further, they are creative in very different ways.

We find something surprising in Ijiri's introduction of triple-entry bookkeeping as a new dimension in accounting. This is accomplished without losing contact with what was accomplished by double-entry accounting in the same way that the latter maintained contact with the preceding accomplishments of single-entry accounting. How was this change accomplished and why was it undertaken only now at this stage of history? It is not too much to say that Ijiri's introduc-

59

tion of triple-entry bookkeeping represents the first advance in accounting per se since Pacioli's introduction of the principles of double-entry bookkeeping nearly 500 years ago in the appendix to his treatise *Summa de Arithmetica, Geomatria Proportioni et Proportionalita*, which was published in Venice in 1494. Ijiri's extension from double- to triple-entry accounting also does something more. It opens the way for still further extensions into more general multi-dimensional developments in accounting that were previously concealed from view.

I asked Ijiri how he came to have these ideas, after prefacing my question with the statement that, like many others, I was as aware as he of the basic connections between balance sheets and income statements, connections that had been noted by many others since Pacioli. Ijiri's reply was that he was motivated by his dissatisfaction with "the state of multi-valued logic." Maybe this is explanatory to some, but not to me. I found his answer to my question illuminating only to the extent that it reminded me that Ijiri, in an unusual role for an accountant, had served as an abstract writer for the mathematical logic section of *Zentralblatt für Mathematik* for many years.

Using the precept "Go where the action is," Kaplan directs attention to business firms where creative and innovative responses to contemporary problems in accounting are occurring, where new developments in accounting are being produced—without benefit of continuing attention or even any evidence of awareness by members of the research arm of the accounting academy. As a member of the research arm and as the newly appointed director of publications of the American Accounting Association, I can attest to the impact of Kaplan's work, which is now being felt with increasing force and which may yet turn the body of accounting research in some of the new directions he is exploring. Kaplan's work is directed toward the issue of relevance as well as validity in scientific research and his chapter is in a long-standing tradition of research in which issues of relevance are raised by a combination of compiling and presenting evidence in a challenge–response mode. Kaplan's work will have its desired impact only when research attention is turned in this way from the present direction of accounting research. I would urge Kaplan to carry this one stage further moving from observation and interpretation to use of his own creative and innovative abilities to provide some of the new developments needed to deal with the problems he is studying and thereby add to the present state of accounting in the spirit of invention as well as discovery.

Kaplan and the companies he is studying are working with new uses of double-entry accounting while Ijiri is concerned with moving from double-entry to triple-entry accounting. Ijiri is concerned with the form and Kaplan with the content of accounting, but creativity and innovation are possible in either case. Kaplan is concerned with creative and innovative responses to problems in accounting while Ijiri has directed his energies to opening new opportunities for uses of accounting in all sorts of contexts.

I turn to yet another way of looking at this topic by directing attention to the common sources of both Ijiri and Kaplan in their experiences at Carnegie-Mellon University's Graduate School of Industrial Administration (GSIA). The nondepartmentalized character of GSIA made it possible to create and innovate from the start by replacing separate courses in accounting and statistics and other mathematical-quantitative techniques in management with one unified course called "Quantitative Controls," which Ijiri and Kaplan helped to develop into its present form. Here I can do no better than to quote from a recent *GSIA Magazine,*

> Quantitative Controls is a discipline in which quantitative methods are used to control resources and influence people in an organization or a society. Accounting is taught along with statistics and other mathematical techniques as a part of the overall framework of quantitative controls. While this dimension relies heavily on mathematics, the resource and people dimensions are also fully integrated. Accounting work at GSIA has [thus] been interdisiplinary from the beginning. The three dimensions of quantities, resources and people characterize the ways in which accounting interacts with other disciplines.

One might be tempted to say that given this context and the close interaction between research and teaching at GSIA, it would be almost impossible to *avoid* being creative and innovative in accounting. This would, however, recognize the creative and innovative environment provided by GSIA at the expense of Professors Ijiri and Kaplan, who have contributed so heavily to that environment.

This brings me to the chapters by George Geis and Sara Kiesler, which are both concerned with the issue of individual and organizational interactions in furthering or stifling creative and innovative activity. Both are also concerned with the opportunities provided by microcomputers, and related network and communication developments, for the study of such situations.

As a coplanner of the antecedent conference, I would find it awkward to criticize either Geis or Kiesler for adhering so well and faithfully to what was planned. After reading the Ijiri and Kaplan papers, however, I realize that we focused too much on the "outside-in" approach in which a scientist seeks to "understand" the phenomena being studied. In retrospect, I wish we had been prescient (or creative) enough to invite more activity by participants in exploring "inside-out" approaches to "control" as well as "understand" what is to be studied.

I can perhaps best illustrate what I am talking about by referring to the 1987 book by George Geis and Robert Kuhn titled *Micromanaging* and subtitled *Transforming Business Leaders with Personal Computers*. With disk included, it comes close to teaching or providing opportunities for managers to learn to be creative. It thus opens new opportunities for management development and thus for management education. It also opens opportunities for research into creativity that the authors should push forward soon.

An example of what I am suggesting is provided by the now classic *Leadership and Decision Making*, by Vroom and Yetton. This reference is appropriate to cite here because the approach it uses came out of Vroom's experiences at GSIA when he modified his original "psychology-only" approach to include decision trees, networks, and like devices that he had learned from his cross-discipline interactions with other GSIA members when he was on the faculty. Incorporating these devices in their studies, Vroom and Yetton were able to provide a method of self-diagnosis for managers that at the same time yielded data they needed to study and subsequently dislodge long-standing positions in psychology that disjointly categorized leadership styles of managers in classes such as authoritarian or democratic. The decision trees, networks, and like devices used by Vroom and Yetton made it possible to generate new data over a great variety of situations, showing that most managers (and especially successful ones) used styles that varied according to such factors as the nature of the decision, the desired form of action, the cooperation needed from others, and the information available at the time of decision. Armed with what they have already done, Geis and Kuhn should be able to go still further in the directions they have already opened in order to *improve* both management practice and management-science knowledge.

If we were to focus entirely on the individual psychology, individual decision maker approach of Vroom and Yetton, however, we would be victimized by discipline myopia that could cause us to miss important opportunities. As Kiesler notes, "Each social science tends to specialize at a particular level and to promulgate different concepts"; for example, industrial psychology works at the individual level, using concepts like "attitudes" and "satisfaction" whereas organization sociology works at the organizational levels and uses concepts like "hierarchy" and "social structure." Even more important, as Kiesler notes, "This specialization extends to research methods as well." I am hopeful that we can use the opportunities provided by studying new topics to develop new methodologies, too, so that we can begin to do what new methodologies nearly always do: 1) blur the boundaries between disciplines and 2) promote the development of new disciplines.

Just as in the comments I offered on the studies by Geis and Kuhn, I would also like to encourage Kiesler to go a step further and explore possible extensions along the lines indicated in the studies she cites as having already been undertaken with Timothy McGuire and Jan Siegel. In particular, I would like to see more inside-out invention instead of only outside-in discovery. The Kiesler-McGuire-Siegel observations on risk-taking behavior by groups as contrasted with risk-taking behavior by individuals in the group might then be extended to consider what organization designs might be used to induce desired types of risk-taking behavior. This in turn could be extended to studies of how to go about inducing organizations, even very old and staid ones, to become more creative and innovative.

Work like this has been undertaken by Rosabeth Kanter and reported in her book, *The Change Masters* (1983), but much more is needed and can surely be undertaken with benefit to science as well as to management. A case in point is the collaboration of Joyce Elam at The University of Texas with the MCC Corporation, a company charged by its supporting companies with responsibility for creating and innovating in microelectronics and computer technology, on the development of new group-workbench approaches to encourage creativity and productivity in new software development. As another opportunity for movement in these same directions, I point to the opportunity provided by this book. Contributors like George Kozmetsky are well known change masters who are interested in both research and practice. Don Gamache, Richard Harriman, and William C. Miller are all associated with organizations that specialize in inducing creativity and innovation in other organizations. After reading their chapters, one feels compelled to ask why none of them cite any of the social science research reported here; or vice versa, one might also ask why the activities cited by these practitioners are not cited in any of the social science research commonly reported. Can it be the case that this research and these activities are unknown to each other? If so, this book may have helped to plug a gap in current activities, but I hope that matters would not end there.

I still would like to see something more stimulated in the way of scientific research directed to improving rather than only studying these practices. This can produce good science as well as improved practice. All of this can be accomplished in a manner akin to the way medical science has long since learned to respond to the problems and opportunities in medical practice with benefit to both science and practice. See W.W. Cooper and S. Zeff, "Kinney's Design for Empirical Accounting Research," *The Accounting Review* for a discussion of the role of the teaching hospital as a means for ensuring relevance as well as testing the results of research in medical science. Maybe something akin to this kind of creative-innovative idea that flowed from the Flexner Report on medical education in the early part of this century could provide similar help in the areas of management education, practice, and research that we are considering here.

5 CREATIVITY AND ACCOUNTABILITY IN MANAGEMENT

Yuji Ijiri

RESEARCH IN CREATIVE AND INNOVATIVE MANAGEMENT

New directions for research in creative and innovative management can be explored in many fields related to management. Accounting is certainly one of them. It should be noted, however, that accounting serves management in two entirely different ways. One is that it helps the management with information useful for making decisions by themselves, while the other is that it helps those for whom the management is accountable with information useful in evaluating the performance of the management. The distinction between the two may be characterized by such terms as *accounting for planning* versus *accounting for control* or *decision-oriented accounting* versus *accountability-oriented accounting* (Ijiri 1975, 1983).

Some studies on creative and innovative management focus on the former type of accounting. Such studies include attempts to understand the characteristics of creative and innovative management by examining the kinds of information management requires for making decisions and comparing them with the information required by less creative, less innovative management. For example, in creative and innovative management, is information presented in a more timely manner, in more details, in greater accuracy, and in a manner more tailored to specific decisions? Although many observations and theories that may be derived from observations are likely to be applicable not just to accounting information but to information systems in management in general, the field does present important issues that benefit accountants in designing and implementing accounting systems for managerial decisions.

Studies on creative and innovative management may also focus on their interaction with the accountability-oriented side of accounting. Here, information on management is collected and reported not for the use by the management but for the use by their superiors or outside parties to whom the management is accountable. The underlying accountability relationship requires the "accountor," in this case the management, to report his or her activities and their consequences to the "accountee," in this case their superiors or outside parties such as the shareholders and creditors as well as the government (Cooper and Ijiri 1977, 1979).

Because information is collected and reported not for the use by the management but by someone else, the managers tend to view this part of accounting as a nuisance that prevents them from using their time more productively. The conflict between management and the accountability system may even be more severe in creative and innovative management.

Therefore, as one of the new directions for research in creative and innovative management, it seems worthwhile to examine the interaction between creativity and accountability in management. In terms of their relationship with accountability, creative management and innovative management seem to stand together. Therefore, the issue will be examined by contrasting creativity and accountability in management.

CREATIVITY

Creative activities must have two basic ingredients. First, creative activities must be novel, different from an established way of doing things (whether creativity is carried out by the humans or by the computers; see Newell 1984 and Simon 1986). Second, they must produce better results. Being not only different but better is essential to creative activities.

To recognize activities as being creative, there must be an established way of doing things and an established value by which to evaluate activities. These ways and values form an established means-ends hierarchy that becomes a benchmark for judging creativity. Activities may also be judged creative if they are in an area so new that there is no established way of doing things. This is because they, too, must achieve a better value without the help of an established way. Such activities are often observed in emerging industries such as software, genetic, and space engineering.

Creativity is distinguished from productivity in that productivity gets things done by following an established way, while creativity does so by not following the established way. Productivity means moving along the learning curve; creativity means a shift in the learning curve. They both try to achieve the same objective: to get a result that is better in terms of the established value. Experts and creative persons are not the same. Experts get to be experts by following an established way but doing it more efficiently through practice. Creative persons get to be what they are by not following the established way but by finding better ways to do things.

Creative activities must not only be different from an established way but also they must be better than those that follow the established way. This requirement presumes an established value by which to evaluate and compare the results. Creative activities challenge established ways but accept established values. Such activities are praised because, in spite of their tentative departure, they eventually join the accepted norm of the organization or the society. Otherwise they cannot be distinguished from destructive activities that are different and worse.

Creativity may be directed toward the lower end of the means-ends hierarchy, say, in management a fresh way of cutting costs on the factory floor, or toward its higher end, say a novel way of contributing to a social goal. It is important to identify what segment of the means-ends hierarchy the creative activities are directed toward. By knowing what such activities challenge and what they accept, they can be better understood and evaluated.

Creative activities may be directed toward finding a means that will improve the value directly above in the hierarchy of values. They may on the other hand be directed toward finding a path that will worsen several intermediate values but will improve a value at a higher level in the hierarchy. The latter, a roundabout method, is more difficult than the direct method because deliberate worsening of intermediate values require courage, persuasion, and understanding. Yet, if successful, it is the roundabout method that often leads to a significant improvement in the organization's value at the higher level by letting the organization move out of a local optimum.

If creative activities are viewed as achieving a better established value by means of an unestablished way, innovative activities may be viewed as implementing the heretofore unestablished way by a collection of established ways in the lower level of the means-ends hierarchy. The similarities between creative activities and innovative activities seem to outweigh their differences as far as their relationship with accountability is concerned. Hence, they will both be referred to as creative activities.

Risk is inherent in creative activities. Only a small fraction of creative attempts may succeed. But they must succeed from time to time in order to receive a continual support from the environment in which these activities take place. How long failures can be tolerated is an important characteristic of the environment in which creative activities take place.

Creative activities are intricately related to the environment. The environment supplies the problem in the form of an established hierarchy of means and ends and the resources by which creative persons may challenge the hierarchy. The environment accepts or rejects the new, unestablished ways developed by them. The creative process is in fact a process of action and reaction—creative persons on one side and the environment on the other. Creativity cannot be appreciated by focusing on one side only.

ACCOUNTABILITY

Accountability is the focal point of the intersection between creative persons and their environment if the creative person is held accountable for the use of the resources in the environment. Unfortunately in accountability, emphasis is normally on observing the established way, the standard operating procedures, the very same item from which the creative person tries to deviate. Accountability presumes that a better value is achieved by conforming to standards than by departing from them, especially for average persons. The creative person must challenge this presumption.

To illustrate the point, let us examine a simplified version of an old puzzle originally published by Henry E. Dudeney in 1903 (cited in Gardner 1961). Consider a room with square walls and long rectangular side walls, say, a room of dimensions 10 X 10 X 20 feet. Right in the middle of the square walls are two doors to the room facing each other. Directly underneath one of the doors is an ant nest. A food source of the ants lies at the top of the opposite wall, directly above the other door. What is the shortest path ants can take to reach the food? (See Figure 5-1.)

Average ants follow the shortest path, crawling straight up and straight across the room or crawl straight across the floor and then straight up (the solid lines in Figure 5-1.) More productive ants may crawl faster but by following the same paths. Perhaps ants deviating from the established paths are held accountable for not following them. In a heavily accountable ant colony, every ant may be forced to follow the paths. In a less accountable colony, deviations may be tolerated, accepted, or even encouraged.

Figure 5-1. Paths of Ordinary, Creative, and Uncreative Ants.

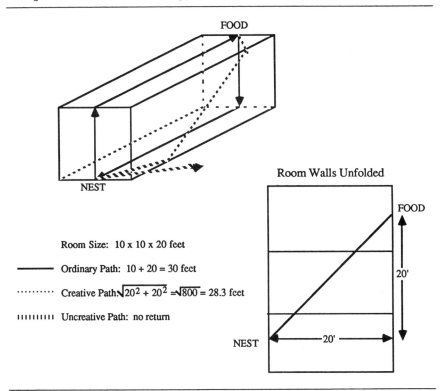

FOOD

NEST

Room Walls Unfolded

FOOD

20'

NEST

20'

Room Size: 10 x 10 x 20 feet

————— Ordinary Path: 10 + 20 = 30 feet

·········· Creative Path: $\sqrt{20^2 + 20^2} = \sqrt{800} = 28.3$ feet

ıııııııı Uncreative Path: no return

In the latter case, creative ants might challenge the established paths by crawling toward a side wall diagonally, climbing up the side wall diagonally, and then crawling the ceiling diagonally to the food source (the dotted line in Figure 5-1.) In fact, it can be proven that if the length of the room is half again longer than the width or the height of the room, there is always such a path that is shorter than the "established paths." Not being mathematically oriented, a creative ant must experiment to find the best path and then convince others that what was found was indeed better than the established ones. An even more difficult task for creative ants (and humans) is to convince others before a success is achieved that their exploration is worthwhile.

Creativity and accountability, therefore, share the same value to be attained (the shorter, the better) but differ in the means to attain it. If in fact it is demonstrated that a better value is achieved by departing from the established way, which is what creativity is trying

to demonstrate, then the established way should change and accountability should likewise adapt to the change. Furthermore, even before a better value is demonstrated, a deviation from the established
way should be made acceptable for the sake of making progress.

But this is not necessarily true in practice for two reasons. One is
that a change in the established way takes time. The other is that
creativity does not always produce what it is trying to produce.
Quite often it is difficult to distinguish between a creative ant on its
way to finding a successful path and an ant that is simply goofing off
in the name of creative exposition (the broken line in Figure 5-1).
Creativity is much more probabilistic than productivity when it
comes to generating successful results. Faced with frequent failures,
the accountability to follow the established paths may be enforced
even more rigorously.

The change element in creativity is indispensable in considering
its relationship with accountability. Once a creative attempt succeeds
in generating something that is better with respect to a given value,
the fact that its process deviated from the established way is often
tolerated or excused. The conflict between creativity and accountability occurs because the matter must be evaluated before a demon-
strable success has been achieved.

The conflict with accountability may be financial or nonfinancial
in nature. Creative attempts consume resources. If the person making
the attempt owns the resources, consuming them does not create nay
financial accountability. It is when someone else supplies the resources for creative attempts that the issues of financial accountability arise. In addition, creative attempts may conflict with nonfinancial accountability. This occurs when such attempts are made in
violation of nonfinancial rules and regulations that are intended to
protect other members of the organization or the society.

The main tools used in implementing the accountability relationship are records and reports. Accountability reports summarize the
activities of the accountor and are presented to the accountee. Accountability records detail the activities of the accountor. Such records are not normally presented to the accountee but serve as documents that support the reports in case questions are raised by the
accountee.

Because creative attempts must necessarily deviate from established ways and because creative attempts must, by nature, frequently fail, accountability records and reports on creative activities
should be different from those on productive activities in two major
aspects: namely, the former should focus on aggregates and on higher
goals.

First, accountability should be focused on aggregates, covering longer periods and diverse activities. It is perfectly sensible to report daily the performance of productive activities because they are mature activities for which standards can be established reliably. Quality control systems can be implemented daily or hourly or even on the basis of continuous time. Such a system does not make sense in regard to creative activities. Detailed time records on how researchers spent their time each day can stifle their motivation to experiment with new approaches.

On the other hand, accountability records and reports must exist in some form on creative activities as long as they are not toally exempt from accountability. The dilemma must be solved by emphasizing accountability on aggregates over time and across different types of activities. Implementing this concept in practice means that records on creative activities should be much less detailed than those on productive activities and provided much less frequently.

Second, accountability on creative activities should focus on higher values or goals in the means-ends hierarchy than accountability on productive activities. The latter may emphasize observance of established ways, because such observance has been proven over time as being a way to achieve the best value. Creative activities challenge this theory by deliberately deviating from established ways in search of better values. Accountability on creative activities, therefore, must recognize their contributions at a higher level of goals.

History of accounting shows a shift in emphasis from stewardship of individual assets to the achievement of better income for the business. It may be an established way of doing business not to waste any resource the business has. But sometimes a greater benefit can be brought to the business by temporarily wasting resources, by making what are investments.

The emphasis on income in current accounting in effect says the following. "You may use the individual resources of the business in any way you like, as long as their total value is increased." The increase in the total value of the wealth of the business is measured as income. There is much more room for creative activities under such a broad notion of an accountability than under the strict stewardship notion on individual resources.

Although accountability based on stewardship of individual resources, accountability can be brought to an even higher level of goals, namely accountability based on what can be called the "impulse measurement." This will be elaborated on below.

ACCOUNTABILITY ON MANAGERIAL IMPULSES

The basic bookkeeping framework in accounting shifted from a single-entry system to a double-entry system in the late fifteenth century in Italy. Under a single-entry system, accounts were kept for assets and liabilities, classified by the types of assets as well as by the identities of debtors and creditors. These accounts, which may be called "wealth accounts," were joined by "income accounts" when the double-entry system was introduced. The essential change in the bookkeeping framework was brought about by linking wealth accounts with income accounts so that every change in net wealth was accounted for by one or more income accounts (Ijiri 1982, 1986).

To state the matter more concisely, let $w(t)$ be the net wealth of an entity at time t and $w(t + 1)$ be the net wealth of the entity at time $t + 1$. Here, w's are the sum of amounts in various asset (positive) and liability (negative) accounts. Contributions by or distributions to owners of the entity can be handled separately, but for ease of explanation, assume that there were none between time t and $t + 1$, then, the difference between $w(t + 1)$ and $w(t)$ is income during the period, denoted by $\Delta w(t)$.

The expression $w(t + 1) - w(t) = \Delta w(t)$ seems to be merely a definitional identity. Nevertheless, it is in this expression that the true significance of the double-entry system is hidden. It expresses the equality of income computed from the beginning and ending balance sheets and income computed from the income statement for the period.

Income accounts are established to account for the reasons for changes in net wealth. The significance of the preceding expression is not that $\Delta w(t)$ is computed as the difference between $w(t + 1)$ and $w(t)$, which can certainly be done under a single-entry system, but that $w(t + 1) - w(t)$ is fully accounted for by a collection of income accounts that sum to the same amount.

This linkage between the explanandum (things that need to be explained) and the explanans (things that explain; see Hempel and Oppenheim 1948) is what was missing in the single-entry framework and what was brought about under the double-entry framework. Such notions as debtors and creditors, which are often associated with the double-entry system, existed long before the double-entry system was introduced.

The focus of accountability shifted gradually from safeguarding of individual resources to improving their aggregate value. The double-entry system and the resulting income statement allowed a further shift in the focus of accountability to reasons for the change in the aggregate value. Instead of merely ascertaining the amount of net change in wealth, income statement and accounts contained in them made it a routine part of discharging one's accountability to explain the net change in wealth by a set of explanatory accounts.

Having considered the change in accountability as a result of a change in the bookkeeping framework from a single-entry system, it is interesting to see what it might mean in the relationship between creativity and accountability in management for the bookkeeping system to move further, to a triple-entry system.

In triple-entry bookkeeping, we consider net wealth change as the explanandum and income accounts as the explanans. A logical extension of this relationship would be to make income as the explanandum whose change over time is to be explained by another set of accounts. There is, however, a problem that needs to be resolved. This is because income is a flow concept and as such requires two points in time to be specified for measurement, unlike wealth, which is a stock concept measurable at any single point in time.

For this reason it is convenient to introduce a new kind of accounting called "momentum accounting" as against conventional wealth accounting (Ijiri 1987, 1988). Unlike wealth accounting, which records and reports wealth (positive or negative) and account for their net change by income accounts, momentum accounting records and reports revenue and expense "momenta" of the business and account for their net change by what will be explained later as "impulse accounts."

Momentum accounts are similar to income accounts except that the measurement unit is all expressed in a time-rate of earnings such as dollars per month or per year. A momentum statement is therefore also similar to an income statement, except for the difference in the measurement unit. However, while income accounts show the amounts of flows between two points in time, momentum accounts show the amounts at a given point in time, the rate at which net wealth is changing at time t, denoted by dw/dt evaluated at time t or more concisely $\psi(t)$. Momentum accounts are, therefore, stock accounts, just as wealth accounts are, yet they are very similar to income accounts in terms of the classification scheme. The hybrid nature of momentum accounts allows us to develop momentum accounting under a double-entry framework and then use it as a basis for extending conventional wealth accounting to a third dimension as explained later.

Various revenue and expense momentums can be "inventoried" and listed on a statement similar to a balance sheet at a given point in time. Interest income or expenses are being earned or expended at a given rate; rental income flows in at a stable rate over time; salaries are also paid at a reasonably stable rate. There are, of course, revenue and expense items whose rates fluctuate significantly. Sales may vary from day to day, week to week, month to month. But their fluctuation may be reflected in momentum accounts under some basic accounting rules.

Comparable issues of measurement exist in conventional accounting. The market value of assets fluctuates daily just as sales fluctuate daily. In wealth accounting the need to revise book values daily is avoided by the so-called historical cost principle, under which the cost of acquiring the asset is used as the book value unless a specific event occurs that mandates a revision in the book value. Analogously, a "historical momentum principle" may be adopted, under which a conservation of momentum is assumed unless a specific event occurs that mandates a revision in its book value. Like depreciation in wealth accounting, dissipation of momentum may be introduced based on some formulas in areas where market assessment is difficult. First in, first out (FIFO) and last in, first out (LIFO) can also be applied in assigning pooled momentums between those that are given up and those that still remain in the business.

A momentum statement, once prepared under a given set of measurement rules, offers a basis for constructing a double-entry framework in a manner analogous to what happened historically in wealth accounting. If we let $\psi(t)$ be the net momenta at time t and $\psi(t + 1)$ be the net momentum at time $t + 1$, then the change in the net momentum, denoted by $\Delta\psi(t)$, is the explanadum, an item to be explained by a set of reasons, the explanans, that are considered to be the factors contributing to the change in net momentum. Accounts designed to explain the momentum change are called *impuse accounts*, borrowing from the momentum-impulse principle in mechanics. The double-entry system between momentum accounts and impulse accounts is an exact analogue of the same system in wealth accounting, the only difference being the unit of measurement. Table 5-1 compares statements from the two systems of accounting using a simple example (Ijiri 1988).

Before we examine the notion of accountability based on impulses, the relationship between the two systems of accounting, wealth accounting and momentum accounting, should be explained. Since momentum dw/dt is a derivative concept, it should equal the amount in the corresponding income account when the momentum is integrated over the entire period. On the other hand, when impulses are integrated over rhe same period, a new concept, called *actions*, arises that may be denoted as $\Delta^2 w(t)$.

This is where the benefit of the hybrid nature of momentum accounts is realized. Since momentum accounts are stock accounts just like wealth accounts, the double-entry bookkeeping framework can be used in momentum accounting on a daily basis. Yet, since momentum integrates to income, impulse integrated over time does not generate old income accounts but creates a new dimension in wealth accounting. (This may in fact be what is called *bisociation*, a term coined by Arthur Koestler, 1964, p. 35, in his discussion of the act of creation. I am indebted to Professor William W. Cooper for this insightful reference.)

As income accounts explain reasons for changes in net wealth, action accounts explain reasons for changes in net income. In this way the double-entry system ties w and Δw, and $\Delta^2 w$ altogether.

Table 5-2 describes the mathematical relationship among these concepts (Ijiri 1988). The table also shows that in addition to wealth accounting under a triple-entry system and momentum accounting under a double-entry system, it is also possible to consider *force accounting* under a single-entry system. This can be done without introducing any new concepts but simply by focusing on the rate of change in impulses.

Just as income accounts opened a whole new framework of accounting, impulse accounts bring accounting to an entirely new dimension. Let us now examine accountability on impulses. What it means and how it can relate with creativity can be understood more easily if we compare an income-based performance measurement and an impulse-based performance measurement.

An impulse-based performance measurement recognizes the fact that income may be earned by doing nothing, simply as a result of riding on the momentum created in previous years or by the previous management. It considers that the contribution of management should be based on what the management did to the momentum, more specifically what actions, impulses, or forces (incidentally, they are all the same concept differing only in measurement units) they exerted to improve the net momentum of the business during a given period.

Changes in net momentum may be attributed to introduction of a new product, an improvement in the production process, or new financing that saved interest cost. They may also be attributed to external factors over which management had no control such as changes in the rate of interest or inflation and other economic and market factors.

Accountability based on impulses therefore means that what needs to be accounted for is management actions to maintain and improve the net momentum of the business, not how much income it earned,

Table 5-1. The Conventional and Proposed Measurement Systems.

Conventional Measurements (Wealth w and Income Δw)		Proposed Measurements Momentum ψ and Impulse $\Delta\psi$		
(Balance Sheet) Wealth Statement as of 1/1/87		*(Balance Sheet)* Momentum Statement as of 1/1/87		
Cash	$ 150	Sales		$125/mo
Receivables	300	Cost of sales		-85/mo
Inventories	450	Operating expenses		-10/mo
Fixed assets	900	Depreciation		-5/mo
TOTAL ASSETS	$1,800	Interest expenses		-5/mo
Payables	-400	Income Taxes		-8/mo
Loans	-500	NET MOMENTUM		$ 12/mo
OWNERS' EQUITY	900			
Less: Owners' net contribution	600			
NET WEALTH	$ 300			
(Change Sheet) Income Statement for 1987		*(Change Sheet)* Impulse Statement for 1987		
Sales	$1,800	New product	(4/1/87)	$ 5/mo
Cost of sales	-1,200	Its tax effect	(4/1/87)	-2/mo
Operating expenses	-180	New product	(7/1/87)	10/mo
Depreciation	-60	Operating staff addition	(7/1/87)	-10/mo
Interest expenses	-60	Manufacturing cost cutting	(10/1/87)	5/mo
Income taxes	-120	Its tax effect	(10/1/87)	-2/mo
NET INCOME	$ 180	Net Impulses		$ 6/mo

(Balance Sheet) Wealth Statement as of 12/31/87		*(Balance Sheet)* Momentum Statement as of 12/31/87	
Cash	$ 200	Sales	$175/mo
Receivables	360	Cost of sales	-115/mo
Inventories	600	Operating expenses	-20/mo
Fixed assets	840	Depreciation	-5/mo
TOTAL ASSETS	$2,000	Interest expenses	-5/mo
Payables	-420	Income taxes	-12/mo
Loans	-500	NET MOMENTUM	$ 18/mo
OWNERS' EQUITY	$1,080		
Less: Owners' net contribution	600		
NET WEALTH	$ 480		

Table 5-2. Differential and Difference Relationships among Six Basic Measurements.

	Six Basic Measurements and Their Classifications		
Classification of Accounts by:	Conventional Wealth Measurements	Proposed Momentum Measurements	Possible Force Measurement
Types of wealth (assets, liabilities)	Wealth w		
Reasons for wealth change (revenues, expenses)	Income Δw	Momentum ψ	
Reasons for income or momentum change (actions resulting from impulses created by forces)	Action $\Delta^2 w$	Impulse $\Delta \psi$	Force $\ddot{w}$

Relationships among the Six Basic Measurements

Wealth: Income: Momentum: $w(t+1) - w(t) = \Delta w(t) = \int_{t}^{t+1} \psi(\tau)d\tau$

Momentum: Impulse: Force: $\psi(t+1) - \psi(t) = \Delta \psi(t) = \int_{t}^{t+1} \psi(\tau)d\tau$

Income: Action: Impulse: $\Delta w(t+1) - \Delta w(t) = \Delta^2 w(t) = \int_{t}^{t+1} \Delta \psi(\tau)d\tau$

which may be merely a realization of momentum with passage of time.

Benefits of creative activities quite often take the form of improved momentum that can last long into the future. Under the income-based accountability notion, gains from a new product, for example, may be credited to the responsible creative activity in that year but are soon forgotten and future gains are atrributed to future management.

In an impulse-based system, contributors to a increase in momentum have a claim on its future realization, just as contributors to a increase in wealth have a claim on its future distribution. The contributed momentum may be systematically dissipated in the future, just as contributed wealth may be reduced systematically through depreciation. But at least the contribution is recognized on a long-term basis. Its impact on net momentum is recorded in an impulse account identifying the contributor. The realization of the momentum increase as the momentum actually increases wealth by the passage of time is accumulated in an action account identifying the contributor.

As bookkeeping moved from single-entry to double-entry, the focus of accountability also shifted from safeguarding individual resources to a more abstract notion of performance based on income and its components. A move in bookkeeping toward a triple-entry system will enable a further shift in the focus of accountability to managerial forces exerted, managerial impulses created, and managerial actions taken to which wealth increases should be attributed.

Accountability need not and should not impede creativity in management; instead it should foster creative activities by properly accounting for their contributions in the aggregate, in the long run, and at a higher level of managerial goals. In order to accomplish this coordination between creativity and accountability in management; however, the framework of accounting must be brought to a higher dimension than the level at which it has been developed traditionally.

A final remark: It is interesting to note that this need to expand accounting at a higher dimension is itself an issue in research methodology. Just as developing new statistical techniques is a research methodology issue, constructing a measurement system in accounting that can handle higher level performance concepts is indeed a research methodology issue. But the construction of a new accounting system is not a purely methodology issue, because the system has to gain acceptance by the business community. The latter is, of course, a far more difficult and time-consuming matter than developing a measurement methodology itself.

REFERENCES

Cooper, William W., and Yuji Ijiri. 1977. "From Accounting to Accountability: Steps to Corporate Social Report." In N. Bedford (Ed.), *Accountancy in the 1980s: Some Issues.* New York: Arthur Young, pp. 105–57.

_____. 1979. "Accounting and Accountability Relations." In W.W. Cooper and Y. Ijiri (Eds.), *Eric Louis Kohler: Accounting's Man of Principles.* Reston, Va.: Reston, pp. 191–207.

Gardner, Martin. 1961. *The Second* Scientific American *Book of Mathematical Puzzles and Diversions.* New York: Simon and Schuster.

Hempel, Carl G., and Paul Oppenheim. 1948. "Studies in the Logic of Explanation." *Philosophy of Science:* 135–75.

Ijiri, Yuji. 1975. *Theory of Accounting Measurement.* Sarasota, Fla.: American Accounting Association.

_____. 1982. *Triple-Entry Bookkeeping and Income Momentum.* Sarasota, Fla.: American Accounting Association.

_____. 1983. "On the Accountability-Based Conceptual Framework of Accounting." *Journal of Accounting and Public Policy* (Summer): 75–81.

_____. 1986. "A Framework for Triple-Entry Bookkeeping." *Accounting Review* (October): 733–47.

_____. 1987. "Three Postulates of Momentum Accounting." *Accounting Horizons* (March): 25–34.

_____. 1988. "Momentum Accounting and Managerial Goals on Impulses." *Management Science* 34, no. 2 (February): 160–66.

_____, and James Noel. 1984. "A Reliability Comparison of the Measurements of Wealth, Income and Force." *Accounting Review* (January): 52–63.

Koestler, Arthur. 1964. *The Act of Creation*. London: Hutchinson.

Newell, Allen. 1984. "On Computers, Creativity, and Management." In A. Charnes and W.W. Cooper (Eds.), *Creative and Innovative Management: Essays in Honor of George Kozmetsky*. Cambridge, Mass.: Ballinger, pp. 213–37.

Simon, Herbert A. 1986. "What We Know about the Creative Process." In R.L. Kuhn (Ed.), *Frontiers in Creative and Innovative Management*. Cambridge, Mass.: Ballinger, pp. 3–20.

6 MICROCOMPUTER ENHANCEMENT OF CREATIVE MANAGEMENT

George T. Geis

Few would dispute the thesis that personal computers (PCs) have had a dramatic impact on managers and organizations. Terms such as spreadsheet, database, desktop publishing, RAM, and laser printer are now common office parlance. However, the issue of whether or not personal computers have enhanced (or have the potential to enhance) organizational creativity would undoubtedly engender more debate.

Some would argue that a machine with input and output as precise and literal as an army sergeant barking out cadence calls to marching troops has little chance of promoting innovative solutions to business problems. Others would counter that, despite their literality, PCs can be partners in creativity, although the dynamics of their influence on the process may be more subtle than direct. The latter could contend that personal computers often trigger creative managerial responses to organizational problems and opportunities.

This chapter suggests a model for studying the influence of personal computers on creativity both at the individual (managerial) level and at the work group (team) level. The effect of PCs on work groups appears to be of growing interest in light of current buzzwords and slogans (such as "connectivity" and "getting those who work together to work together") used by major hardware manufacturers to promote their new generation of equipment.

PERSONAL COMPUTER ANTECEDENTS
OF CREATIVITY

In this section, antecedents of managerial or group creativity commonly reported in organizational psychology (or other) literature are presented. These antecedents are not intended to be a list of necessary and sufficient conditions for creativity, but rather variables impacting creativity that in turn are hypothesized to be influenced by the use of personal computers in organizations.

Hypothesis 1: Personal computers promote a sense of playfulness. Introspective accounts written by highly creative people have commonly stressed the importance of intellectual playfulness, free from external control, in the creative process (Einstein 1949).

Playing with raw data, words, or ideas on a personal computer can be a personal brainstorming, with free-flow generation of concepts and testing of assumptions. Selecting, combining, and manipulating patterns and relationships in a private, yet high-feedback environment could be a powerful trigger for creative insight.

Evidence exists that creativity flourishes when one is motivated by intrinsic aspects of a task and not by external factors (Amabile 1983). Does the gamelike use of a PC promote an intrinsic desire to solve business problems and probe company opportunities?

Hypothesis 2: Personal computers provide relief from the routine, thus allowing more time for creative tasks. If PCs are used to routinize that which can be routinized, is more time and energy utilized for creative exploration? For example, in spreadsheet modeling does computational relief (left brain, to use the popular metaphor) promote more creative patterning and problem solving (right brain)?

On the other hand, does relief from one routine task simply lead to doing (or being assigned) another? Or is relief from the routine an end in itself with little if any additional time or energy being spent on creative tasks? For example, does one simply spend less time working?

Hypothesis 3: Personal computers provide rapid feedback for scenario building and problem solving. PCs enable the processing of assumptions more immediately, allowing one to see creative possibilities in a situation more rapidly and efficiently.

Does the use of PCs encourage action-oriented managers to behave more like scientists, testing hypotheses, running simulations and observing outcomes? Does the rapid feedback obtainable, from a PC model promote experimental insight?

The importance of rapid, repeated feedback in promoting insight was recently brought home to me. I had driven the same route to UCLA at least 200 times and had commonly experienced severe bottlenecks at two consecutive traffic lights along my established route. Beyond these two lights the main road curved through a glen. I noticed cars were merging onto this main road from a small side road. Yet it had never occurred to me that I could somehow access this side road prior to the bottleneck lights. After maneuvering this traffic maze the same way hundreds of times, it dawned on me that perhaps there was an alternative solution. So I backtracked on the side road and discovered that it completely bypassed the two bottleneck lights. Taking this alternative route would cut about five minutes off my travel time to work.

Would I have discovered the alternative route sooner had I been able to quickly simulate this travel experience? Does rapid, repeated feedback enable more experimentation thereby stimulating managerial or team creative problem solving? On the other hand, is there a danger that specific equations and relationships in quantitative models will be mechanically relied upon thereby actually hindering an innovative breakthrough?

Hypothesis 4: Personal computers build confidence by enabling risk to be contained. Highly creative ventures almost always require a calculated gamble (Simon 1985). There also appears to be a strong relationship between risk containment and risk taking. If managers or work groups feel they can get their hands around (understand and contain) risk, they will be more likely to take risk. Furthermore, if they feel the odds are somehow stacked in their favor (because of superior knowledge or analysis) they will be especially inclined to venture forth.

A personal computer can allow one to experiment cheaper and faster, examining alternatives using the most recent and relevant data. Doing sensitivity analysis for central outcomes can allow creative managers to understand the range of possible outcomes. Developing strategies for containing the downside can give one more confidence to go for the upside.

On the other hand, can the artificial (and all too easy) manipulation of model inputs and the attribution of a higher reality to model output give false confidence and promote false starts?

Hypothesis 5: Personal computers can support incubation of ideas. A number of highly creative people have stressed the importance of a period of incubation where conscious work on a problem ceases and after which an apparent flash of illumination occurs (Poincaré 1924). In a classic description of the creative process, Wallas (1926) listed the following sequence of steps: preparation, incubation, illumination, and verification (validity checking).

Personal computer databases have been used by managers to support the incubation process (Geis 1987). Systematic input and retrieval of data and ideas relating to problems and opportunities is facilitated. The incumbation (brewing) process commonly associated with creative illumination is allowed for, respected, and promoted.

Hypothesis 6: Personal computers promote graphic imagery. A keen sense of visual, auditory, or kinesthetic imagery is often related to creativity in a given domain (Feldman 1980). Thus Einstein reported seeing himself traveling alongside a beam of light, Mozart reported hearing in his imagination all musical parts at once, and Gretzky attributed his great success in hockey to his ability to picture and then skate to where the puck will be.

Personal computers enable one to recast data from tabular to graphic form. Creative presentations can be designed, featuring aspects of the data most important for conveying key issues or trends. Do graphic images also have the potential to trigger mental sparks, igniting creative insight that would be unrealized had the data been presented in absolute numerical or percentage form only?

Hypothesis 7: Personal computers promote information flow and availability. Domain-relevant skills are a major component of creative performance (Amabile 1983). This involves mastery of the domain in question and includes understanding the facts, methods or "chunks" (Simon 1985) necessary to solve problems in a given domain. Creative and innovative managers commonly display an obsession for raw data, keeping themselves in close contact with virtually all firsthand data reflecting competitors' positions and customers' needs. Personal computers can provide a manager or work group with efficient access to such data for ad hoc query or manipulation.

Furthermore, PCs can support the flow of information needed to solve problems and take advantage of opportunities. Innovative companies have been characterized as having freely flowing information channels, with requests for needed information requiring only minimal justification (Kanter 1983). Discovered problems are more likely to be solved creatively than presented ones (Getzels 1975). Truly "connected" work environments can facilitate discovery of organi-

zational problems and opportunities, thereby increasing the likelihood of innovation.

PERSONAL COMPUTER/USER
SYSTEM VARIABLES

Certain personal computer or user system variables are important in
promoting the antecedents of creativity discussed in the previous section. A number of these variables are suggested by Bjorn-Andersen,
Eason, and Robey (1986) in their study of the impact of computer
systems on managers.

Ease of use measures the degree of difficulty experienced by a
manager in attempting to use a PC or specific software packages.

Match with roles/tasks measures the fit between the services provided by the personal computer and needs arising out of managerial
roles and responsibilities.

User support measures the extent to which there is formal or informal organizational infrastructure to provide a manager with
needed hardware, software, data, systems, or training.

Connectivity measures the degree to which individuals can communicate with data sources or other individual or groups important
for organizational solving problems or scanning opportunities.

ORGANIZATIONAL CONTEXT

It is evident that the model components—PC or user system variables,
antecedents of creativity, and managerial or group creativity—all
occur within a given organizational context. Figure 6-1 provides a
model for studying the impact of personal computers on creativity,
including the central role played by a given organizational context.
The organizational context includes aspects such as the nature of
the business, organizational structure, leadership style, power structure, as well as other environmental variables important in determining the influence of personal computers on organization creativity.

FURTHER DIRECTIONS

The model presented in this chapter is intended to provide a conceptual framework for future studies investigating the role of personal computers in organizational creativity. The most productive
first line of inquiry will be to study innovative organizations that
heavily use personal computers and have strong expectations that

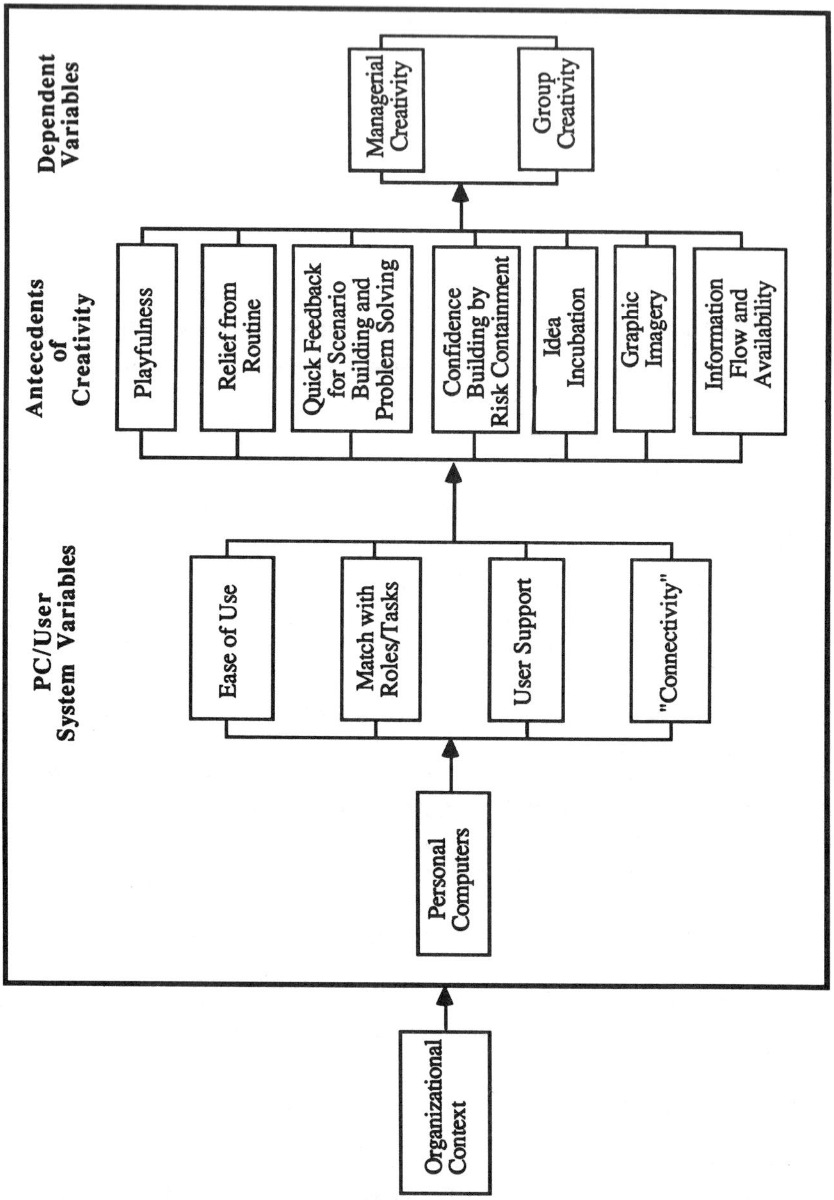

Figure 6-1. Model for the Impact of Personal Computers on Creativity.

creative responses to company problems and opportunities will emerge from multiple levels of the organization.

We should look first at organizations where what we are seeking is likely to be occurring. Later studies can investigate why the conjoining of personal computer and creativity may not be happening everywhere.

REFERENCES

Amabile, T.M. 1983. *The Social Psychology of Creativity.* New York: Springer-Verlag.

Bjorn-Andersen, N., K. Eason, and D. Robey. 1986. *Managing Computer Impact.* Norwood, N.J.: Ablex.

Einstein, A. 1949. Autobiography. In P. Schilpp, *Albert Einstein: Philosopher-Scientist.* Evanston, Ill.: Library of Living Philosophers.

Feldman, D. 1980. *Beyond Universal in Cognitive Development.* Norwood, N.J.: Ablex.

Geis, G. 1987. Databases for Managerial Creativity. *Ashton-Tate Quarterly* (April/May/June): 31-22.

_____ , and R. Kuhn. 1987. *Micromanaging: Transforming Business Leaders with Personal Computers.* Englewood Cliffs, N.J.: Prentice-Hall.

Getzels, J. 1975. "Problem-Finding and the Inventiveness of Solutions." *Journal of Creative Behavior 9*: 12-18.

Kanter, R. 1983. *The Change Masters.* New York: Simon and Schuster.

Poincaré, H. 1924. *The Foundations of Science.* New York: Science Press.

Simon, H. 1985. "What We Know about the Creative Process." In R. Kuhn (Ed.), *Frontiers in Creative and Innovative Management.* Cambridge, Mass.: Ballinger, 1985.

Wallas, G. 1926. *The Art of Thought.* New York: Harcourt, Brace.

7 TECHNOLOGY AND THE DEVELOPMENT OF CREATIVE ENVIRONMENTS

Sara Kiesler

A paradoxical goal of research on creativity in organizations is to discover predictable conditions, rational strategies, and learnable attributes that we typically associate with unpredictability, intuition, and unlearning. The paradox is resolved if we view creativity as one facet of organizational change, and organizational change as arising from mundane processes (March 1981). During the last several years, my colleagues and I have been studying one aspect of organizational change—the introduction of new computer technologies into organizations. We have studied how managers introduce technology and the effects of technology on the organization. In this chapter I discuss only one aspect of our work: the effects of computers and computer networks on organizational communication. Managers spend the majority of their time communicating: talking on the telephone, attending meetings, reviewing and writing reports, visiting and being visited. Because managers stand at the intersection of the organization and the environment, and of different subunits and jobs, communication is an important part of their role. Although the incentive structure, slack resources, and other noncommunication factors determine in large part whether managers act creatively, a communication environment that affords free exchange of data, ideas, and feelings is one which creative management is made more possible.

Computer communication technologies include some that facilitate intentional human-to-human interaction, such as computer mail, and some for linking humans with stored information, such as database information systems. Because these technologies transmit more information faster, they enable managers to work more efficiently.

But they have a social effect also: They deregulate the communication environment. The manager who has access to an information database and uses a spreadsheet can work out an almsot infinite number of questions, allowing fine-tuning and innovative decisionmaking that was simply not available a decade ago (Sandberg-Diment 1987). Even more revolutionary in this respect is the development of computer mail, about which most of our research is concerned. Computer mail not only changes access to information, but interaction itself.

The following excerpt is from a computer bulletin board that is used by a group of professionals for a variety of purposes, ranging from "Can you answer this technical question for me?" to "Someone with a green Toyota in parking lot has left his lights on." The message was inspired by rumors of a new organizational policy:

> I cannot resist fanning the flames of discontent. Under the kindest interpretation, the motives of the administration were to view the . . . issue as an adversary conflict, send up a trial balloon taking an extreme hardline stance. Then, any amount of yield gives a false appearance of conciliation . . . regardless of whether their next proposal is almost as ludicrous as the present one. It is also possible that the administration actually mean to ram through their policy with minimal notice or comment. . . . I propose we draft a statement.

This message illustrates "flaming," a phenomenon we observed when, five years ago, we began experiments on the effects of computer communication on interaction and decision making. We observed behavior that was quite unlike what we had been conditioned to expect from literature extolling the improvements possible from computerized Delphi techniques and command and control communication systems. However, our colleagues in computer science were not surprised; for years they had been using the word *flaming* to describe forceful or opinionated messages on the Arpanet. In our initial experiments, people who discussed decisions quietly and politely when they were face to face, were more extreme, impolite, intimate, excited, and in other ways uninhibited when they communicated using computer conferencing or computer mail. This led us to ask how interactions might change when computers and computer networks are ubiquitous in organizations, as seems likely.

THE REGULATED COMMUNICATION
ENVIRONMENT

As suggested by the aphorism, "Birds of a feather flock together," all communication is subject to regulation. Physical location, individuals' positions in time and space, affect the opportunity and obligation to communicate. Those who use the same water cooler tend to share the same gossip (Newcomb 1961; Festinger, Schachter, and Back 1950; Sykes, Larntz, and Fox 1976; Monge and Kirste 1980). Social location refers to individuals' positions in the social order, for example their place in the status hierarchy. Like physical location, social location affects the opportunity and obligation to communicate. People who occupy similar social locations tend to communicate with one another. People who belong to the same groups, particularly if those groups are cohesive, tend to communicate with one another. And people who have stature, who occupy valued social location, communicate more than people who do not. When people with prestige or authority are interacting in a group, their stature generalizes the group situation. They talk more often than others, speak more frankly, control the agenda, and have more influence; these behaviors are expected and lead to group satisfaction (Berger, Fisek, Norman, and Zelditch 1977; Weiner and Goodenough 1977; Strodtbeck and Lipinski 1985; Holtgraves 1986).

The organizations in which we live and work regulate communication. Within organizations, two kinds of variables affect physical and social location, organizational structure, and routines. Organizational structure consists of organizational units, chains of command, the status hierarchy, and job categories. These structural dimensions of organizations determine who works near whom, which people share similar attributes and perspectives, and which people occupy valued positions. People who work in the same department tend to do work that requires interaction, hence close contact leads to sharing of goals, interests, group identification, and personal attributes. Their proximity and similarity affords them opportunities and obligations to communicate (Monge and Kirste 1980). People who occupy high social positions (for example, high socioeconomic status, male gender) tend to communicate more than people who occupy low positions, and those in positions of authority or status communicate commands, desires, personal questions, self-congratulation, negative feedback, and bad news more freely than those in positions with lesser stature (Carli 1982; Stein and Heller 1979; Wood and Karten 1986). Routines such as copy distribution lists frequently reinforce these effects.

Perceptions of organizational structure and routines are conveyed through social context cues. It is not sufficient for people simply to hold different social positions for communication between them to be constrained; they must be aware of this difference between them. Static social context cues emanate from peoples' appearance and artifacts such as private offices and clocks. Dynamic cues emanate from verbal and nonverbal behavior, such as nodding approval and frowning with displeasure. When static and dynamic social context cues are strong and salient, they influence who communicates with whom and what is said. But when social context cues are weak, reminders of structure and norms become less salient, and peoples' behavior becomes less well regulated. Considerable research in laboratory settings shows that when social context cues are removed, individuals' perceptions of their location vis-à-vis social structure and norms are clouded. They feel anonymous, don't care about making a good appearance, and behave more extremely, more impulsively, and with less respect for social differences (Cottrell, Wack, Sekerak, and Rittle 1968; Diener, Fraser, Beaman, and Kelen 1976; Singer, Brush, and Lublin 1965).

TECHNOLOGY AS DEREGULATOR

In nature, the correlations of actual and perceived physical and social location are high. In a world without elevators, telephones, railroads, automobiles, and other technologies that reduce physical distance, a person's temporal and physical proximity with others tends to correlate highly with his perceptions of closeness, which in turn correlates with his group memberships—family, friends, work groups, neighborhood, tribe, Belonging to these groups correlates with other dimensions of similarity, such as race, age, income, political attitudes, and social status. Also, levels of certain attributes, such as age, income, and gender also command high status in the eyes of others.

All modern communication technologies attenuate these correlations to at least some degree. They do so, first, by separating the opportunity and obligation to communicate from the fact of physical propinquity. Before the telegraph was invented, foreign ambassadors were virtually their own bosses once they set sail from the home country. But the telegraph drastically reduced ambassadorial autonomy by providing a continuing connection between the ambassador and the officials he was meant to represent. In other words, physical presence of the officials was no lonter a requirement of interaction.

Computer communication contributes to the independence of actual physical location from effective proximity. A message can be sent across the world in minutes or seconds and lie in waiting for the recipient to read at his convenience. Time zones, office hours, and geography are irrelevant to the exchange. The president of a large firm in Pittsburgh tells us that he sent a request for a status report to Singapore at dinnertime and expected a reply by breakfast. For the president, his man in Singapore is right at hand, day *and* night.

The second way that communication technologies attenuate the correlations of actual and perceived physical and social location is by reducing social context cues that convey social structure and norms. As compared with face-to-face conversation, the telephone reduces dynamic and static cues by eliminating visual information about communicators. Letters and memoranda reduce static cues by imposing standardized format conventions; they eliminate dynamic cues altogether. The relatively low level of social context information in written communication can produce interaction that is less well regulated than face-to-face communication. Surveys printed on paper elicit more antisocial opinions and more personal revelations than do face-to-face interviews (Sudman and Bradburn 1974); written notes elicit more swings of opinion than face-to-face discussion (Festinger 1950, p. 278).

Computer communication attenuates social context cues even more than do other communication technologies. It is written communication, as letters are, and it also lacks static cues of physical proximity, organizational position, level of the hierarchy, departmental affiliation, race, age, appearance, and often even gender. Furthermore, a situational definition is missing. When using electronic communication across a network, one does not encounter reminders of the situation in which the communication is generated or received and interpreted, as one does using other communication technologies. Corporate memoranda, for example, are generated and read in some settings but not others, by some people and not others, and are about some topics but not others. The absence of situational cues is important in electronic communication because electronic communication can be used to exchange so many different kinds of information, from cafeteria menus to corporate strategy documents to love notes, all of which are conveyed within the same message format. People make announcements and suggestions using electronic mail, just as they do paper memos, but people also carry on conversations, discussions, and exchanges of affection or hostility using electronic mail, just as they do in face-to-face conversation.

ORGANIZATIONAL RESEARCH STRATEGY

Our strategy for studying the impact of computer communication in organizations is illustrated by a study of electronic mail that I carried out with Lee Sproull (1986) in a Fortune 500 electronics manufacturing company we call "PHC." The primary purpose of this study was to examine the external validity (the generality) of the idea of technological deregulation. Would we be able to observe overcoming

Figure 7-1.   Distribution List Message I: PHC.

Date: 12-April-83 10:47 PST (Tuesday)

From: Sam Jones

Subject: ViscalcInterest

To: OSBU.es

Reply to: Sam

This is to announce the start of a new distribution list.
VisicalcInterest.es and to solicit your input. We want to
design a spreadsheet-like capability in [new product under
development]. If you would like to participate in the
discussion, let us know and we'll add you to the list.

One of the biggest functional gaps that now exists in
[new product] (compared to other personal computers)
is an adequate computational facility such as Visicalc.
How can we best respond to this demand? We would
like to advance the state of the spreadsheet art, rather than
just imitate what already exists. We welcome your ideas.

---

of physical and social location in the computer communications of
employees? To do so convincingly, we would have to gather more
than just self-reports of employees; this study represents the first
time actual computer messages have been analyzed. A representative
organizational sample of 96 people saved their electronic mail for
three days prior to being interviewed. We then evaluated the characteristics of 1,248 messages that we collected (as many as 15 from
each person). Based on the idea that using a computer to communicate reduces constraints of physical and social location, we measured
boundary spanning and uninhibited behavior in the messages.

The evidence of boundary spanning was marked. The employees in
this firm received 26 messages a day. There were no differences due
to gender and hierarchy—an equalization of participation that is a
absent or rare in other communication modes. Fifty-two percent of

Figure 7-2. Distribution List Message II: PHC.

Date: 5 May 1983 9:06 am PDT (Thursday)

From: [technical professional]

Subject: Damage to my Scooter

To: Bldg35 + .es

cc: Motorcyclists + .es

Yesterday, some nameless obscenity moved my scooter.
Since the handle bars were locked, this involved dragging
my Vespa sideways. This was done with enough vigor to
break off one of the rubber molding strips protecting the
foot platform.

Whoever you are, LEAVE MY MACHINE ALONE.
LEAVE MY MACHINE ALONE LEAVE MY MACHINE
ALONE. I AM ANGRY AT THE M*****FER WHO
F***KED WITH MY MACHINE.

This is my basic transportation. I don't own a car.
If you destroy my machine, you deprive me of my mobility.
If I discover anyone tampering with my scooter again, I
will cheerfully re-arrange your face w/the "generic blunt
object" I carry with me.

Note: This message was sent to everyone who worked in Building 35, about 300 people
(including the president of the division).

---

the messages were from unknown senders at unknown sites. Many of
the messages consisted of distribution list group mail; a phenomenon
that electronic mail created was an expanded, routinized way to dis-
seminate information. Figure 7-1 shows a message from a technical
professional who had an idea for developing a new product. Within
two days, he received 25 messages from 22 people in five cities. He
had never met most of these people, yet now they would provide
feedback and help or hindrance on his product idea. This is one example of deregulation of physical location. At PHC, 4 percent of the
message traffic was nonwork communication. Many of the messages
exhibited flaming and upward communication. Figure 7-2 illustrates
flaming and deregulation of social location.

It was impractical but unfortunate that in the PHC study we did not compare electronic mail with paper memos, telephone discussions, and face-to-face meetings. Even had we done so, we would not have been able to rule out self-selection effects (maybe employees who send messages to bosses are a special breed). We have conducted a series of experiments, however, that permit comparisons across technologies and also enable us to rule out self-selection effects.

EXPERIMENTAL RESEARCH STRATEGY

Our experimental research falls into two categories: 1) comparisons of computer-administered surveys with paper-administered surveys, and 2) comparisons of computer-mediated decision making with face-to-face decision making. Our choices of these research settings reflects the fact that we are not primarily interested in technology per se. (If technology had been our primary interest, we would have compared computer communication with telephoning, writing on paper, and so on.) Instead, our research focuses on the potential effects of computer technologies as they may actually be used in organizations. Further, we view technological interventions as a way to study organizational processes themselves.

Our research on the "electronic survey" was stimulated by our learning about attempts of organizations to administer on-line questionnaires. Early reports indicated that responses to a computer survey or interview differed from responses to interviewers or paper questionnaires (Greist, Klein, and Erdman 1976). We and others have confirmed these reports experimentally. The computer survey does produce different responses than the paper and pencil survey (Sproull and Kiesler 1986; Kiesler and Sproull 1986; Waterton and Duffy 1984). This research, some of which is summarized in Table 7–1, shows that responses to a computer are more extreme, more revealing, and more self-centered than responses to a paper questionnaire. Although we have not tested the mediating process directly, we explain these results as a consequence of reduction of social context cues in electronic communication—where not even the respondent's own handwriting provides distinctive situational cues.

Our experiments on group decision making have employed a strategy of comparing computer communication effects as against known effects of face-to-face interaction. For example, uninhibited behavior increases when the communication situation is anonymous or impersonal (Williams 1977; Diener, Fraser, Beaman, and Kelen 1976). Equality of communication increases when status and other social cues are dampened. Shifts of decisions toward the extreme advocated initially by others occurs when people discuss decisions in a group.

Table 7-1.   Reduced Social Context Cues in the Electronic Survey:
Response Effects.

	Paper	Computer
Extreme opinions[a]	27%	73%
Positive remarks[b]	38%	26%
Personal remarks[b]	2.8	4.9
Socially desirable self-ratings[b]	72%	62%
Alcohol use reported[c]	19.1	26
Drug use reported[d]	3%	14%

a. From Sproull 1985.
b. From Kiesler and Sproull 1986.
c. From Waterton and Duffy 1984.
d. From Hartman, Sproull, and Kiesler, unpublished data.

From our "deregulation" hypothesis, we predicted that communicating by computer as compared to communicating face to face would increase uninhibited behavior, equality of participation, and decision shifts. Our experiments have supported these predictions.

In an experiment conducted by Timothy McGuire, Jane Siegel, and me (1987), university administrators and corporate managers were asked to make investment decisions both as individuals and as members of a three-person group. The executives made half the decisions face to face and half using a computer-mediated communication program that allows people to talk simultaneously, each using one "window" on the computer screen. In this experiment the choice we gave the groups was of a type that has been studied extensively by psychologists Amos Tversky and Daniel Kahneman (1981): Suppose you have a choice between a safe investment that is guaranteed to return $20,000 over two years and an investment that has a 50 percent chance of returning $40,000 and a 50 percent chance of returning nothing. Which would you choose? In general, most people are risk aversive and choose the safe $20,000.

In our experiment, groups that met face to face were risk averse for gain choices and risk seeking for loss choices. In fact, they were much more biased in this direction than they were as individuals and more than individual managers had been in previous research. When the same group met using the computer, however, they were slightly risk seeking no matter what the choice was. Yet they were every bit as confident of these decisions as they were of the more conventional decisions they made face to face. We performed extensive analyses of the group discussions. These indicated that the group decisions could be predicted in large part by what was proposed by the first manager in the group to offer a proposal. However, in the face-to-face conditions, the initiating manager proposed a "conventional" solution whereas in the computer communication condition, the initiating manager proposed an unconventional solution. A number of differences between the face-to-face and computer communication situations might account for this effect. Discussions in the computer communication condition were shorter and less elaborate and tended to get to the point (managers made proposals without full discussion of their merits). Discussions in the communication condition were also somewhat more equal and more uninhibited. These findings support our thinking that computer communication is deregulating. We are now conducting further research on the different attributes of computer communication that might account more exactly for the effects we observed.

NEW TECHNOLOGY AND CREATIVE MANAGEMENT

If computer technology has a deregulating impact on the communication environment of managers, their interactions will change in three ways. First, managers will have new information sources, both databases and people. Their acquaintance networks, what has been called their "weak ties," will expand. Computer distribution lists and bulletin boards will offer the possibility of broadcasting throughout the organization: "What do you think of this idea?" "Does anyone know an expert car mechanic in Pittsburgh?" "So-and-so is visiting from Australia. Would you like to meet him?" Second, managers will give and receive new kinds of information and find out things they would not have discovered otherwise: "Unit X is about to release a new product." "Did you hear the rumor about the takeover of Company A?" "I have just solved the infamous valve problem and wish to let everybody know." "Third, managers will use different information exchange procedures, and some information gathering that was done informally will be routine. The computer laboratory notebook is an example of managers' having access to information routinely that they used to receive only when they took the trouble to visit their laboratories.

What would make these changes really significant is if they were to lead to kinds of social arrangements and social structures that promote creativity: diversified networks, long-distance project groups, virtual neighborhoods, and desktop information systems. However, the development of creative environments from applications of technology will depend on management decisions and policy. It is not technology but management that in large part determines how a technology will be used. Should the policies be to restrict access to computers, to leave computing to specialists, or to implement a monolithic "system," the result will be a constriction of the interaction environment. By contrast, should the policies favor open access, distributed computer skill, all-channel networks, and decentralized information storage, creativity will be stimulated.

Authorities and elites frequently try to maintain control over use of new technologies and to implement policies that promote conformity. The Egyptian scribes tried to keep writing for themselves. The initial users of telephones were businessmen who envisioned telephones as an instrument of authority. Doubtless computer technologies, in some organizations, will be used mainly to routinize interactions, to monitor performance, and to control access to data. Proponents of centralized systems will contend that employees waste time when they can interact freely with people and data. They will develop or buy software designed for broadcasting rather than conversation, for carrying out "company business" instead of "irrelevant experiments." Should this bottom-line ideology determine the introduction of computer technology, the consequence will be less rather than more creative environments in organizations.

Our research shows, however, that computer technology as such provides the wherewithal to transfer control to individuals and nonelites, and to allow more democratic or laissez-faire social arrangements. Some organizations have experienced these effects inadvertently. Managers acquired personal computers, and suddenly they were free to explore information unconstrained; they acquired access to a network and interacted with whomever they chose. In high-technology firms and universities, the culture has encouraged wide access to computing and few rules for its use. Whether the same will be true in other kinds of organizations is an open question.

IMPLICATIONS FOR FUTURE RESEARCH

Our experience suggests that research on creative management must include research on the organizational processes and settings that foster creativity. Since the dependent variables of interest exist both at the individual level (number of patents; introduction of new products), the ideal approach is to work at different levels all at once. However, the processes and setting lead to individual behavior are not generally examined in the same way as the processes and settings that lead to organizational effects. Each social science tends to specialize at a particular level and to promulgate different concepts. For example, industrial psychology works at the individual level, using concepts like attitudes and satisfaction, whereas organizational sociology works at the level of the organization and uses concepts like hierarchy. Specialization extends to research methods as well.

Difficulties notwithstanding, there are stong conceptual advantages to research that simultaneously explores behavior of individuals and organizations in both preexisting and experimental settings. A major conceptual advantage is to further development of construct validity (Cronbach and Meehl 1955). A given variable, such as creativity, may refer to both an individual-level construct and an organizational-level construct. By working at both levels we address the similarity and differences of process at both levels. For each level, we can ask three questions: Do both individuals and organizations vary on this construct? Are the patterns of covariation between process or environmental forces and this construct the same at both levels? Are the causal connections the same for individuals and organizations?

Many of the effects relevant to creative management refer to both the individual level and to innovation at the organizational level. Flexibility might be measured by nonconformity at the individual level and by adaptability at the organizational level. In practice, organizational researchers often use the same measure to examine constructs at both levels. For instance, a survey question, "How satisfied are you with your ability to respond to new opportunities?" might be used in studies of individual flexibility and of organizational adaptability. In reality, processes at the two levels might be very different. For example, an organization's age tends to be negatively correlated with individual flexibility but positively correlated with organizational adaptability. Simultaneous research on different levels would help to disentangle these conundrums.

REFERENCES

Berger, J., M.H. Fisek, R.Z. Norman, and M. Zelditch. 1977. *Status Characteristics and Social Interaction.* New York: Elsevier.

Carli, L. 1982. "Are Women More Social and More Task-oriented? A Meta-analytic Review of Sex Differences in Group Interaction, Reward Allocation, Coalition Formation, and Cooperation in the Prisoner's Dilemma Game." Ph.D. diss., University of Massachusetts.

Cottrell, N.B., D.L. Wack, G.J. Sekerak, and R.H. Rittle. 1968. "Social Facilitation of Dominant Responses by the Presence of an Audience and Mere Presence of Others." *Journal of Personality and Social Psychology 9*, 245–50.

Cronbach, L.J., and P.E. Meehl. 1955. "Construct Validity in Psychological Tests." *Psychological Bulletin 52*: 281–302.

Diener, E., S. Fraser, A. Beaman, and R. Kelen. 1976. "Effects of Deindividuating Variables on Stealing by Halloween Trick-or-Treaters." *Journal of Personality and Social Psychology 33* (Bibliography B): 178–83.

Festinger, L. 1950. "Informal Social Communication." *Psychological Review* 57: 271-82.

Greist, J.H., M.H. Klein, and H.P. Erdman. 1976. "Routine On-Line: Psychiatric Diagnosis by Computer." *American Journal of Psychiatry 12*: 1405-8.

Holtgraves, T. 1986. "Language Structure in Social Interaction: Perceptions of Direct and Indirect Speech Acts and Interactants Who Use Them." *Journal of Personality and Social Psychology 51*: 305-14.

Kiesler, S., and L. Sproull. 1986. "Response Effects in the Electronic Survey." *Public Opinion Quarterly 50*: 401-13.

March, J.G. 1981. "Footnotes to Organizational Change." *Administrative Science Quarterly 26*: 563-77.

McGuire, T.W., S. Kiesler, and J. Siegel. 1987. "Group and Computer-Mediated Discussion Effects in Risk Decision Making." *Journal of Personality and Social Psychology 52*, no. 5 (May): 917-29.

Monge, P.R., K.K. Kirste. 1980. "Measuring Proximity in Human Organizations." *Social Psychology Quarterly 43*: 110-15.

Newcomb, T.R. 1961. *The Acquaintance Process.* New York: Holt, Rinehart, and Winston.

Sandberg-Diment, E. 1987. "Taking the Personal out of PC." *New York Times*, May 17, 1987, p. 14.

Singer, J., C. Brush, and S. Lublin. 1965. "Some Aspects of Deindividualation: Identification and Conformity." *Journal of Experimental Social Psychology 1*: 365-568.

Sproull, L., and S. Kiesler. 1986. "Reducing Social Context Cues: Electronic Mail in Organizational Communication." *Management Science 32*, no. 11 (November): 1492-1512.

Sproull, L., D. Zubrow, and S. Keisler. 1985. "Socialization to Computing in College." Working Paper of the Committee on Social Science Research in Computing, Department of Social and Decision Sciences, Carnegie-Mellon University, Pittsburgh, Pa.

Stein, R.T., and T. Heller. 1979. "An Empirical Analysis of the Correlations between Leadership Status and Participation Rates Reported in the Literature." *Journal of Personality and Social Psychology 37*: 1993-2002.

Strodtbeck, F.L., and R.M. Lipinski. 1985. "Becoming First among Equals: Moral Considerations in Jury Foreman Selection." *Journal of Personality and Social Psychology 49*(4): 927-36.

Sudman, S., and N.M. Bradburn. 1974. *Response Effects in Surveys.* Chicago, ill.: Aldine.

Sykes, R.E., K. Larntz, and J.C. Fox. 1976. "Proximity and Similarity Effects on Frequency of Interaction in a Class of Naval Recruits." *Sociometry 39*: 263-69.

Tversky, A., and D. Kahneman. 1981. "The Framing of Decisions and the Psychology of Choice." *Science 211*: 453-58.

Waterton, J.J., and J.C. Duffy. 1984. "A Comparison of Computer Interviewing Techniques and Traditional Methods in the Collection of Self-report Alcohol Consumption Data in a Field Survey." *Institutional Statistical Review 52*: 173-82.

Weiner, S.L., and D.R. Goodenough. 1977. "A Move Toward a Psychology of Conversation." In R.O. Freedle (Ed.), *Discourse Production and Comprehension*. Norwood, N.J.: Ablex, pp. 213-25.

Williams, E. 1977. "Experimental Comparisons of Face-to-Face and Mediated Communication: A Review." *Psychological Bulletin 8*: 963-76.

Wood, W., and S.J. Karten. 1986. "Sex Differences in Interaction Style as a Product of Perceived Sex Differences in Competence." *Journal of Personality and Social Psychology 50*: 341-47.

8 ORIGINALITY IN MANAGEMENT ACCOUNTING SYSTEMS
Field Studies of the Processes

Robert S. Kaplan

Creativity and accounting is a combination that most reasonable people would believe is either illegal or oxymoronic. Nevertheless, I am pleased to report that the opportunity for creativity and innovation in management accounting—the field dealing with the production and consumption of information internal to the firm—is at a level not seen for almost a century. Before describing this opportunity, and the methods by which creativity and innovation in management account can be studied, I will set the stage by providing the historical context for the radical changes now underway.

In its early days (1825-1905), management accounting innovation paralleled the innovation in the organization of economic activity. (The historical developments are documented in Chandler 1977 and Johnson and Kaplan 1987.) As organizations became more hierarchical-by internalizing activities that formerly had been conducted through market transactions—and more dispersed—through the expansion of activities made possible by the railroad, telegraph, and telephone, the demand arose for information about the efficiency of internally managed activities. Summary activity measures, such as cost per pound, cost per ton mile, and inventory turn ratios, were developed to motivate and evaluate the efficiency of internal operations.

Further demands for management accounting information arose as firms began to produce multiple types of products and product lines within the same organization. Product diversity created a demand for information on product costs to aid pricing decisions and to measure profitability across product lines. Already in existence by 1910 were sophisticated systems for measuring the performance of decentralized units (especially the return on investment (ROI) criterion developed at the Du Pont Corporation) and for measuring product costs through intensive study of production processes (the standard cost system, an outgrowth of the scientific management movement).

This flurry of creative management accounting activity seemed to stop in the early part of twentieth century. While individual companies made significant changes in their management accounting systems throughout the twentieth century, these changes usually just succeeded in bringing them to the level of sophistication of the 1925 systems at Du Pont and General Motors. Using the terminology established in earlier books in this series, companies may have been *innovative* during the past sixty years, but *creativity* mostly stopped with the new management accounting schemes devised by the engineers of the scientific management movement, and the engineers who became the financial and chief executives of the early twentieth-century Du Pont and General Motors corporations.

Only in the past several years has the virtual cessation of creative activity in management accounting been noted. (Kaplan 1984; Johnson and Kaplan 1987.) More intensive study by accounting historians will be needed, first, to confirm the existence of this cessation, and, second, if confirmed, to study in detail the reasons why it occurred. At this time, we can offer only informed speculation and tentative hypotheses, and though the focus of the book is to study creative and innovative management, I believe it is appropriate to learn more about the conditions that fostered a sixty-year void in creative and innovative activity in an important managerial function.

FACTORS INHIBITING CREATIVITY
IN ACCOUNTING

The cessation of management accounting creativity occurred at about the same time as the public accounting profession became recognized and regulated as the primary auditors of financial statements for external constituencies.[1] In principle, the separate accounting information demands by both internal and external constituencies could have been handled independently from each other. In practice, however, several forces combined to coalesce the two separate demands for accounting information into a single system.

First, both internal and external systems had apparently similar interests in cost information. I have already noted the internal (management accounting) demand for information on performance measurement and for product costs. The external, financial accounting demand arose from the need to apportion periodic production costs between two financial statement accounts: cost of goods sold (on the income statement) and inventory (on the balance sheet). The latter demand required a system to allocate factory overhead when measuring product costs. Thus two different functions, measuring product costs for internal managerial purposes and valuing inventory for financial statement purposes, could apparently be met with a single system. Given the high cost of collecting, processing, and reporting information in the early decades of this century, firms decided to use, for internal purposes, the same product cost information that had to be produced to value inventories for external reporting.

With only one system for both internal and external reporting, and with external reports having to satisfy a host of regulatory principles for consistency, conformance, objectivity, and auditability, the opportunity for creativity and experimentation in the measurement of product costs became severely limited. The opportunity for creativity and innovation was further constrained, until the early 1980s, by the severe limitations imposed by information processing technology. Embedding cost accounting systems into computer code, a trend that started in the mid-1960s, produced systems even more inflexible than the manual ones they replaced. Only with the advent of inexpensive microcomputers coupled to powerful spreadsheet languages has the technology for creativity and innovation in management accounting become available.

The previously diverse fields of financial and management accounting became linked together early in the twentieth century by a specialty field known as cost accounting. Cost accounting provides the rules and procedures by which all production costs, direct and indirect, become attached to products so that external reporting requirements may be satisfied. Understood in this context, it is clear that cost accounting is a subset of financial accounting and in reality has little to do with management accounting.[2] But in practice, management accounting did not develop as a separate field. It became an offshoot of cost accounting. Accounting students first learn how to allocate costs for inventory valuation purposes. Then they learn how to undo the allocations in order to produce data for managerial decisions and control.

The primacy of cost accounting became further institutionalized when problems of cost allocation were included on the certified public accountant's examination. The demand for straightforward, easy-to-grade questions further relegated product costing to detailed procedures for cost allocation. Since much accounting education is designed to prepare students for the CPA examination, the opportunities for creativity and innovation in management accounting education also diminished.

During the past sixty-five years, many academic economists and accountants noted that the product costs produced by the cost accounting system to value inventories were irrelevant for managerial decisions and control. Concepts like direct costs, contribution margin, breakeven analysis, and flexible budgeting became part of the teaching and practice of management accounting. But these concepts were relatively small perturbations of the basic cost accounting system, to guide short-term incremental product decisions.

Given the creativity-inhibiting effect from satisfying inventory valuation demands for external statements, one might have expected management accounting creativity and innovation to arise in organizations that did not have to value inventories. Service organizations, which deliver a great diversity of products, should have been intensely concerned with the measurement of product costs. With no inventories to value, service organizations would not have been constrained by accounting and auditing principles when designing procedures to measure products costs. Why then did creativity and innovation not come from this large and important sector?

The lack of interest in measuring the product costs of service companies can be explained by the extensive regulations of the activities of complex service organizations until the late 1970s. The regulations frequently dictated the method of reporting in order that prices could be set, by regulators, to allow a "fair" rate of return. Thus three-letter agencies such as the ICC and TCC, established complex reporting schemes that determined the chart of accounts and allocation procedures for regulated service companies. Prices were set to permit cost recovery across the entire product line of a service company, with little concern about the profit or loss on individual products. Thus, the lack of pricing freedom and protection from price competition within and outside the industry produced an environment where there was little demand for accurate product costs in financial institutions (banks, thrifts, insurance firms, stock brokerages), transportation companies (railroads, airlines, trucking firms, bus lines), health services (hospitals, clinics), and telecommunications companies.

As the practice of accounting, for both manufacturing and service organizations, became dominated by the regulatory demands for external reporting—to investors, creditors, regulators, and tax authorities—the teaching of accounting came to emphasize highly detailed rules and procedures. Most creative and innovative undergraduate students do not find themselves highly stimulated by their first accounting course (or the second, in the unlikely event they get that far). Conversely, students who enjoy a well-defined, tightly constrained subject, where there is little premium for creativity, are likely to find that financial and cost accounting courses meet their preferences. Thus, the field may be systematically self-selecting among the least creative and innovative segment of the student population.

CONDITIONS FOR CHANGE

What has occurred in the environment such that creativity and innovation in management accounting is now not only possible but actually occurring? Three forces have emerged during the past decade that have stimulated the great renaissance of interest in management accounting. First, U.S. manufacturing environment has changed. Simplistic overhead allocation schemes, based on direct labor, gave increasingly inaccurate product costs. Also, with aggressive overseas competitors selling into the traditional markets for U.S. manufacturers, the adverse consequences from misestimating product costs or not promoting manufacturing efficiencies rose considerably.

For service companies, deregulation brought new freedom for pricing, for product innovation, and for entry by new types of competitors. Products whose profitability had previously been assured by regulatory actions and restrictions suddenly had to be costed accurately and priced competitively. The information technology revolution that made available low-cost powerful computers and software for collecting, processing, and reporting information provided the third stimulus for change.

Given the previous somnolence in the field, it is remarkable how rapid and widespread has been the recognition for major changes. Conferences titled "Cost Accounting for the 1990s" or "Cost Accounting in Advanced Manufacturing Environments" are oversubscribed and virtually no dissent is heard to the speakers' proposals or examples of new systems.

HOW TO STUDY CHANGE

The challenge now is to determine how to study the creativity and innovation bursting upon the management accounting discipline. To me the answer is obvious. Creativity and innovation in management accounting must be studied where they are occurring: in creative, innovative organizations. In some fields creativity can be studied in the laboratory or library. Experiments in the natural sciences are performed in laboratories and successful outcomes disseminated in the professional literature. Some creativity in the natural and social sciences is the outgrowth of formal mathematical analysis that can be performed in the researcher's office.

But there are no laboratories for management accounting. The demand for management accounting information arises only in complex, hierarchical organizations. When a major paradigm shift is underway, all the previous models of how management accounting information is generated and used become open to serious question. The new ideas can be studied only by close observation of the creative people in organizations who are rethinking the old approaches and devising new schemes that are more compatible with the current realities and challenges.

Short plant visits, conversations at professional meetings, and extensive reading of conference papers provide only a limited view of the innovations now underway. I will describe the process I have used for the past three years, with my colleague Robin Cooper of Harvard, to study and document the new approaches to management accounting. I am not claiming that this is the only method that works, or would have worked; but I can attest that it worked extremely well for us. We are quite confident that our current writing and teaching capture well the leading edge practice in management accounting in the United States.

We started by developing a coherent set of entirely new teaching cases that document innovative management accounting systems. The teaching case, a long-established tradition at Harvard that permits extensive class discussion of an administrative issue, has highly desirable characteristics for studying creativity and innovation in organizations. First, the written case requires an extensive description of the particular organizational environment and context in which the innovation occurs. At this early stage, we cannot be sure which innovations are transferable to other organizations and which are successful only in a specific organizational setting. The teaching case, containing a description of both the innovation and its organizational context, provides sufficient information to permit such an evaluation to be made at a subsequent time.

The rich description in the teaching case includes more information about an organizational innovation than do papers prepared by managers in innovative organizations. The innovating managers take their context for granted and focus almost exclusively on what they have done new in their organization. It would be unusual, from such an account, to learn much about the organization, its history, competitive markets, products, and production processes. Yet these factors must be known if the innovation is to be understood properly.

The researcher as case writer need not fully understand the innovation being documented. The main requirement is to recognize that something interesting and important likely occurred and is worth documenting. If the phenomena are captured well in the case, ample opportunity subsequently exists for interpretation and reinterpretation.

Such opportunities arise initially when having to teach the case for the first time. We all know the old expression about nothing concentrating the mind more than an imminent hanging. Well, preparing a case for discussion in front of 60 to 100 MBA students comes in a close second. We have also found that an active discussion in a class of experienced MBAs and senior executives usually provokes new insights into the organizational phenomena. A third opportunity for concept and theory building occurs when the teaching note for the case is prepared.

Thus as long as the basic and relevant facts in the situation have been documented, one does not need to have a well-specified theoretical framework in advance of performing the empirical work. This somewhat atheoretical approach to empirical investigation strikes me as especially valuable when exploring poorly understood phenomena such as creativity and innovation. If I had been guided in my initial empirical investigations by what passed for existing theory in management accounting, circa 1984, I would have been looking in the wrong places and would have missed important phenomena that were occurring in innovating organizations. Empirical investigations guided by a tightly constructed theory are indeed appropriate in mature fields, where a strong body of knowledge already exists, to test the limits of the theories. In emerging and poorly understood fields, however, the need is greatest to look where the action is, reserving interpretation for a later date.

A third advantage of the teaching case as an exploratory research vehicle arises from the knowledge gained by linking together several such cases studies and attempting to find a common thread. We have gained enormous insights from teaching a sequence of cases about organizations in apparently very diverse settings, production processes, and competitive environments, and discovering the lessons that flow from one case to the next.

As just one example, initially, we thought that we would eventually split our course into two segments, one for manufacturing companies and one for service. This dichotomy seemed appealing because the inventory valuation function that so pervaded the design of cost accounting systems in manufacturing organizations does not exist for service organizations. Our case writing and teaching led us to the opposite course structure. We discovered that we have to teach some of the cases about service organizations to establish a theoretical framework for understanding innovative cost systems in manufacturing environments. While we need to do further work (case writing) on computer integrated manufacturing (CIM), our current belief is that management accounting systems for CIM environments may look more like a new cost system we observed in a railroad that like any traditional cost system found today in a manufacturing environment.

Not all case studies (in fact few done by people outside of business schools) are teaching cases. I am not arguing that all case studies should be done with a teaching purpose in mind. In fact, there is a danger that important details may be suppressed or lost if they are thought not to be important for the class experience. But unlike other case studies, teaching cases tend not to be done once and discarded. They come alive each time a teacher prepares a lecture and an active class participates in the discussion. Also, the demand to link together the knowledge emanating from a sequence of cases forces continual reevaluation of the underlying messages. I have found these to be powerful and important forces in my own learning process about the phenomena described in our cases.

Regardless of all these merits, teaching cases cannot be the final research product. Researchers must eventually build theories (not necessarily mathematical ones) about the observed phenomena. Theory building is a major comparative advantage for academic researchers. Creative and innovative managers know well what they did in their organizations. They are not able, however, with their small sample size to understand what was unique to their circumstances and what was generic. This is the difficulty that many business people have when they try to teach an entire course in a business school. War stories, no matter how entertaining, wear thin after a while. Academic researchers can use their access to many organizations to construct organizing, conceptual frameworks (theories) that can explain generic phenomena; they learn under what circumstances a given procedure is likely to work and when it is unlikely to work. Therefore, we should expect and demand that research, while grounded in organizational phenomena, go beyond mere description to provide theoretical frameworks to explain the phenomena.

One final note before leaving this subject of teaching cases: Robin Cooper and I have introduced an innovation of our own by using many multiple-session teaching cases. Usually, a business school case is prepared for discussion and *analysis* of a single, well-defined managerial issue. We found that when shifting from a focus on *analysis* to an emphasis on the *design* process, we need at least a two-class sequence. We start with one session to discuss the company environment, the nature of the old cost system, its strengths and weaknesses, and some design concepts being thought about for the new system. After this session, a second case is distributed that describes both the design details of the new system and the method of implementation. This two-part series (one case series extends to a four-session sequence) helps us to capture the demand for creativity as well as the innovation process in the organization. Perhaps this multiple-session approach will work well in capturing other examples of creativity and innovation. Our experience is too specific to one type of innovation to permit us to generalize.

Implicit in this discussion is the guideline we have used to find interesting organizations to study. Initially we were just lucky in finding innovating organizations that permitted us to work with them to document their experiences. Subsequently we realized that any organization that has made a major change in its cost system would be highly fertile for our research. The politics and disruption from designing and installing a new cost system are so significant that that old system had to be dysfunctional for such an effort to be undertaken. Learning why people in the organization thought the system was inadequate or had failed gave us many insights into the demand for innovative systems. Also, when the major new system was installed, we could work closely with the system's designer, the creator, to learn about the underlying design principles and philosophy. Finally, by interviewing a variety of people after the system has been installed, we learned about innovation and implementation process and how the new system has affected decision making in the organization.

Still to come in our research are longitudinal studies of companies that have implemented new cost systems. We want to be able to determine whether the new systems have had an impact on company decisions. This is the point where case writing transforms into more traditional forms of field research. The initial set of teaching cases provides the baseline from which we can assess future actions and performance. Of course, companies rarely do just one thing. Many cost system innovations are triggered by significant changes in production processes and competitive environments that made the limitations of the old cost system painfully obvious. It could be difficult to disentangle the effect of the cost system from changes in production processes, in corporate strategy,[3] and in the competitive environment. Cooper is just starting this aspect of our research and we will have to wait a few years before we determine whether we can sort out such simultaneous and cofounding effects.

FACTORS CONTRIBUTING TO INNOVATION

Several themes were present in all the organizations where innovation occurred (innovation being defined as the successful introduction of a creative, novel cost system). First, each organization faced radical change in some form: in its operating environment (deregulation of interest rates for a commercial bank, deregulation of pricing for a railroad); in its competitive environment (sharply declining profitability, or threats from overseas competitors); or in its production processes (a shift from manual to computer-driven machines). We studied one situation where a highly creative system was eventually rejected by operating managers who did not feel the organization was in a crisis situation requiring a radical rethinking of its product strategy. Sharply declining profitability was attributed to a recession-induced slowdown in sales and not to fundamental problems with the company's manufacturing and product strategy.

Second, all the innovations had the active support of senior management, who saw the new system as critical to the organization's ability to survive and prosper in the 1980s competitive environment. The innovation failure mentioned above occurred when the new system was designed by managers on the corporate planning staff. The planning managers initiated and performed the study for an operating division that didn't think its current system was dysfunctional. Overcoming the primary American management philosophy (If it ain't broke, don't fix it) is likely the highest barrier that cost system innovation must hurdle.

Third, successful innovation occurred when the new system was run side by side with the existing system. In no case did the innovators attempt to replace the existing system until a degree of comfort and credibility had been obtained with the new system. Frequently the old system was retained to perform the periodic financial reporting function while the new system was operated for decision purposes only. This parallel functioning would have been difficult to implement or justify before personal computers and spreadsheet software became widely available. In one other innovation failure we observed, the newly designed cost system was turned on and, within one month, the old system turned off. Three years later, the organization was still engaged in heated debate about the now three-year-old system. It eventually had to be redesigned to incorporate features from the old system that had been dropped when the new system was designed.

Finally, all successful implementations occurred when the design team and operating people worked closely together. The two implementation failures we observed occurred when a design team did not interact closely with the eventual users of the system.

Whether all these factors for innovation—radical change in the environment, active senior management support, good parallel computing facilities, gradual phase-in of the new system, and close interaction between creative design people and operating managers—are necessary can be explored on wider samples and in other settings. I suspect that the successful introduction of any new information system, not just an accounting system, would require all these factors.

FINAL REMARKS

This chapter has been a personalized account of the rationale and methods Robin Cooper and I have used to study management accounting creativity and innovation in organizations. Not being a student of the creativity and innovation literature, I have little idea as to whether our experiences are idiosyncratic or whether they are consistent with the methods and findings of others. In retrospect, we were fortunate to have used a mechanism that forced us to document systematically and analyze organizational innovations that were occurring in actual practice. I can think of no other research method that we could have used, or that we could use in the future, to understand the creativity and innovation in management accounting practice now underway.

NOTES

1. A fascinating account of the issues surrounding the emergence of the public accounting profession appears in Miranti (1986).
2. For management accounting, product costs should represent the demands that products make on all of the organization's resources. While this purpose may sound similar to that of cost accounting, to attach production costs to products, it is philosophically entirely different.
3. Of course, a change in corporate strategy could also be triggered by the output from the new cost system.

REFERENCES

Chandler, Alfred D., Jr. 1977. *The Visible Hand: The Managerial Revolution in American Business.* Cambridge, Mass.: Harvard University Press.

Johnson, H. Thomas, and Robert S. Kaplan. 1987. *Relevance Lost: The Rise and Fall of Management Accounting.* Boston: Harvard Business School Press.

Kaplan, Robert S. 1984. "The Evolution of Management Accounting." *Accounting Review* (July): 690–718.

Miranti, Paul J. 1986. "Associationalism, Statism, and Professional Regulation: Public Accountants and the Reform of the Financial Markets, 1896-1940." *Business History Review* (Autumn): 438–68.

Discussion

Moderator: William W. Cooper

Question: Bob Kaplan mentioned factors that inhibited innovation. As I look at those, they seem to be largely, although not exclusively, a function of this country's economic development. Is this fifty-year malaise purely a function of what has gone on in cost accounting in this country or is it a worldwide phenomenon? Do we see innovation in other countries in cost accounting?

Kaplan: You don't see much in the English-speaking countries. The English-speaking countries (England, Scotland, Australia, South Africa) tend to have a very strong financial accounting tradition and very powerful chartered or certified accountants. The innovation that seems to occur is more in West Germany. In Japan there are innovative ways. They haven't thought much about accounting measures to stimulate performance. They have used production measures, quality measures, and time measures. There is some degree of performance measurement innovation going on in Japan, which has not been accounting oriented. There is a lot we can learn. The scenario I played out is institution-specific and by going international, you have the opportunity to see how these forces play within a different institutional structure and a different set of regulations.

Question: For a number of years in our service company (consulting, computer processing) we have not really believed the conventional accounting data. We have got it and we try to interpret it. I think we have been groping. Is everybody still groping?

Kaplan: Unlike financial accounting, there is no particular reason why a company that has successfully introduced a management accounting innovation needs to write about it. In terms of getting these cases released, a process by which you have to get the company to sign off to allow you to use it, we have found increasing resistance to granting that release. Even after we disguise the numbers and so forth, they say, "You have captured so much of our strategy and the way we are thinking that we just don't want that showing up." In one case we actually had to completely disguise the industry. For the first time in a long time, these systems are getting much closer to managerial significance because managers are feeling a proprietary right to them.

You will not see too much writing about management accounting. I can identify the companies that are feeling good about themselves and wanting to go public with it. They are starting to appear in journals like *Management Accounting*, which is a practitioner's journal. However, there are not a lot of them. There may be ten or twelve companies that I keep my eye on and follow. That is not to say that these are the only companies that are doing these innovative things. A lot of companies are now reexamining their ideas, rethinking, and forming task forces. I think that in the next five years we will start to see a lot of new ideas and systems being developed.

Question: Every month we have a traditional accounting presentation made by our vice-president-financial controller, who is supposed to point out to us anything that he thinkg we are doing wrong. Then individual groups analyze and defend and show why any change wouldn't lead to the right decisions. We have not had enough of a structure to really see how to go.

Ijiri: It is clear that we are liberated from the notion of stewardship of assets to the income notion. Very few of us have been liberated from the notion of income. We are still constrained by the traditional notion of income. It is easy to say that we need to be liberated from that, but the question is, What is an alternative or a higher level objective? I think that the notion of impulse will be the one that logically follows the notion of income.

Question: In our research we have become interested in how to account for creativity. That is, when we look at organizations that have innovated a lot technologically, one of the key elements in that innovation is the existence of slack—not just slack in terms of money, but also time. My question is whether any of these new accounting procedures can account for slack.

Ijiri: Normally the way that it is done is to provide a cost/benefit relationship under a longer and a larger framework. Unfortunately, accounting is done on the one-year basis or one-quarter basis or one-month basis. It does not recognize the benefits of new products developed for the life cycle of the product. I think that if proper matching of cost and benefit is done, there is a way to recognize and promote creativity. I want to emphasize that accountability has to be there on the creative activities. Otherwise, you can recognize unconventional activities but can't determine whether they are creative activities or destructive activities. I think that we have to have a longer timeframe, a larger grouping of the activities than is traditional. Unfortunately, the direction has been more and more toward minute reporting. Television commentator John Chancellor once said, "We have more reports and less knowledge." That is the kind of thing we have to worry about.

Question: The symptom of the problem is the monthly review. This is a financial accounting story. There is no reason why the cycle of business is one month. There are some things that you should be reporting on daily. With the new technology, maybe we issue reports every minute or even every second about how well we have been cutting metal. There are certain activities that have a cycle of eight months or thirteen months. As Yuji Ijiri said, we must budget, evaluate, and monitor on that basis. I fully agree that if you put very tight controls on creative people, you tend not to get a lot of creativity. They are filling out their time cards and thinking about performance at the end of the day or the end of the week. It is this financial accounting mentality that says that we have to report every period that forces us into the monthly or quarterly cycle. I would advocate recognizing that that work that has periodicity to it (day or batch) should be reported that way. But for creative activities, where you have set milestones and want to look every eight months, then look every eight months to see how well you have done, instead of every month or every week.

I have had companies call me and say that they want me to install a productivity measurement system in their R&D lab. I ask, "Why would you want to do that?" They reply that it is the most important aspect of their business and that they are going to live or die as a result of the R&D lab. They want it to be productive. I don't take those assignments. They want [R&D workers] to be filling out reports to show exactly how much time they put in. That kind of mentality of control [may work for] structured repetitive activities but doesn't transfer very well [to creative activities]. What I do is say, "Turn off the system."

Geis: I have seen numerous cases, going back to the personal computer environment, where people become obsessed with this easy control. In particular, creative environments need a longer periodicity to be able to get meaningful results. It is so easy to control now. You can build a spreadsheet or database very quickly, so now you have this control. I have even seen it a personal budget in a home, controlling every element, including the kid's clothing budget. But it can have some negative side effects as well as highly creative opportunities. One of dangers that we have to be very careful about is the cost/benefit dynamics of information. We should not employ the technology, particularly in creative environments, to go counter to the goals and purposes of the system.

Question: I think Sara Kiesler's point [on organizational slack] is important. There is a connection between allowing the occurrence of slack resources (people's time and coordinating units of the organization as well as money to gamble with) and the inclination or the ability of the organization to experiment or to innovate. Unfortunately, this process has not been very controlled. Other research shows how managers appropriate the slack in order to protect themselves from an isometric reward system in an organization. You want to have these slack resources so that you can cushion unexpected nonperformance in an organization. Some cultures of organization have, in fact, the opposite, which addresses the specific question that Sara Kiesler raised.

Question: In Andrew Van de Ven's project [see Chapter 13], there was a story of a particular company that installed a more refined financial control systems and the bootlegging of the experimentation that was going on began to diminish. This is because a new system enabled monitoring of what they were doing with the resources and drove away that slack. Now the slack was siphoned through the higher level. Whatever sort of innovation that was occurring or bubbling up is being stifled.

Ijiri: On this issue of slack, I would like to add a few tidbits I learned many years ago on a National Geographic program on TV that dealt with various nature events. I was so impressed when they said that about 5 percent of pine cones never open. They drop on the ground but never open to spread the seeds around. Yet, pine cones are fire resistant and when there is a forest fire and other pine cones die, these special cones are the ones that carry the seeds to the next generation. I thought that this is what research is really all about. When you talk about slack, why did nature choose 5 percent instead of 50 percent or 7 percent? I bet nature is so adaptive that when the environment is changing rapidly, the proportion will become larger to prepare for diversity. When the environment is very stable, the percentage will tend to shrink. That is the kind of adaptivity that we need in management as well.

Kozmetsky: When you put your accounting hat on, you have to think of three things in parallel. You have to think of financial accounting. Second, I happen to use the phrase "operational accounting." I want to distinguish between the creative operation and the innovative one. The third one is accounting for investment decisions such as capital budgeting. So you get a confusion between the three aspects of accounting and it is breaking apart creative and innovative management.

When you talked about the fifty years of nothing being done, you are absolutely right as a professional. Those of us who happened to have been involved in the so-called aerospace industry were creative as all get out in managerial accounting. As a matter of fact, we found that we could ignore the accounting precedents. When an environment is changing rapidly, you have actual data. I never could use models for operational control in the first two years when I was production manager at Teledyne, where I had to oversee 250 jobs. I had no production clerks or accounting systems. Every morning, I added on my worksheet 250 job data. It took me an hour to run through. With the computers that George Geis is talking about, we can get lots of these things. I think what we are really talking about here is that we are getting into a whole new way of looking at integrating these things.

Kaplan: George Kozmetsky rightly corrected me. I think there have been two significant innovations in the last sixty years, one of which is discounted cash flow techniques for capital budgeting. The second one is the project management ideas that were developed in the aerospace industry. In the interest of a fast talk and glib generalities, I omitted both of those exceptions.

Geis: Well, we are going into using parallels [parallel processors] and supercomputers now for accounting. There is now a business book on parallels. That is the research side.

D. Morgenthaler: As one who about twenty-five years ago introduced a marginal cost accounting system into the American subsidiary of a British publicly held company and introduced it over the dead bodies of the English and Scottish accountants to whom we had to report, I thoroughly appreciated the difficulty of introducing these systems into English-speaking countries. My question has two parts. First, what is the basic objection of the accounting profession to using a marginal costing kind of system? Second, are the business schools today teaching this [marginal costing] to students?

Kaplan: The objection of the profession was that all of the cost had to be traced to products, not just the short-term variable costs. That was the regulation both for financial accounting and for tax reporting. The answer to the second part is yes, they are teaching marginal costing now, but I am going to try and put a stop to it.

Morgenthaler: Why?

Kaplan: It is O.K. for short-term performance measurement, but it is a disaster for making product decisions. One of the things that I have learned in recent years from some of these new environments is the extreme difficulty that you get into with incremental costing. Correctly specifying marginal costing is fine. The problem is that we have never understood what most of the costs in the organization vary with. Just identifying marginal costs as those costs that go up and down with the volume of production will lead a company to follow a very disastrous product strategy. Some of the new ideas that have emerged are actually getting back to full costing, but in a different way than the way it is done with a single overhead rate.

Morgenthaler: This is precisely the reason the British gave us twenty-five years ago, saying, "We can't trust management with a tool this powerful. They will get themselves in trouble with it every time." So, are you saying that this is still the theory?

Cooper: I would like to throw in a question to Bob Kaplan at this point. I was fascinated with your answer when you were asked to set up a system to measure R&D productivity. I gather that your answer is that they were trying to translate a rather strait-laced concept and set up procedures. My answer would have been, "I don't know how to do it." That seems to me to be a research question that requires invention. I missed that invention in all of the chapters with the exception of Yuji Ijiri's. You are describing what other people did, yet you have made your reputation on the ability to innovate in response to unsolved problems.

Kaplan: You have this whole system out there that is broken in a major way. This little 3 percent problem, the measurement of R&D productivity, comes along and you only have so much time and energy to work it. I don't work on the 3 percent problems, I work on the big problems. It was a matter of allocation of my time. R&D productivity is an interesting problem and someone should work on it. I just assigned somebody to write a case about it so that we could understand the situation.

Cooper: Let me look at this in a different way. I listened to a talk by a social anthropologist who had been studying mediums—people who read ouija boards and tell your future. I asked the anthropologist how she knew if she really understood what that medium society was about. Her answer was that she actually went into the society and performed as a medium and was accepted as a medium by the others. I would still say that that isn't good enough. Could she go into that world and innovate something that the other mediums would, in fact, accept. That seems to me to be a missing element in most of the chapters. That is a real test, both for science and management.

Kaplan: We are doing it. One of the prices that we get companies to pay is that when we go in and study their existing system and make recommendations for change, they have to institute the system and allow us to stick around and watch what happens.

Yuji Ijiri has some incredibly creative ideas. There is a legacy that goes back to some of his colleagues. Sterling and Chambers also do innovation in financial accounting. They write papers and books on it and mail them to people. Then they become angry when the people don't accept it. If you really want to show that your stuff is more than just creative, but also innovative, you should find some organizations that are willing to say, "Yes, exit value is exactly the way that I want to evaluate my decentralized divisions." Or, "I am really going to try momentum accounting for measuring these two divisions." The traditional academic mode of writing papers and distributing them is not enough. We have to try to get these organizations to accept our ideas. You don't need a lot of them, as you know from your own rich experience. If you have a few companies who do it and feel good about it, they will broadcast it to the world. It is very powerful.

Kiesler: I am not sure what it is that you are saying. I hope you are suggesting that if I want to study drugs, I have to be able to take them. I can understand a system without being immersed or doing it myself. I can understand how people make money without making a lot myself. I think the research process is completely different from the process of actually producing. I know that the tradition in business schools is for people to go out and do consulting and tell businesses how to apply research. I don't think that it is absolutely necessary. Some of the best researchers in the world couldn't actually start a company and make it successful because it is not just a matter of understanding that process, it is a matter of a myriad of other things needed for success.

Another point is that in order to study creativity, you can study people and do measurements at the individual level. You can say, "Is this person's product different from the others?" To study innovation, which is an organizational level of analysis, you do not ask if this person is creative, but rather, "Is this organization turning out x number of new products more than other organizations?" Immediately, when you jump up to that level of analysis, you have to make comparisons among organizations. You can't just inquire, "How many new products is this corporation producing?," but "How does it compare to competitors' behavior?" You can measure innovation by counting patents. But you have to do comparative analysis with other organizations. After you start measuring behavior at the organizational level, the problem then becomes how to infer what caused those differences to occur. Once you go up to the organizational level, a number of different things could have happened. It could be the environment, the accounting department, the people in R&D, or a number of things that caused the effect. The problem is that if you want to study innovation, you immediately get out of the laboratory and get into real organizations. You have to do comparisons. The problem is that you can't understand what is causing what. It is messy and very complex. Our problem, as researchers, is to shift back and forth. We do some experiments on individuals and look at what affects creativity and what doesn't in a certain experimental laboratory condition. When we jump up to the organizational level, we have a problem of analysis.

Kaplan: I agree with the complexity and the confounding factors. Sara Kiesler's response reminded me that I neglected to say something that is perhaps the most important aspect of our work, which may be unique to accounting. I think that the biggest change in my own teaching since 1984 has been the shift away from analysis (here is the situation, what is going on, and how do you analyze it). We now teach design, which is a much more creative process.

In Herbert Simon's book about the design of business school and the sciences of artificial intelligence [*The Sciences of the Artificial*, 2nd ed. (Cambridge, Mass.: MIT Press, 1981)], he makes the point that it is really a terrible mistake for business schools to think of themselves as social scientists. Social scientists tend to study the world as it is and try to understand it, such as the impact of drugs and the like, but you don't sit there trying to change it. We have the opportunity of changing organizations, changing the measurement system, and changing the incentive system. That is part of the design process. We have not typically exploited that. We have taught students how to analyze situations. I believe that we must train students so that when they get out in the world, they will be able to see what is wrong with the system in an organization and they will be able to design a system that is appropriate for that organization. They can actually institute change.

To me, it is terribly important to shift our research and teaching from analysis to design. We get to set the rules. In accounting, we can change the rules and design and install new systems. In principle, we may be able to do it in a way that some of the confounding factors may not occur. It is a longitudinal study; you can do the before and after. It will never be completely clean; there are too many other things changing.

Gamache: I am very intrigued and impressed by Yuji Ijiri's discussion on momentum and impulse accounting. Does implementing that system require judgment and opinions? The accounting part is numbers and is very precise. When we get into momentum and impulse, we are really submerging into a more intangible, touchy-feely area that requires opinions on the ultimate efficacy of the creativity or innovation. Is it implementable?

Ijiri: The principles that I have been putting together are objectively definable relative to the existing accounting. If you criticize various techniques used in existing accounting and throw them away and start from scratch, then I have a harder task of building things objectively in terms of measurement and allocation. For example, the notion of momentum dissipation has to be introduced at some stage. Otherwise those who initiated the momentum will get the credit forever. There is some notion of product cycles and momentum dissipation patterns. Do we have something comparable in the existing accounting? Sure enough: We have "depreciation." Depreciation is one of the greatest innovations in accounting. The notion makes it possible for accountants to measure this year's income without really knowing what might happen in the future. You just depreciate, say, one-twentieth of the cost each year. Similarly, by introducing a set of reasonable conventions or a set of reasonable patterns of momentum dissipation, we can develop standards in momentum measurements. William Cooper's teacher, Eric Kohler, president of the American Accounting Association in 1936, took a great initiative in standardizing the accounting procedure overcoming many political difficulties. Perhaps the same initiatives are needed in establishing standard for momentum accounting. With such efforts, momentum accounting is definitely implementable.

Cooper: I would like to close with a story that gets back to the disagreement between Sara Kiesler and me. Many years ago when I was a student at the University of Chicago, I took a course that was for beginning medical students. The professor, a world-famous physiologist, began with the following experiment. He took a bowl of urine and said, "The first job of a medical scientist is to be willing to experiment or experience." He dipped his finger in and licked it. He passed it around the class and asked us all to do that. We all did and the bowl finally went back to him, then he said, "The second job of a scientist is to be a very careful observer. If you were a careful observer, you will notice that I dipped my forefinger in the urine and licked my middle one."

IV BEHAVIORAL DIRECTIONS AND METHODOLOGY

9 AREA INTRODUCTION AND OVERVIEW

Karl Weick

Part IV has a more behavioral cast to it than the other parts of this book. It has a more methodological cast than the previous part. Methodologists sometimes feel a little out of place, something like the man from Toronto whom Warren Bennis ran into a few years ago. Warren Bennis has been through several incarnations, first as a university president at the University of Buffalo and then at the University of Cincinnati. He is now a faculty member at the University of Southern California. While he was at Buffalo, he had an unusual experience. Jascha Heifetz was to present a concert at the Buffalo Civic Auditorium, which holds around 4,500 people. Bennis was supposed to introduce Heifetz for the concert. When Bennis got to the concert, there were exactly six people sitting in the audience because of a blizzard. Heifetz came out on the stage and looked at the six people scattered around and said, "Let's just go over to my hotel room and have a drink and talk about music. It really doesn't make any sense for me to have a concert tonight." One person at the back of the room held up his hand and said, "Hey, I drove here all the way from Toronto to hear you sing and, by God, you are going to sing."

What are some things that you should look for in the following chapters? One of them is odd events or procedures that don't quite fit into the setting. Such events are often triggers, as we have already seen, for certain kinds of stimulation and ideas and twists on creativity and innovation.

You will also want to look for trade-offs. Consider product innovation. The standard heiristic that happens when you engage product

127

development people is that you are told, "O.K. Do you want it fast? Do you want it cheap? Do you want it good? Pick two." You can never get all three of those things in a product. If you get it cheap and fast, it will not be good. If you get it fast and good, it will not be cheap. If you get it good and cheap, it will not be fast. You have these kinds of trade-offs in product development.

You will see the same set of trade-offs in the following chapters on methodology. They are trying to do an impossible task. They are trying to describe a methodology that has simultaneously: *generality* (they cover all of your problems), *accuracy* (they cover each of your problems in fine detail), and *simplicity*. If you think general, accurate, and simple, what tends to be true of these characteristics is that any explanation will have two of them and be as far from the third as possible. If a chapter heroically discusses a point that is general and accurate, it is not going to be simple. If a chapter presents something that is simple and accurate because it fits your situation, your neighbor will probably say it is irrelevant. It will not have generality and won't fit his.

There is no way to finesse the issue, other than to be conscious of all three of these bases. In these chapters one of these components is always missing—but that goes along with the turf.

Do we really need methodological innovations to get hold of problems of creativity and innovation? Division 14 of the American Psychological Association, which studies industrial and organizational problems, recently completed a task force cosponsored by the Office of Naval Research and the National Institute of Education titled, "Innovations in Methodology for Studying Organizations." It is the same kind of topic we are concerned with here. The ongoing debate in trying to set up the conference and the books and the papers that grew out of that particular agenda was over the question, "Does the field really need new methodological innovations if it is to become a better field, or do we rather need not new methods but patient, thorough, and informed use of the methods we already have?"

That is not as simple and straightforward a question as it may sound. Tension exists between the two options. If you look at the six books that have come out of that American Psychological Association project, it is interesting that they never resolved the issue. Three of the six books propose new innovations in the field. The other three books say that if only we understood the existing methodologies, this field would be in terrific shape. So, as you read the chapters in this part, consider whether we need new methodologies or whether, in fact, we need more patient, thorough, and informed understanding and applications of the methods that already exist.

Everybody has remedies for methodological problems in a field. That is certainly true for our cast of authors. Their chapters represent quite a striking diversity of approaches, sets of assumptions, and ways of tackling these sorts of problems. If you ask the generic question of how to improve a field or what the problems are right now, thinking about the discipline of creative and innovative management, the arguments tend to fall into three categories. Here are the three that you might want to keep your eye on:

One of the arguments that is often made in any kind of methodology discussion is that things are going a little slow on the creative and innovative management front because data gathering and data analytic techniques are insensitive to important features of the databases, such as the level of analysis that Sara Kiesler was talking about or the context dependency discussed in George Geis's chapter. If you have that family of problems or if the problems are methodological problems, then the remedy is to *beef up* the field by improving technique.

Another kind of argument you will hear is what we may call an anormative argument. This argument goes essentially that it is the personal and social influences of academics, researchers, and so forth that have an adverse effect on research activities. Here, the organization theory, the research, the work on creativity and innovation flounders because researchers are incompetent or they are poorly trained or they are so concerned with professional advancement that they put style over substance, quantity over quality, and easy, trivial problems over hard, important ones. If you use that line of analysis, then the remedy is for the field to *grow up*.

Finally, there is a third argument. If you get in close as Bob Kaplan does, you will find that most organizations are pretty chaotic. If that is the case, then the fact that we have chaotic subject matter in the field is simply a reflection of the actual chaotic reality of organizations. So, if organizations are overdetermined and generally disorganized and have a lot of shifting cause-and-effect relationships, then it is impossible to explain them in any other way than by being situationally specific and context specific. If that is your analysis of the situation, then since there is nothing stable to study, your advice is to *give up*.

So we have three kinds of alternative prescriptions that people have in the back of their minds: 1) beef up, 2) grow up, or 3) give up. Watch for these three elements. Let me preview the chapters.

Arie Lewin, of the Decision Science Group of the National Science Foundation and of Duke University, is starting up a journal that promises to be a major voice in organizational studies. Arie wears several hats, which leads him to spot several kinds of blindspots that exist when you try to improve the way to study creative and innovative management. He will comment from those several perspectives on traps that can ensnare us.

Scott Isaksen from the State University College at Buffalo has done a lot of work with creativity and problem-solving groups, constantly shuffling through different methods, both to examine these groups and to examine the methods that he has those groups try out. He will be our eye on that particular literature.

Chapter 12 is derived from the work on creative leadership at the Center for Creative Leadership at Greensboro, North Carolina. This chapter looks at how to assess organizational climates for their degree of creativity and innovation. Robert Burnside, Teresa Amabile, and Stanley Gryskiewicz, bring a crisp set of perspectives to bear on this issue.

Chapter 13 is presented by Andrew Van de Ven. His group, the Strategic Management Research Center at University of Minnesota, is conducting the largest scale ongoing project on organizational innovation. His material is a gold mine of information on what is being discovered about sources of innovation in organization. He deals with how we might be able to develop some sensitivities toward innovation processes, the same methodologies that he has been able to use to get fresh insights into these organizations.

The final chapter of this part is by Stephan Chorover from MIT. He is in the psychology department, but his images of the human mind are wide ranging and extraordinarily stimulating.

10 RESEARCH ON CREATIVE AND INNOVATIVE MANAGEMENT
An Evaluation of Research Strategies

Arie Y. Lewin

Understanding processes of creativity and innovation within organizations and knowing how to design innovative organizations implies the development of processual descriptions and explanations of how creativity and innovation occur within organizations (for example, business firms), as a basis for deriving normative theories that affect the practice of management. Processual research implies finding out how creativity and innovation happen by observing and tracking the occurrence of innovations longitudinally in real time, by interviewing participants and learning what they do and how they do it, by studying archival data, and ultimately tying it all together through retrospective sense making and inductive theorizing.

This approach to processual empirical research on organizations, emphasizing the rationality of organizations in terms of their information-processing, problem-solving and decision-making behavior began at Carnegie-Mellon in the 1950s (March and Simon 1958), it has revolutionized the field of organizations and with the publication of *The Behavioral Theory of the Firms* (Cyert and March 1963) became the stimulus for behavioral research in economics (Williamson 1975; Scherer 1980; Nelson and Winter 1982). One of the major contributions of Cyert and March was the specification of organization learning and adaptation models as integral elements of the behavioral theory of the firm and the extension of the theory to account for investment in and the occurrence of innovation in organizations (Cyert and March 1963, pp. 278–79).

This chapter reviews the challenge to organization researchers to undertake empirical research on learning adaptation and innovation processes in organizations, and it discusses promising research approaches for studying creativity and innovation within organizations.

THE CHALLENGE FACING RESEARCHERS ON ORGANIZATIONS

At the Second International Conference on Creative and Innovative Management (November 1984), Herbert Simon noted, in response to a question from W.W. Cooper, that "we do not yet have a full or satisfactory theory of how we design organizations to be creative" (Kuhn 1985, p. 21). A similar observation regarding the state of theory on organization innovation is made by Van de Ven (1986) in his description of the Minnesota Innovation Research Project. However, the lack of theories of innovation, or of organization design in general, can be traced to the state of theorizing and empirical research on organizations as well as to indifference on the part of management practitioners to become partners in research on organization effectiveness and design, which could lead to increased effectiveness of management practice in managing and designing organizations.

Concern with designing organizations for greater effectiveness has served as the unifying theme for a century of research on management and the design of organizations (Lewin and Minton 1986). However, any review of the relevant literatures must conclude that this research effort has resulted in consistent disappointments for practitioners and academicians alike. The recurrent disappointments can be attributed to the relative lack of progress on such issues as how to design effective, innovative or highly reliable organizations, despite varied and extensive efforts to be successfully prescriptive (Lewin and Minton 1986b).

To a great extent the lack of prescriptive progress can be traced to the scientific management movement (Taylor 1911) and classical management theory (Fayol 1949 (originally 1916-1925; Urwick 1938; Dale 1952; Davis 1951; Koontz and O'Donnell 1959). The theory was inductive and intuitive in nature. It concerned itself with a simplistic search for a universalistic set of management principles regarding the "logical" arrangement of activities and functions with a great emphasis on ensuring unity of command, defining authority relationships, and determining optimal span of control. The theory had no empirical basis; however, its concerns reflected the applied managerial problems of the times. As the influence of classical management theory declines it is interesting to note that no new all-encompassing prespective theory emerged to take its place (Lewin and Minton 1986b). Yet the last three decades resulted in an enormous outpouring of research on organizations.

The prescriptive theories that have been advanced during the period were mostly motivated by particular beliefs and values (for example, to be effective organizations should be more human and participative). To a great extent the application of the new theories by managers was a function of the fit between their management philosophy, values, and management styles and the beliefs embodied within particular theories. Although during the last several decades of research and theory we have learned more about what does not work (Perrow 1978), it should be noted that in the fifties and sixties the managers of American enterprises did not perceive a need for academic theorizing or research on designing effective organizations, perhaps because their management practices were held up as models of excellence in management for the rest of the world as a means to improve their ability to effectively manage and design organizations. Also, during this period, organization researchers were largely unconcerned with drawing out the prescriptive implications of their descriptive research.

The deepening concern with the decline of U.S. competitiveness, the industrial hollowing of America, and the general skepticism of the public at large regarding the ability of American management to adapt, innovate, and to reliably and consistently manage high-consequence organizations (such as those involving complex technologies) has clearly permeated the popular culture. It has put pressure on management and organization scholars to concern themselves with the applied problems of managers and organizations and it has resulted in a greater receptivity by practitioners to research on organization design.

Organization design has often been equated with the design of the organization structure. However, a more encompassing view treats choices about structure or structural relationships as only one variable of many that the organization designer needs to consider. Certain attributes of organization effectiveness may be more prominently associated with certain features of organization design and in real life organization design is a never-ending process involving choices or trade-offs that attain certain effectiveness attributes and deemphasize others. This iterative trade-off process has been referred to as "the management of paradox" (Cameron 1986), and thus the domain of research on organizations on such matters as problem solving and decision making; learning, adaptation, and innovation; strategy formulation and environmental scanning; planning, goal setting, and evaluation; as well as the organization structure, culture, managerial leadership, socialization, recruiting, and management of human resources.

Organization textbooks provide certain insights as to the perceived state of knowledge of the field and the type of prescriptive conclusions being drawn. The volume of research being covered is vast and the order of subject presentation varies greatly. However, with rare exceptions the phenomena being discussed are treated as a main effect and there is little recognition that the designing of organizations in practice involves trade-offs among a multiplicity of interacting variables and perspectives (Lewin and Minton 1986b).

The challenge for researchers on organization effectiveness extends beyond classification and interpretation of prior research on organizations as it relates to organization design and effectiveness. It involves structuring the research to capture interaction effects as well as focusing on variables and processes that have not been well studied empirically. Examples include the role of organization structure on the framing of problems and solutions of unstructured problems; the fit between the organization's design and its values; predispositions as well as management style of the leaders of the organization as a determinant of effectiveness; the relationship between organization culture and effectiveness; and, the central concern of this book—learning, adaptation, and innovation in organizations. To a great extent the gaps in the empirical knowledge base about organizations and its relevance to design and effectiveness can be attributed to research strategies that have not captured rich processual descriptions, which are not designed to yield causal explanations and to the fragmented disciplinary perspectives that guide these strategies.

RESEARCH ON CREATIVITY AND INNOVATION

The challenge that organization scholars face in devising approaches to studying variable rich phenomena such as creativity and innovation processes in organizations is widely recognized (see, for example, Van de Ven 1986). Triandis (1966) estimated that at least 200 key variables can be identified (many of them interacting) that affect the performance of organizations. The study of creativity and innovation may not involve all 200 variables, but in reality research on innovation is not less complex. This complexity clearly emerged during the discussions at the workshop reviewing results of four years of research from the Minnesota Innovation Research Project (MIRP). The following is a classification of research questions most of which were raised at the workshop and each of which is important in understanding the creativity and innovation process within organizations.

A. The Origin of Innovation. Innovation is the result of 1) a shock (a major failure) to the system, 2) problemistic search, 3) random variability or experimentation, 4) deliberate decision to invest in learning, 5) match between a need and ideas which already exist, 6) formal vehicles for stimulating innovation such as research and development units or internal venture funds, 7) managerial risk seeking or risk averse behavior, 8) availability of slack resources, 9) management philosophy and organization climate, 10) customer needs.

B. Reasons for Success or Failure. Certain events, managerial actions, organizational processes, or other variables account for the successful occurrence of innovation. 1) Innovations terminate because they run into resource constraints. 2) Innovations fail because of commitment to old ideas or, existing products or technology. 3) Innovations fail because of conflict over ownership. 4) Innovations succeed because they enhance or complement existing products, processes, or technologies. 5) Innovations succeed because they satisfy a perceived need or fit the organization strategy.

C. Processes of Innovation. Processual descriptions of innovation require explanations of 1) decisions to begin, continue, or terminate an innovation, 2) when the innovation process is considered complete, 3) outcomes describing success or failure, 4) how an innovation or the innovation process changes the organization, 5) how organization learning occurs as result of innovation activity, 6) leadership processes that facilitate or impede innovation, 7) the linkage between uncertainty, avoidance behavior, and innovation activity, 8) the innovation process as uncertain, unpredictable, nonlinear or rational, planned, and deterministic, 9) the adoption and diffusion of innovations.

D. Macroorganizational Variables. Organization design variables are considered to affect innovation. Thus it is considered important to understand 1) the strategic centrality of innovations, 2) structural, control, or operational features of the organization design that facilitate or impede innovative processes, 3) which organization designs satisfy requirements of operational efficiency that also embody a capacity to innovate and adapt, 4) the relationship between organization size and capacity for innovation and adaptation.

E. Other Issues. Also suggested were the research questions on 1) relationship between the organization and the highly innovative person, 2) cultural characteristics of experimenting or bootlegging organization, 3) causal linkages between innovation and organization effectiveness, 4) the appropriate unit of analysis, 5) explanations for barriers to innovation, and 6) contingent explanations of the innovation process as a function of whether the innovation is normal and incremental or revolutionary and discontinuous.

The foregoing classification and listing of research questions is not intended to be exhaustive or indicative of what variables should be researched or which ones interact. This compilation of questions, however, clearly indicates the magnitude and complexity of the task of developing a descriptive knowledge base about learning, adaptation, and innovation processes in organizations that could serve as a basis for prescriptive theorizing. The research is made even more difficult because the field is in poor paradigms and lacks developed frameworks to guide empirical research. The section that reviews research strategies that can result in a cumulative body of knowledge on creativity and innovation and that also have the potential to produce robust heuristics to guide management practice.

RESEARCH APPROACHES TO STUDYING CREATIVITY AND INNOVATION

It is clear that the study of a phenomenon as complex as creativity and innovation requires research strategies which go beyond studying a few variables at a time, and which aim at identifying variables, actions, and processes upon which managers can act (identifying causal linkages for variables that managers can influence or control). Most of the research on creativity and innovations in organizations can be described as exploratory pilot studies, stimulation experiments, or questionnaire surveys (Schon 1963; Maidique 1980; Maidique and Zirger 1984; Rubenstein et al. 1976) and most prescriptive theorizing as intuitive and anecdotal (Marquis 1969; Galbraith 1982; Kanter 1983). The intuitive theorizing reflects the pressing needs of organizations and their managers for conceptual ideas and heuristic guidelines as well as the lack of strong explanatory processual theories. The small scope and exploratory nature of most empirical research to a large extent reflect the limitations arising from the bounded rationality of researchers and limited disciplinary perspectives (Lewin and Minton 1986b). In other words the scope and direction of research projects are often constrained by the research capacity of a single investigator with limited access to research sites (for the conduct of questionnaire survey or retrospective case study, for example). In what follows we shall examine some research approaches for studying creativity and innovation in organizations, placing emphasis on contextual research strategies.

HYPOTHESES-TESTING RESEARCH

The lack of comprehensive theoretical frameworks on creativity and innovation in organizations would suggest that, given the current state of knowledge, hypotheses testing will not prove fruitful. Indeed, that has been the working assumption underlying the Minnesota Innovation Research Project (Van de Ven 1986). However, it is not at all clear that the empirical literature on creativity and innovation to date (with all its limitations), partial theories that have been advanced, and existing theories of organizations cannot serve as a basis for generating hypotheses for guiding research on innovation. The recent volume of metaanalyses papers suggests that new insights and hypotheses for guiding research can be obtained from integrative literature reviews. Metaanalysis offers a statistical procedure for making some sense (under certain conditions) and gaining new insights out of a collection of empirical studies often reporting contradictory results (Lewin and Minton 1986b). Although metaanalysis cannot be a substitute for good theory and its findings cannot contribute causal explanations, it does offer an approach to integrative literature reviews not previously possible from qualitative reviews. Such metaanalytic integrative reviews will very likely yield some new insights into theory building and for guiding empirical research.

Another approach to hypotheses testing involves making implicit theories and concepts explicit by generating research questions on the basis of intuition, managerial experience, and anecdote, or on the basis of partial theoretical paradigms. The list of research questions enumerated earlier contains examples of both. The following is an illustration of generating a proposition regarding managerial decision making to invest in an innovation project based on preference reversal research and on the concept of organizational slack (Cyert and March 1963).

Payne, Laughhunn, and Crum (1981) reported that risk-seeking or risk-averse behavior by managers when making capital investment decisions was a function of their aspirations for absorbing a loss. In other words if the potential loss exceeded the managers' aspiration level for loss, managers chose risk-averse outcomes. When the potential loss was below the level of aspiration for loss, managers were risk seeking in their behavior. Organization slack can serve as a moderator variable in such behavior. Cyert and March (1963) have argued that innovation, in particular the allocation of resources to learning (such as to basic research) is a function of the perceived level of organization slack. Thus an interesting proposition regarding managers' willingness to invest in innovation could be summarized as follows: All else equal, the higher the perceived level of organizational slack the greater the risk-seeking behavior of managers in making initial decisions to invest in innovations. This proposition is not stated in a form that leads to direct empirical testing. However, it can serve as the basis for the derivation of several hypotheses that can guide data gathering and empirical testing. More generally the literature on managerial risk taking (MacCrimmon and Wehrung 1986; March and Shapira 1987) has important implications for research on organizational decisions to invest in innovations. Yet this literature has had scant influence in research on creativity and innovation.

LONGITUDINAL FIELD STUDIES

Large-scale real-time longitudinal field studies across several organizations represent an alternative, grounded-theory research approach for studying creativity and innovations. The objective of field studies is to observe in a natural setting how innovation occurs in organizations. The focus is on developing detailed process descriptions by, for example, tracking innovations from their inception to termination. Such a research strategy is based on long-term access to participating organizations; it involves the collaboration of interdisciplinary teams; it requires the collection of a vast array of every conceivable data using multiple means of data collection (nonparticipant observation, interviews, surveys, and archival data). The data analyses are directed at empirically deriving theories about the innovation process.

Such studies are rare in the annals of organization research. Of three longitudinal field studies currently underway, the Minnesota Innovation Research Project (Van de Ven 1986) is the only one focusing on innovation. It is longitudinal, it involves thirteen organizations, and its objective is the understanding of how innovations actually develop over time and the determination of factors that influence the successful development of innovations. The research, which was initially funded by the Office of Naval Research, is being undertaken by an interdisciplinary team of thirty investigators and is likely to contribute to the building of theories about processes of innovation, learning, and adaptation in organizations. The MIRP project, however, also illustrates the difficulties and complexities of real-time longitudinal research. The project has followed, to date, fourteen different innovations. However, the researchers have no baseline on which to judge whether their findings will illustrate effective or ineffective innovation processes. Similarly, since the research is not motivated by a priori research questions or hypotheses it is possible that certain data necessary for the testing of specific research issues will not have been obtained. Finally the task of making sense out of the vast and diverse array of data that has been collected will be very difficult. The other two large-scale longitudinal field studies are experiencing similar methodological obstacles (see Lewin and Minton 1986b for descriptions of the Army Research Institute (ARI) supported organization design study and the study supported by the Office of Naval Research and by the National Science Foundation on high-reliability, high-consequence organizations).

Field studies are complex, expensive, and relatively inefficient approaches to research. To increase their success and efficiency there is need to train researchers in the methodology and there is a need to incorporate the discipline of conceptualizing research in terms of hypotheses testing in the initial design of the research project. Nevertheless it is a strategy with high promise; it involves real organizations; it is real time and longitudinal; it is based on a close relationship between the subject managers and the researchers; and the research can be focused on finding causal relationships. Unlike retrospective case research or surveys, real-time observation is more likely to yield realistic processual descriptions of the innovation process. Van de Ven and his associates, for example, were able to characterize the innovation process as nonlinear, discontinuous, having many false starts or as stop-and-go. Furthermore, they illustrate how a retrospective analysis, as described by a manager, presents the innovation process as rational, planned, and linear. Thus, real-time field studies need to become an important element in the research portfolio on innovation and on organizations as the only basis for robust, grounded theorizing.

REPLICATED CASE STUDIES

Another potentially promising research strategy involves the building of a cumulative knowledge base about creativity and innovation in organizations through clinical research cases. Case research, like field studies, requires access, often multiple access, to organizations. Unlike longitudinal field studies, case research in general does not require long-term access. For that reason case research represents, perhaps, a more feasible research methodology to most researchers. Case research could be "real time," in particular if the research is observing a short-term phenomenon. However, retrospective data gathering and analyses seem to be the norm.

Successful case research follows several stages. It includes an early phase of identifying research questions and generating propositions. As a rule, case research is qualitative and it does not involve hypotheses testing in a statistical sense. The research questions and propositions serve to clarify the problem to be investigated and to guide data collection such as the gathering of archival records, direct observations, interviews, business plans, financial records, and surveys. Case research provides a good means of obtaining in a relatively efficient manner, within the bounded rationality constraints of a small research team, rich contextual data from multiple sources about specific research questions. It also yields varied unexpected qualitative descriptions that relate to the phenomenon of interest.

Good case research requires the involvement of trained clinical researchers with an appreciation of the managerial and organization situations being researched. It requires subjective judgment of significant events, careful triangulation of multiple sources of information, and making sense of meanings and of objective reality. Case research provides an opportunity to confirm or disconfirm specific questions or generalized theory in a specific instance. Methodologically its greatest weakness is its reliance on retrospective data collection and analyses that often tends to describe events as more rational, intended, and coherent.

Yin (1984) has described a multiple-case research approach that allows for replicating the study of the same specific research questions by the same research team across a large number of organizational settings. This approach allows for the cumulating of results and under certain conditions could permit hypotheses testing and more robust generalizations. Replicated case research is not in wide use. It is a methodology of high promise that should become more prevalent and that should be taught to organization researchers in doctoral programs.

ENGINEERING INNOVATION RESEARCH

Action research and intervention in organization has the potential for undertaking research that can contribute to theory building as well as be immediately useful to the practitioner. Innovation or creativity events can be engineered in such a way as to reveal useful case information for theory building or validation (see for example Nystrom and Starbuck 1977 and Lewin and Minton 1986a). In this usage the term *engineering* has two purposes. For the practitioner it involves the redesign, or construction and management of organization activities (a change or an innovation) to achieve improved outcomes according to contextually determined criteria. However, the engineered event must be approached in such a way that it provides an empirical basis for theory induction or theory testing. In practice it means that the researcher is involved with the practitioner in defining the problem and in designing the intervention.

In this book, Robert Kaplan describes an extremely relevant example of engineering innovations in management accounting systems that affected the practice of managerial decision making as well as providing an empirical basis for describing and theorizing about innovation processes in organizations. Three other chapters (by Gamache, Harriman, and Miller) each illustrate cases of innovation interventions. These case interventions indicate that the client managers were concerned with the instigation and management of innovation events, and that they perceived certain problems and expected certain innovation outcomes from these interventions. It seems that these client managers are good candidates for administrative experimentation (Berlin 1978) or for the engineering of innovation research.

Success in engineering innovation research requires access go real situations and a receptivity on the part of managers to structure the engineering of the innovation event as an administrative experiment or as a research case. This could be achieved through a research practitioner partnership that results in immediate benefits for the subject organization but also provides for the collection of the data necessary for understanding, describing the engineered innovation event as a basis for processual theory building and prescription for guiding managerial practice (Lewin and Minton 1986a).

SUMMARY

This chapter has reviewed the complexity of the task and the challenge of undertaking research on creativity and innovation in organizations. The topic of organization's learning, adaptation, and innovation is not well understood; it is underresearched and it is fundamental to the evolution of theories about organization design and effectiveness. This chapter advocates contextual research strategies and considers in turn real-time longitudinal field studies, replicated research cases, and the engineering of innovation events. The expected outcome of contextual research could lead to rich contextual descriptions with causal linkages, diagnostic research cases, integrative replicated research cases involving hypotheses testing and ultimately structured theories of innovation based on metaanalyses across cases, engineered events, and field studies. This approach to research on creativity and innovation, however, is very much contingent on a researcher/practitioner partnership. Contextual research cannot be done without the support and participation of organizations and their managers. Long-term success depends on managers perceiving payback in the form of problems solved, achievement of successful innovation interventions, or the learning of innovation heuristics as well as on researchers gaining data and insights necessary for theory building, testing of ideas, or describing and explaining innovation processes.

REFERENCES

Berlin, V. 1978. "Administrative Experimentation: A Methodology for More Rigorous 'Muddling Through'." *Management Science 24*: 789–99;

Cameron, K. 1986. "Effectiveness as Paradox: Consensus and Conflict in Conceptions of Organizational Effectiveness." *Management Science 32*: 539–53.

Cyert, Richard, and James March. 1963. *A Behavioral Theory of the Firm.* Englewood Cliffs, N.J.: Prentice-Hall.

Dale, E. 1952. *Planning and Developing the Company Organization Structure.* New York: American Management Association.

Davis, R.C. 1951. *The Fundamentals of Top Management.* New York: Harper.

Fayol, H. (Storrs, Trans). 1949. *Administration Industrielle et Generale.* London, UK: Sir Isaac Pitman and Sons.

Galbraith, Jay R. 1982. "Designing the Innovating Organization." *Organizational Dynamics* (Winter): 5–25.

Kanter, R.M. 1983. *The Change Masters: Innovations for Productivity in the American Corporation.* New York: Simon and Schuster.

Koontz, H. (Ed.). 1964. *Toward a Unified Theory of Management.* New York: McGraw-Hill.

Koontz, Harold, and Cyril O'Donnell. 1959. *Principle of Management: An Analysis of Managerial Functions.* New York: McGraw-Hill.

Kuhn, Robert L. (Ed.). 1985. *Frontiers in Creative and Innovative Management.* Cambridge, Mass.: Ballinger.

Lewin, Arie Y., and John W. Minton. 1986a. "Determining Organizational Effectiveness: Another Look, and an Agenda for Research." *Management Science 32*, no. 5 (May): 514–38.

_____ . (1986b) forthcoming, *Organizational Science*, Institute of Management Science, 1989.

MacCrimmon, Kenneth R., and Donald A. Wehrung. 1986. *Thinking Risks: The Management of Uncertainty.* New York: Free Press.

Maidique, M.A. 1980. "Entrepreneurs, Champions and Technological Innovations." *Sloan Management Review 21*, no. 2 (Winter): 59–76.

Maidique, Modesto A., and Billie Jo Zirger. 1984. "A Study of Success and Failure in Product Innovation: The Case of the U.S. Electronics Industry." *IEEE Transactions on Engineering Management EM-31*, no. 4 (November): 192–203.

March, James G., and Zur Shapira. 1987. "Managerial Perspectives on Risk and Risk Taking." *Management Science 33*, no. 11 (November): 1401–18.

March, James G., and Herbert A. Simon. 1958. *Organizations.* New York: John Wiley & Sons.

Marquis, D. G. 1969. "The Anatomy of Successful Innovations." *Innovation 1*: (November): 28-37.

Nelson, Richard R., and Sidney G. Winter. 1982. *An Evolutionary Theory of Economic Change.* Cambridge, Mass.: Belknap Press of Harvard University Press.

Nystrom, P. C., and W. H. Starbuck (Eds.). 1977. *Prescriptive Models of Organizations: TIMS Studies in Management Sciences*, vol. 5. Amsterdam: North Holland.

Payne, John W., Dan J. Laughhunn, and Roy L. Crum. 1981. "Further Tests of Aspiration Level Effects in Risky Choice Behavior." *Management Science* 27: 953-58.

Perrow, C. 1978. "The Short and Glorious History of Organizational Theory." In H. L. Tosi and W. C. Humner (Eds.), *Organizational Behavior and Management: A Continuing Approach*, rev. ed. New York: Wiley, pp. 8-18.

Rubenstein, A. H., A. K. Chakrabarti, R. D. O'Keefe, W. E. Souder, and H. C. Young. 1976. "Factors Influencing Innovation Success at the Project Level." *Research Management 19*, no. 3 (May): 15-20.

Scherer, F. M. 1980. *Industrial Market Structure and Economic Performance.* Boston: Houghton Mifflin.

Schon, D. A. 1963. "Champions for Radical New Inventions." *Harvard Business Review 41*, no. 2: 77-86.

Taylor, F. W. 1911. *The Principles of Scientific Management.* New York: Harper & Row.

Triandis, H. 1966. Notes on the Design of Organizations. In Thompson, J. (Ed.), *Approaches to Organization Design.* Pittsburgh: University of Pittsburgh Press.

Urwick, L. 1938. *Scientific Principles of Organization.* New York: American Management Association.

Van de Ven, Andrew H. 1986. "Central Problems in the Management of Innovation." *Management Science 32*, no. 5: 590-607.

Williamson, Oliver E. 1975. *Markets and Hierarchies: Analysis and Antitrust Implications.* New York: The Free Press.

Yin, Robert K. 1984. *Case Study Research: Design and Methods.* Beverly Hills, Calif.: Sage Publications.

11 INNOVATIVE PROBLEM SOLVING IN GROUPS
New Methods and Research Opportunities

Scott G. Isaksen

Despite many difficult obstacles, creativity and innovation are becoming important concepts for individuals, groups, and organizations (Charnes and Cooper 1984; Isaksen 1987a; Kuhn 1985, 1988). The actual study of creativity, from a psychological perspective, is a relatively recent phenomenon. Many writers on creativity identify Guilford's (1950) presidential address to the American Psychological Association as the cornerstone of research and psychological inquiry into this concept. Since this beginning, a substantial body of literature regarding creativity has grown and spread. As Treffinger (1986, p. 19) indicated: "Through more than thirty years of research and development, creativity has continued to be a topic of considerable interest to educators as well as social and behavioral scientists." Although the field seems to be fairly young, creativity research has been reviewed and summarized by various writers (Raina 1980; and Taylor and Getzels 1975). There are also many edited collections of important contributions to the literature (Anderson 1959; Ghiselin 1952; Parnes and Harding 1962; and Rothenberg and Hausman 1976). The purpose of this chapter is to place research and inquiry into creative problem solving in groups within the larger context of creativity research.

MYTHOLOGY, DEFINITIONS, AND APPROACHES TO CREATIVITY

The definitions of creativity are numerous. Some seem grounded in research or common sense. Others seem to be based on beliefs and

145

assumptions that need to be questioned or examined. Anyone interested in the concept of creativity must deal with a series of myths in order to make productive and lasting connections. It is essential to deal also with the problem of semantics and the ambiguity that a variety of definitions for the same word will cause.

Creativity has been viewed as a mysterious or mystical phenomenon because no one seems able to offer a universal definition or explanation. People who view creativity in this manner suggest that fruitful inquiry and discussion of it are not possible due to this ambiguity. These critics scoff at the vagueness and looseness of the concept. They recommend the abandonment of this work for more productive, concrete, or tangible lines of thinking. These critics overlook the fact that it is the very nature of creativity to appear to be ambiguous and challenging to study. Those who choose to make progress into understanding the applications of creativity often make their own distinctions and assumptions. For example, Charnes and Cooper (1984, p. xvii), in setting forth the framework for the inquiry into creative and innovative management, indicated:

> For purposes of creative and innovative management, we need to begin to drop old distinctions, and the distinction between entrepreneur, manager, and administrator is surely a candidate for elimination. Thus, by creative management, we refer to new conceptions and new ideas, new entities and new methods that can also be used to provide new directions or new modes of operation for already existing organizations and activities. By innovative management we refer to the ability to implement such new ideas and/or to move successfully in such new directions. Making things work successfully is an old and abiding task of management. It is the coupling of this task with new ideas, directions, and the like that makes it innovative and creative. Finally, it is the ability to induce these kinds of activities in others in an organized way that makes it an act of management rather than only the act of an individual.

There are many theories, definitions, and means of assessing creativity. Despite this profusion, there does appear to be some agreement on key attributes of definitions among investigators most closely associated with work in the field. Welsch (1980) reviewed twenty-two sources that presented definitions of creativity. She analyzed the relevant concepts included in these definitions and found considerable agreement on the key elements. The definition that reflects this agreement was (Welsch 1980, p. 110)

> creativity is the process of generating unique products by transformation of existing products. These products, tangible and intangible, must be unique only to the creator, and must meet the criteria of purpose and value established by the creator.

The analysis of twenty-two authorities' definitions supports this definition. I am sure that another twenty-two authors could be found who would disagree with an element or two, but the definition does seem to address most of the critical elements of creativity. Creativity is a subject that is complex, multifaceted, and dynamic. If one can look beyond the vapor and clouds created by such complexity, there does appear to be some productive agreement upon which to build.

Not only is there some basic agreement in terms of definition, but when one examines the vast literature of creativity, basic categories of inquiry do appear. For example, many researchers who have analyzed the literature of creativity describe essentially four basic arenas within which inquiry has occurred. The boundaries around these arenas seem permeable. In fact, when considering the larger concept of creativity, the boundaries seem to disappear. However, when examining experimentation and progress at a more exact or empirical level, the relationship to the arenas becomes more clear. The four broad areas include inquiry into

- The characteristics and attributes of the creative person
- Criteria determining the creative product
- Identification and description of the stages of the creative process
- The nature of the creative environment

Much of the creativity research available in the literature seems to fall within these four broad categories. In short, it does appear possible to make conceptual progress through the confusion and complexity. Much more work is needed here, but there is something upon which to build.

Another rather pervasive myth surrounding creativity is that it is something magical. Only a few people in human history have ever been really creative. These few lucky geniuses were given a special gift. In earlier times they were thought to have a muse or to be possessed. This approach to creativity resists temptations to explain or explore, and promotes the notion that creativity should simply be appreciated or held in awe. Further, if creativity is magic, then like most magic it is based on tricks or sleight of hand. So even if you were able to explain it, you would merely expose the trickery.

This area of mythology has a very early start. It seems to promote the view that creativity is a rare attribute possessed by only a few gifted individuals. Of course, history seems to favor those who are very high on "the creativity scale." We seem to focus on those who are of exceptional ability or talent and on those who break down paradigms and provide new ways of doing things. We seem to reject another entire type of creativity—that which is more widely distributed and focused on doing things better or making adaptive contributions. What appears to be a major difference in "level" of creativity may be more a matter of "style" difference (see Kirton 1987).

An interesting line of work that calls this myth into question is the attempt to have computers recreate scientific discovery. Simon (1985, p. 4) rejects the idea that sparks of genius need to be present in order for creativity to exist.

> As long as we refer to acts of creativity with awe and emphasize their unfathomability, we are unlikely to achieve an understanding of their processes. And without such an understanding, we are unlikely to be able to provide usable advice as to how to encourage and enhance them. . . . Today we have a substantial body of empirical evidence about the processes that people use to think and to solve problems, and evidence, as well, that these same processes can account for the thinking and problem solving that is adjudged creative.

Creativity appears to be accessible by everyone with a modicum of ability. There does appear to be an infrequency of extremely high-level creatives; but if a person is able to think and solve problems, then there does appear to be room for creativity.

A final myth surrounding creativity is that in order to be creative a person must be mad. This myth asserts that creativity is based on the psychological processes of neurosis or psychosis, that it is a function of a troubled mind. According to this myth, creativity is something to be avoided like any other form of pathology or sickness.

Although much popular literature seems to focus on creativity as madness, many believe that creativity is related to the natural development of human potential. Releasing creativity is healthy. Maslow (1959, p. 94) described this aspect of creativity as being related to mental health when he stated:

> Self-actualizing creativeness is hard to define because sometimes it seems to be synonymous with health itself. And since self-actualization of health must ultimately be defined as the coming to pass of the fullest humanness, or as the "Being" of the person, it is as if self-actualizing creativity were almost synonymous with or a sine qua non aspect of . . . essential humanness.

Once it is possible to go beyond the mythology surrounding creativity, various definitions and conceptions can be identified, and means of assessment can be developed. In fact, there is a growing body of literature focused on these issues and supporting the notion that creativity can be reliably and validly assessed (see Gowan 1972; Roweton 1972; Taylor 1976; Treffinger 1986, 1987; and Treffinger, Isaksen, and Firestien 1983).

CAN WE TEACH CREATIVITY?

If it is possible to identify and assess creativity, it is possible that something can be done to deliberately nurture it. But it is not necessary to wait for a precise, universal definition of creativity; the concept can be approached as a natural human characteristic upon which people differ. As a natural human characteristic it can be deliberately nurtured and developed. As Gowan (1977, p. 89) put it:

> Heretofore we have harvested creativity wild. We have used as creative only those persons who stubbornly remained so despite all efforts of the family, religion, education, and politics to grind it out of them . . . as a result of these misguided efforts, our society produces only a small percentage of its potential of creative individuals (the ones with the most uncooperative dispositions). If we learn to domesticate creativity—that is, to enhance rather than deny it in our culture—we can increase the number of creative persons in our midst by about fourfold.

The need to do something deliberate to nurture creativity appears to be supported by many. But what about the evidence? Torrance (1981, p. 99) reported:

> A few years ago, it was commonly thought that creativity, scientific discovery, the production of new ideas, inventions, and the like had to be left to chance. Indeed many people still think so. With today's accumulated knowledge, however, I do not see how any reasonable, well-informed person can still hold this view. The amazing record of inventions, scientific discoveries, and other creative achievements amassed through deliberate methods of creative problem solving should convince even the most stubborn skeptic.

The research on the deliberate nurturance of creativity begins with about six studies on the effects of training specific techniques (Taylor 1959). By the early seventies, a number of studies were conducted that took a more comprehensive research approach. The largest single summary included 142 individual research studies on deliberate training and their outcomes (Torrance 1972). These studies were published from 1960 to 1972 and encompassed a wide range of training approaches including facilitating testing conditions, motivation, the creative arts, and the Osborn-Parnes Creative Problem Solving Approach. All the approaches investigated had a better than 60 percent success rate with a range of 67 percent for motivation and 91 percent for the Osborn-Parnes program. Follow-up on this line of investigation has included a metaanalysis of long-term training effects (Rose and Lin 1984). In addition, more comprehensive reviews of more studies done since the 1972 review have been reported by Torrance (1986, 1987).

One of the most comprehensive studies of the development of creative thinking abilities was the Creative Studies Project. Parnes and Noller (1972) designed a two-year program to enhance the creativity of college students. They hypothesized that those students completing a four-semester sequence of creative studies courses would perform significantly better than control group students on measures of creative application of academic subject matter, non-academic areas calling for creative performance, personality factors associated with creativity, and selected tests of mental ability and problem solving. (For the most comprehensive reports of the results of this line of research, see Parnes 1987; Reese, Parnes, Treffinger, and Kaltsounis 1976; and Torrance 1986, 1987.)

Some of the criticism surrounding this research (see Mansfield, Busse, and Krepelka 1978, for example) raises questions about research methodology, test validity, and the general construct of creativity. Rather impressive explanations have been provided by Torrance and Presbury (1984) and other researchers who indicate the criteria of success can go far beyond tests of ideational fluency.

It seems that we can do something to deliberately improve the skills of creative problem solving. In concluding a report of their metaanalysis of creativity training effects, reported (Rose and Lin (1984, p. 22)

> The overall results of this metaanalysis suggest that training does affect creativity. While it seems obvious to state that training and practice develop skills, the obvious often needs to be stated. Creative thinking is at once a skill that can be developed through various teaching methodologies and an innate ability that some individuals have in greater abundance than others. This dual nature of creativity is not a contradiction of human development but an affirmation of the flexibility and maleability of individual potential. Through education and training the innate creative thinking ability of individuals can be stimulated and nourished.

If creativity can be identified and assessed as well as nurtured, then it is important for managers, teachers, or anyone who is responsible for accomplishing tasks or managing resources to develop creative problem solving (CPS) skills in themselves and those with whom they work. This assertion is supported by a study done by Johansson (1975) in which it was found that 7 percent of the corporations surveyed offered training courses in creativity, innovation, problem solving, or related fields. Additional support for expanding this type of activity is provided by Drucker (1985) and Basadur and Thompson (1986).

THE CREATIVE PROCESS

Research into the creative personality has provided information about the motivations, styles, abilities, and other characteristics of highly creative individuals (Guilford 1977; MacKinnon 1978). Creative products have been examined in an effort to determine the criteria differentiating the degree of creaticity they manifest. This approach has also provided some promising developments with regard to some basic definitional elements of creativity (Besemer and O'Quinn 1987; Besemer and Treffinger 1981). The environment conducive for creativity has also been the subject of much recent research and inquiry. The focus has been on attempting to understand the attributes of the environment that release and support, as well as hinder or stifle, creative behavior of individuals and groups (Amabile and Sensabaugh 1985; Ekvall and Arvonen 1983). The fourth major category of creativity research, the creative process, provides information into an aspect of creativity that seems to be most amenable to deliberate development.

Early inquiry into the nature and nurture of the creative process began with examinations of the mental activities and processes of highly creative individuals. These studies have yielded a variety of models of the creative process. One model was originally outlined by Osborn (1953) and modified by Parnes, Noller, and Biondi (1977). The current version of the model of creative problem solving is described in Isaksen and Treffinger (1985). The current view of the model is provided in Figure 11-1.

The creative problem-solving process is a model that organizes a variety of specific methods and techniques. When this model is focused on providing acceptable solutions to specific opportunities or challenges it can also be called innovative problem solving. The model, or general system, is based on a series of stages of mental activity consisting of alternating phases of divergent and convergent thinking. Although the graphic depiction of the model may lead to an observation that the process is neat and inflexible, real creative problem solving is rather "messy" and flexible. The user need not sit down and follow this process as though it were a recipe for successful or effective thinking. The actual use and application of the process is quite dynamic, iterative, and expandable. Depending on the specific task and the orientation of the problem solver (among other variables), some aspects of the process will be more fully and appropriately utilized while others may not be used at all (or as much).

In examining the graphic design of the process, it is easy to see that there appears to be an opening up to generate and develop alter-

Figure 11-1. Creative Problem-Solving Process.

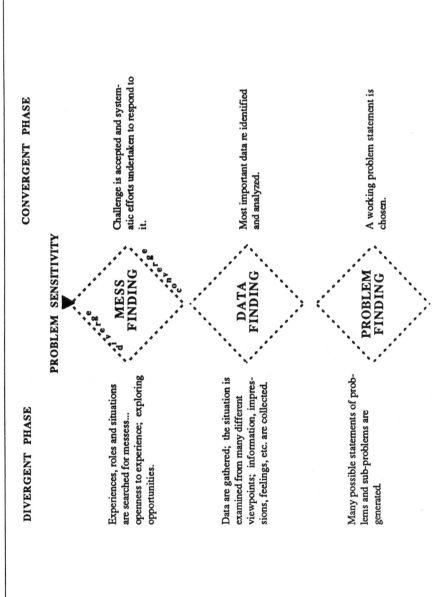

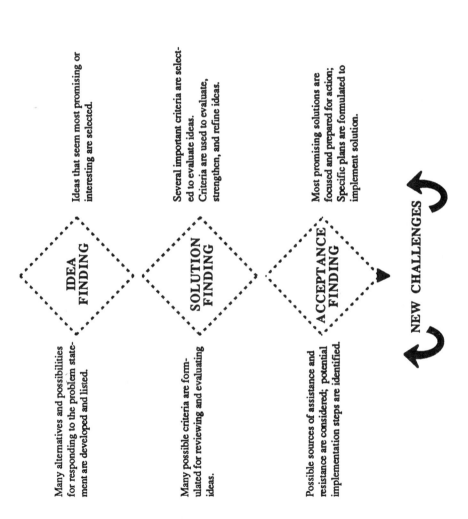

Many alternatives and possibilities for responding to the problem statement are developed and listed.

IDEA FINDING

Ideas that seem most promising or interesting are selected.

Many possible criteria are formulated for reviewing and evaluating ideas.

SOLUTION FINDING

Several important criteria are selected to evaluate ideas. Criteria are used to evaluate, strengthen, and refine ideas.

Possible sources of assistance and resistance are considered; potential implementation steps are identified.

ACCEPTANCE FINDING

Most promising solutions are focused and prepared for action; Specific plans are formulated to implement solution.

NEW CHALLENGES

natives followed by a selecting, choosing, or narrowing down of the alternatives. In each stage, two complementary types of thinking are necessary. The current model is built on the belief that effective problem solving relies upon both creative and critical thinking. Creative thinking is defined as making and communicating meaningful new connections to

- Think of many possibilities
- Think and experience in various ways and use different points of view
- Think of new and unusual possibilities
- Guide in generating and selecting alternatives

The basic principle underlying this type of mental activity is referred to as critical thinking. Critical thinking is defined as analyzing and developing possibilities to

- Compare and contrast many ideas
- Improve and refine promising alternatives
- Screen, select, and support ideas
- Make effective decisions and judgments
- Provide a sound foundation for effective action.

The basic principle underlying this type of thinking is affirmative judgment. These dynamics, guidelines, and the specific methods and techniques that provide the basic tools for the two different types of thinking are described more completely in Isaksen and Treffinger (1985).

Creative problem solving (CPS) does not mean merely rattling off one novel idea after another without ever judging or evaluating the options. The ability to make novel associations is important, but it is equally important to be able to make good decisions and choices about ideas. Therefore, in learning CPS it is important to learn and use effective methods for generating and evaluating ideas. This suggests a reasonable and delicate balance between creative and critical thinking. This balance also implies the need to see creative and critical thinking as mutually important components of effective problem solving. More detailed information regarding the general rationale for learning creative problem solving is provided in Appendix 11-A.

CPS provides a systematic and deliberate application of thinking strategies to ensure a productive balance between creative and critical thinking, it mediates natural blocks or unproductive patterns of thinking, and it provides a common language to help individuals and groups describe and plan their mental activities. As such it can be learned and used in a variety of circumstances by individuals and groups. Managers can use CPS skills and methods in a variety of situations with peers, subordinates, and others.

There are at least three different levels of application for CPS. The first is learning the basic tools of divergent and convergent thinking. These tools can be taught in a condition that is removed from the daily, real-life context of the learners. After learning the basic principles and skills, the techniques can be woven together to form some meaningful problem-solving event. This can take the form of simulations, role playing, and practicing the process on presented challenges and opportunities. A third level of use is applying CPS on real challenges and opportunities. The fact that these are real opportunities means that the application of the skills and techniques is embedded in the context of the problem owner. This model of learning CPS is depicted in Figure 11-2.

The manager may be seen as a teacher or trainer when providing basic awareness and facility with the tools of divergent and convergent thinking. Managers will need to provide a more situational type of leadership as individuals with whom they work begin to practice these skills as meaningful units. The manager who is involved in real applications will find the role of facilitator to be productive.

If a decision is made to involve a group in real applications of CPS, it is helpful if the style of leadership is consistent with the notion of group participation. It would be counterproductive if the leader were to autocratically order all group members to participate and to insist that they enjoy it. It is also important to understand the unique style and skills necessary for effective facilitation. This special type of group-oriented leadership role focuses on the release and effective utilization of group resources.

During a typical CPS session, a group is led by someone called the facilitator. The facilitator is the person who takes primary responsibility for the process and procedures with which the group will be involved. The facilitator structures and prepares the environment, acts as a catalyst for releasing and focusing the efforts of group members, uses appropriate methods and techniques, and is sensitive to the variety of group dynamics. (For more information regarding the role and responsibilities of the facilitator of a CPS session see Isaksen 1983, 1986, and Parnes 1985. Appendix 11-B provides some helpful information for facilitators of small group CPS sessions.)

It is important for group members to know that their efforts have some meaning and relevance. This can be achieved only if someone within the group has a sincere interest in implementing the solutions the group helps create. Thus, the facilitator interacts with a client. This is the individual (or group in some cases) who has decision-

Figure 11-2.   A Model for Learning Creative Problem Solving.

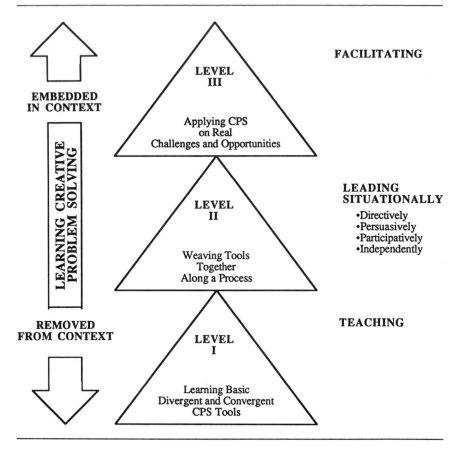

making authority or ownership over a particular situation or challenge. The role of the client in CPS groups supplies content-related expertise and provides convergence and decision making during the session. The client helps to keep the group on track by clarifying the situation, choosing directions and approaches, and participating in the session. In the final analysis, it is the client who needs to have a problem solved or an opportunity reached. Therefore, the role of the client is an important one in determining the effectiveness and productivity of the group's efforts.

Clients need guidance from the facilitator in making choices and judging at appropriate times, and they need to have support for permitting, encouraging, and participating in the divergent activities of the group. For clientship to be present, there must be room for a new approach or fresh ideas that the client is willing and able to implement. This type of ownership builds commitment to the group process and helps in the development of effective groups. The client's role helps to provide the group access to a clear definition of the task at hand. During the session, for example, the client shares the most important data and provides other information the group needs to know before proceeding. Elements of the client's task must be specified and have clear connection to his or her responsibilities.

The other members of the CPS session are called participants and they function collectively as the resource group. These group members suggest options and provide a wide range of alternatives during the session. Effective resource group members show an interest in the client's content, but do not make decisions for the client. They support the decisions the client makes and provide a divergent range of possibilities from which the client can choose.

Resource group members provide energy, diversity of experience, and a variety of viewpoints. The facilitator's challenge is to capitalize on the group's assets and limit their liabilities by providing the necessary balance of creative and critical thinking processes in meeting the needs or goals of the client.

Another major challenge to the facilitator of CPS sessions is to effectively balance and reinforce the roles of facilitator, client, and resource group. Part of this responsibility includes making these roles explicit for all group members so that everyone knows what is expected of him or her. These three roles provide the basic interpersonal framework for CPS in groups.

All group members need to have some basic information regarding what they are expected to do. Agreement is necessary regarding the procedures and methods used for group activity. It is also very helpful for group members to be aware of their strengths and limitations in using various process technologies, as well as the kinds of blocks to creative thinking that may surface during the session. Some deliberate decisions need to me made regarding the number and type of human resources to be part of the session. Heterogeneity of perspectives and experiences as well as homogeneity of levels of power should be considered. Depending on the purposes of the session, a certain number of participants should be specified for the working group (generally five to seven). Larger groups should provide additional facilitators to allow an equivalent ratio. The facilitator may also want to consider the levels of expertise necessary in dealing with the client's task.

So far this chapter has focused on the definitions and approaches to studying creativity. In addition, some background and description of the CPS model, roles for group sessions, and some of the dynamics of these sessions have been provided. The following section will provide a few of the implications for future research into using this type of problem solving with groups.

SOME RESEARCH IMPLICATIONS

The emphasis of current research and development surrounding CPS consists of better targeting the methods and techniques toward specific types of people under specific circumstances and for specific types of outcomes. The research literature has already made significant progress in answering the more basic question regarding the teachability of creative thinking skills. In short, we think we can do something to deliberately enhance the creative thinking ability of individuals. The more targeted questions regarding which techniques work best for whom under what circumstances remain to be answered.

Process Strategies: Development and Testing

Most previous research and development has focused on divergent creative problem solving methodology. There has been much interest, for example, in the brainstorming technique. One frontier for those involved in researching the effectiveness of creative problem solving is the development and testing of convergent CPS methodology. There are many reasons for becoming more concerned with the dynamic balance and complementariness of creative and critical types of thinking. One major reason has been provided by the research surrounding the Creative Studies Project.

The two-year program was very successful for the experimental subjects who stayed with the entire program. The experimental and control subjects who stayed with the program were comparable on nearly all the personality assessments conducted. There were some interesting findings regarding those experimentals and controls who dropped out. They tended to be more directed toward deviancy or culturally disapproved behavior, in closer contact with their primary processes, freer, more impulsive, more likely to drop out of college, less responsible, and more anxious, and they shared other characteristics. Drop-outs seemed to be more interested in artistic forms of creativity and dropped out because of their disappointment in the nature of the course. The implications and more extensive description of the findings of the drop-outs are reported more extensively in Parnes and Noller (1973).

The authors described a possible explanation for the drop-out phenomenon by describing two very different types of people. They used the terms "lines" and "squiggles" in much the same way Juster (1963) did in his book *The Dot and the Line*. The line was described as being straight, rigid, disciplined, responsible, seeking the ability to bend or twist, and to become more free and open. The opposing type of person, the squiggle, was described as undisciplined, unruly, wild, unconventional, original, and uninhibited. In Juster's story, the squiggle loses out to the line who has learned to merge his innate freedom and spontaneity with his self-discipline and responsibility. The drop-outs seemed more like the squiggles; the stay-ins seemed to be more like the lines. The creative studies program seemed better suited to the needs of the lines. The program's emphasis was on learning and applying many divergent techniques of creative problem solving. Perhaps the squiggles had already mastered these skills and needed some assistance with the convergent techniques. The lines were very likely to have been able to recognize the impact of the learning on broadening their repertoire of skills and abilities.

Questions related to this aspect of the development and testing of process strategies include:

- What kinds of convergent process strategies are appropriate for inclusion in the CPS model?

- How might existing or new strategies be developed or modified for inclusion in the CPS model?

- What kinds of convergent techniques are more appropriate for individual (or group) application?

- What convergent tools are most appropriate for which stages of the CPS process?

- Are there nonverbal or nonsemantic convergent (or divergent) techniques that can be useful for CPS?

Cognitive Styles: A Means to Target Technology

Another implication from the drop-out phenomenon from the Creative Studies Project is that different types of people may have different preferences for learning and applying the various CPS process strategies. Those students with certain kinds of cognitive orientation seemed to benefit from and enjoy learning and applying the divergent process strategies the early Creative Studies Program offered.

A line of research supportive of this connection is the work of Gryskiewicz (1982, 1984, 1987). Gryskiewicz used the Kirton Adaptive-Innovative Inventory to evaluate the outcomes of three different CPS technologies. He found that Kirton's construct was replicated by his research and developed the targeted Innovation Model which is considered to be a goal-referenced model for targeted CPS. Certain CPS techniques were likely to produce certain types of outcomes. These finding have important implications for practitioners and facilitators of CPS groups.

If it is possible to examine an individual's preference for a particular type of process technology, it would be likely to do a much better job of diagnosing and selecting appropriate techniques for personal development and qualitatively acceptable results. Facilitators could help individuals select techniques that broaden their repertoire of skills or that focus more appropriately on the type of outcome desired. Individuals can decide about the appropriateness of their match between their own stylistic tendency and the situational determinants. Planning the membership of a CPS group could be assisted by knowing the type of outcome needed and the kind of preferences most likely to produce those results. In short, knowing more about a person's orientation to the CPS process and the specific types of techniques contained therein can increase the ability to be more targeted or intelligent about the application of CPS technology.

Some of the question for research regarding the use of cognitive styles to target CPS technology include:

- What constructs and instrumentation are most appropriate for use within the CPS process? Which instruments have predictive value?

- What types of people have what types of preferences in learning and applying various CPS methods and techniques?

- Do certain styles have strong preferences for certain stages or phases of the CPS process?

- Do certain mixes of styles have qualitatively or quantitatively different outcomes on CPS methods or techniques?

- Do cognitive styles make a difference in how certain individuals behave in the various roles (facilitator, client, resource group) during a CPS session?

Climate Variables: Understanding the Context

A third major area for future inquiry on the subject of using CPS in groups includes concern for the situational contingencies that make a significant difference in selecting people, process technologies, and solutions for challenges and opportunities.

Ekvall and Andersson (1986) identified the following situational factors that contribute to the generation of a particular working climate: visions and goals, strategies, the style of leadership, the work setting and logistics, the characteristics of the individuals, the type of work, how people organize to get the work done, qualitative features of the context, and the values and norms of the people. Within these broad factors, Ekvall has designed a questionnaire to study the working climate or organizations. He defined working climate as the behaviors, attitudes, and feelings typical of life within the workplace. His instrument seems to be able to discriminate those working climates more favorable to creative and innovative outcomes and climate.

To better understand the context within which CPS exists, it appears that certain climate variables must be identified and described. In addition, the amount of domain-relevant knowledge, the structure of the challenge or opportunity, and the qualitative aspects of the available resources would also be important to consider. It seems reasonable that environmental contingencies like time (how far along the task has come, as well as deadlines), budget, degree of crisis orientation, degrees of freedom within the job, the amount and type of experience individuals and teams have with the task and with each other, and what type of motivation is predominant within the workplace are all important to know about when applying CPS in groups.

- What climate factors are the most significant in relation to the client's ownership of the task and what effects do these have on implementation?

- Should certain factors within the context of CPS play a significant role in selecting and using specific process strategies?

- Do certain diffusion strategies have a stronger likelihood of impact in certain situations? What factors seem to make the difference?

- How might certain domain-relevant knowledge requirements be determined and assessed?

- Which quality, time, cost, or acceptance factors have the most predictive value in determining the approach to CPS (group versus individual; focus on learning the process versus solving a problem) most appropriate for the situation?

CONCLUSIONS

Some progress has been made in terms of creativity research in general. Despite the increased efforts to study creativity, some important challenges continue to exist. As MacKinnon (1978, p. 187), indicated:

> As we have seen, empirical research has shed some light of each of the major facets of creativity—the creative product, the creative process, the creative person, and the creative situation. But its illuminations have been spotty and far from complete. There remain critical issues concerning each of these several aspects of creativity which can only be resolved through the findings of future research.

One of the most important needs for the field is a better conceptual schema of key constructs (see Isaksen, Stein, Hills, and Gryskiewicz 1984). An improved conceptual schema could assist in organizing and evaluating gaps in the literature and could encourage networking among interested researchers.

The focus of this chapter has been primarily on the aspects of the creative process; specifically on innovative or creative problem solving in groups. It would serve the emerging field of inquiry into creative and innovative management well to examine this aspect as well as the other apsects of person, product, and situation in an effort to gain a more comprehensive understanding of the practical implications of creativity theory and research.

APPENDIX 11-A: RATIONALE FOR LEARNING CREATIVE PROBLEM SOLVING

Creative learning has been described as becoming aware of challenges or opportunities; bringing together available information; defining the difficulty; searching for solutions; perfecting them; and communicating the results (Torrance and Myers 1970). Creative learning is closely parallel to the creative problem solving (CPS) process (Isaksen and Treffinger 1985). The rationale for the importance of learning CPS includes the following (see Isaksen 1987b):

The Nature of Knowledge. The accumulation of factual information is growing to the point that total comprehensive awareness is not feasible. More comprehensive states of awareness are possible within selected specific disciplines. This may lead to isolated learning of static information. Data can be "looked up," skills of creative problem solving cannot.

The Importance of Creative Thinking Skills. Since the world is changing so rapidly and it is impossible to predict accurately what knowledge or information will be needed, it is important to focus on the development of skills that help individuals become more adaptable to new and changing circumstances. This focus can help shape alternative images of future circumstances.

The Greater Transferability of Skills than Knowledge. The ability and facility of using knowledge are more generalizable and more widely applicable than memorization of data. Skills and abilities are more permanent and related to the process of solving problems.

The Situational Demand for Creativity. There are many situations where there is no immediate or single right answer. These frequent real-life conditions clearly call for a creative type of thinking.

The Enjoyability of Creative Thinking. Learning that calls for the student to actively produce, rather than passively recall, is more motivating. These situations encourage commitment by providing opportunities for learners to follow through on intrinsically motivated tasks. This increases motivation and relevance for learning.

The Naturalness of Creativity. All students benefit from involvement in creative learning. There may be varying levels and styles in the responses, but all people can use their natural level or style of creativity they have when provided the appropriate opportunity.

Foundation on Knowledge. Creative learning is not an either/or situation. You cannot focus purely on creativity. All creativity has a context and data surrounding that context. Creative learning uses traditional content as raw material when there is some relevance and need. The focus on process is not entirely independent or exclusive of content and may actually increase the retention and transfer of learned data.

APPENDIX 11-B: SOME GENERAL CONSIDERATIONS FOR FACILITATORS OF SMALL GROUP CREATIVE PROBLEM SOLVING

The following general considerations for facilitators are meant to provide selected factors to be aware of when planning to use creative problem solving with groups. Rather than being a comprehensive list, these are springboards for planning and thinking. These considerations may overlap and provide a quick checklist for response to the question: Once I am convinced that I want to use a group for creative problem solving, how do I get started?

The Role of a Facilitator. It is important to understand the unique style and skills necessary for effective facilitation. This special type of group-oriented leadership focuses on the release and effective utilization of group resources.

The Client's Role. Establishing and reinforcing the client's role during creative problem solving is a significant element of a productive session. Clients need to have guidance for making choices and judging at appropriate times; and they need to have support for permitting, encouraging, and participating in the divergent activities of the group.

Resource Group Roles. The members of the group who provide energy, diversity of experience, and viewpoints need to have guidance regarding their role. The facilitator's challenge is to have the group use their assets and limit their liabilities by providing the necessary balance of creative and critical thinking processes in meeting the needs or desires of the client.

Process Technology. Awareness of a variety of methods and techniques for use during a CPS session is an important attribute of an effective facilitator. Having the ability to use a diversity of tools provides the facilitator with an efficient means of meeting the needs of a client by fully utilizing the resources of the group. Knowing the type of outcome (adaptive or innovative) various techniques are likely to produce is another aspect to consider.

Orientation to Process. All group members need to have some basic information regarding what they are expected to do. Agreement is necessary regarding the procedures and methods used for group activity. It is also very helpful for group members to be aware of their strengths and limitations in using various process technologies, as well as the kinds of blocks to creative thinking which may surface during the session.

The Structure of the Environment. The climate needs to be conducive to creativity. Group members need to have a certain degree of trust and safety to make contributions and engage in open communication.

Ownership. It is important for group members to know that their efforts have some meaning and relevance. This can be achieved only if the client has sincere interest in implementing the solutions. The client also needs to possess a reasonable amount of influence to be able to implement the solutions. For a sense of ownership to develop, there must be room for a new approach or idea that the client is willing and capable to implement. This type of ownership builds commitment to the group process and helps in the development of effective groups. Elements of the client's task must be specified and have clear connection to the responsibilities of the client.

Planning for Logistics. Some attention must be focused on assuring that the necessary equipment and resources are assembled for the session. This means setting up visuals, flipcharts with plenty of paper and markers, and a means for affixing these papers in a prominent place for all to see. In addition, the group should be assembled in a place where it is possible to be comfortable to share ideas and engage in effective communication.

Timing. The purpose of the session, as well as the amount of time to be scheduled should be explicitly identified for all group members. Is the purpose of the group meeting to identify the initial statement of the problem (planning meeting), to generate ideas, or to develop and evaluate options? A specific task should be identified and an appropriate amount of time should be set aside for the accomplishment of that task.

Group Composition and Size. Some deliberate decisions need to be made regarding the number and type of human resources to be a part of the session. Heterogeneity of perspectives and experiences, as well as homogeneity of levels of power should be considered. Depending on the purposes of the session, a certain number of participants should be specified (generally five to seven). Larger groups should provide additional facilitators to allow an equivalent ratio. (For additional information, see Isaksen 1983, 1986.)

REFERENCES

Amabile, T.M., and S.J. Sensabaugh. 1985. "Some Factors Affecting Organizational Creativity: A Brief Report." Unpublished paper presented at the Creativity, Innovation, and Entrepreneurship Symposium at the George Washington University, Washington, D.C.

Anderson, H. (Ed.). 1959. *Creativity and Its Cultivation.* New York: Harper.

Basadur, M.S., and R. Thompson. 1986. "Usefulness of the Ideation Principle of Extended Effort in Real World Professional and Managerial Creative Problem Solving." *Journal of Creative Behavior 20*: 23-34.

Besemer, S.P., and K. O'Quinn. 1987. "Creative Product Analysis: Testing a Model by Developing a Judging Instrument." In S.G. Isaksen (Ed.), *Frontiers of Creativity Research: Beyond the Basics*. Buffalo: Bearly, pp. 341-57.

Besemer, S., and D.J. Treffinger. 1981. "Analysis of Creative Products: Review and Synthesis." *Journal of Creative Behavior 15*: 158-78.

Charnes, A., and W.W. Cooper. 1984. *Creative and Innovative Management: Essays in Honor of George Kozmetzky*. Cambridge, Mass.: Ballinger.

Drucker, P.E. 1985. *Innovation and Entrepreneurship: Practice and Principles*. New York: Harper & Row.

Ekvall, G., and J. Arvonen. 1983. *Creative Organizational Climate: Construction and Validation of a Measuring Instrument*. Stockholm: The Swedish Council for Management and Organizational Behavior.

Ekvall, G., and Y.T. Andersson. 1986. "Working Climate and Creativity: A Study of an Innovative Newspaper Office." *Journal of Creative Behavior 20*: 215-25.

Firestien, R.L. and D.J. Treffinger. 1983. "Ownership and Converging: Essential Ingredients of Creative Problem Solving." *Journal of Creative Behavior 17*: 32-38.

Ghiselin, B. (Ed.). 1952. *The Creative Process*. New York: New American Library.

Gowan, J.C. 1972. *The Development of the Creative Individual*. San Diego: R. Knapp.

_____. 1977. "Some New Thoughts on the Development of Creativity." *Journal of Creative Behavior 11*: 77-90.

Gryskiewicz, S.S. 1982. "Creative Leadership Development and the Kirton Adaption-Innovation Inventory." Unpublished invited paper presented at the 1982 Occupational Psychology Conference of the British Psychological Society meeting "Breaking Set: New Directions in Occupational Psychology" at Sussex University, Brighton, England.

_____. 1984. "Uniformity Pressure Revisited: An Evaluation of Three Creative Problem Solving Techniques in an Industrial Setting." Unpublished paper presented as a part of a Division 14 Symposium, "Creativity in the Corporation," at the Ninety-Second Annual Convention of the American Psychological Association, Toronto.

_____. 1987. "Predictable Creativity." In S.G. Isaksen (Ed.), *Frontiers of Creativity Research: Beyond the Basics*. Buffalo: Bearly, pp. 305-13.

Guilford, J.P. 1950. "Creativity." *American Psychologist 5*: 444-54.

_____. 1977. *Way Beyond the IQ*. Buffalo: Bearly.

Isaksen, S.G. 1983. "Toward a Model for the Facilitation of Creative Problem Solving." *Journal of Creative Behavior 17*: 18-31.

_____. 1986. "Facilitating Small Group Creativity." In S.S. Gryskiewicz and R.M. Burnside (Eds.), *The Proceedings of Creativity Week*, vol. VIII. Greensboro, N.C.: Center for Creative Leadership, pp. 71-84.

_____. (Ed.). 1987a. *Frontiers in Creativity Research: Beyond the Basics*. Buffalo: Bearly.

_____ . 1987b. "Educational Implications of Creativity Research: An Updated Rationale for Creative Learning." In G. Kaufmann and K. Gronhaug (Eds.). *Innovation: A Cross-disciplinary Perspective*. Oslo: Norwegian University Press.

_____ , D.J. Treffinger. 1985. *Creative Problem Solving: The Basic Course*. Buffalo: Bearly.

_____ , M.I. Stein, D.A. Hills, and S.S. Gryskiewicz. 1984. "A Proposed Model for the Formulation of Creativity Research." *Journal of Creative Behavior* 18: 67–75.

Johansson, B. 1975. "Creativity and Creative Problem Solving Courses in United States Industry." Unpublished paper supported by the Center for Creative Leadership, Greensboro, N.C.

Juster, N. 1963. *The Dot and the Line*. New York: Random House.

Kirton, M.J. 1987. "Adaptors and Innovators: Cognitive Style and Personality." In S.G. Isaksen (Ed.), *Frontiers in Creativity Research: Beyond the Basics*. Buffalo: Bearly, pp. 282–304.

Kuhn, R.L. (Ed.). 1985. *Frontiers in Creative and Innovative Management*. Cambridge, Mass.: Ballinger.

Kuhn, R.L. (Ed.). 1988. *Handbook for Creative and Innovative Managers*. New York: McGraw-Hill.

MacKinnon, D.W. 1978. *In Search of Human Effectiveness: Identifying and Developing Creativity*. Buffalo: Bearly.

Mansfield, R.S., T.V. Busse, and E.J. Krepelka. 1978. "The Effectiveness of Creativity Training." *Review of Educational Research* 48: 517–36.

Maslow, A. 1959. "Creativity in Self-actualizing People." In H.H. Anderson (Ed.), *Creativity and Its Cultivation*. New York: Harper & Brothers, pp. 83–95.

Osborn, A.F. 1953. *Applied Imagination: Principles and Procedures of Creative Problem Solving*. New York: Scribner's.

Parnes, S.J. 1985. *A Facilitating Style of Leadership*. Buffalo: Bearly.

_____ . 1987. "The Creative Studies Project." In S.G. Isaksen (Ed.), *Frontiers of Creativity Research: Beyond the Basics*. Buffalo: Bearly, pp. 156–88.

Parnes, S.J., and H.F. Harding (Eds.). 1962. *A Sourcebook for Creative Thinking*. New York: Charles Scribner's Sons.

Parnes, S.J., and R.B. Noller. 1972. "Applied Creativity: The Creative Studies Project (Part II: Results of the Two-Year Program)." *Journal of Creative Behavior* 6: 164–86.

_____ . 1973. *Toward Supersanity: Channeled Freedom*. Buffalo: DOK Publishers.

Parnes, S.J., R.B. Noller, and A.M. Biondi. 1977. *Guide to Creative Action*. New York: Charles Scribner's Sons.

Raina, M.K. (Ed.). 1980. *Creativity Research: International Perspective*. New Delhi: National Council of Educational Research and Training.

Reese, H.W., S.J. Parnes, D.J. Treffinger, and G. Kaltsounis. 1976. "Effects of a Creative Studies Program on Structure of Intellect Factors." *Journal of Educational Psychology* 69: 401–10.

Rose, L.H., and H.T. Lin. 1984. "A Meta-Analysis of Long Term Creativity Training Programs." *Journal of Creative Behavior* 18: 11–22.

Rothenberg, A., and C.R. Hausman (Eds.). 1976. *The Creativity Question.* Durham, N.C.: Duke University Press.

Roweton, W.E. 1972. *Creativity: A Review of Theory and Research.* Occasional Paper 7. Buffalo: Creative Education Foundation.

Simon, H.A. 1985. "What We Know about the Creative Process." In R.L. Kuhn (Ed.), *Frontiers in Creative and Innovative Management.* Cambridge, Mass.: Ballinger, pp. 3–22.

Taylor, C.W. (Ed.). 1959. *The Third University of Utah Research Conference on the Identification of Creative Scientific Talent.* Salt Lake City: University of Utah Press.

Taylor, I.A. 1976. "Psychological Sources of Creativity." *Journal of Creative Behavior 10*: 193–202.

_____ , and J.W. Getzels. 1975. *Perspectives in Creativity.* Chicago: Aldine.

Torrance, E.P. 1972. "Can We Teach Children to Think Creatively?" *Journal of Creative Behavior 6*: 114–143.

_____ . 1981. "Can Creativity be Increased by Practice?" In J.C. Gowan, J. Khatena, and E.P. Torrance (Eds.), *Creativity: Its Educational Implications.* Dubuque, Iowa: Kendall/Hunt, pp. 99–108.

_____ . 1986. "Teaching Creative and Gifted Learners." In M.C. Wittrock (Eds.), *Handbook of Research on Teaching,* 3rd ed. New York: Macmillan, pp. 630–47.

_____ . 1987. "Teaching for Creativity." In S.G. Isaksen (Ed.), *Frontiers of Creativity Research: Beyond the Basics.* Buffalo: Bearly, pp. 189–215.

_____ , and J. Presbury. 1984. "The Criteria of Success Used in 242 Recent Experimental Studies of Creativity." *The Creative Child and Adult Quarterly 9,* 238–43.

Treffinger, D.J. 1986. "Research on Creativity." *Gifted Child Quarterly 30*: 15–19.

_____ . 1987. "Research on Creativity Assessment." In S.G. Isaksen (Ed.), *Frontiers of Creativity Research: Beyond the Basics.* Buffalo: Bearly, pp. 103–19.

_____ , S.G. Isaksen, and R.L. Firestien. 1983. "Theoretical Perspectives on Creative Learning and Its Facilitation." *Journal of Creative Behavior 17*: 9–17.

Welsch, P.K. 1980. "The Nurturance of Creative Behavior in Educational Environments: A Comprehensive Curriculum Approach." Unpublished Doctoral Dissertation. University of Michigan, Ann Arbor.

12 ASSESSING ORGANIZATIONAL CLIMATES FOR CREATIVITY AND INNOVATION
Methodological Review of Large Company Audits

Robert M. Burnside, Teresa M. Amabile and Stanley S. Gryskiewicz

PURPOSE

There are three main reasons for assessing organizational climates for creativity and innovation: theory, instrument development, and benefit to society. Comprehensive theories of individual creativity and organizational innovation can be advanced by the hands-on study of living organizations. The assessment tool itself can be further refined through audit-trail application: Does it effectively demonstrate how creativity and innovation are affected by organizational climate? Can intervention prescriptions be developed from it? Can postintervention follow-up accurately assess the changes? Finally, the assessment of organizational climates for creativity and innovation can play a beneficial role in current society: Large organizations are playing an increasing role in the development of society; they have become a primary place where individuals experience (or fail to experience) self-actualization; and the increasing complexity and pace of change of overall society puts great pressure on large organizations to fulfill their missions creatively and innovatively.

BACKGROUND

Our methodology at the Center for Creative Leadership (CCL) to assess organizational climates for creativity fits well within the overall stream of study on organizational effectiveness. Whether it is called "organizational development" and defined as an educational strategy for change (Bennis 1969), or "organizational diagnosis" following the medical model (Levinson 1972), or "organizational assessment" defined as "knowledge about how to collect, understand, and use valid information about the functioning of formal organizations" (Lawler, Nadler, and Camman, 1980, p. 2), the study or organizational effectiveness is aimed at accurately assessing an organization's situation and providing this information to the organization in a manner that it will find useful for improving its effectiveness.

In the study of organizational effectiveness, the concepts of organizational climate and culture have emerged as key functional aspects of organizations. The *1985 Annual Review of Psychology* section "Organizational Climate and Culture" (Schneider 1985) notes that researchers are distinguishing between climate and culture. Climate generally refers to interpersonal practices (the social climate as reflected in facets of policies and activities) and is associated with quantitative research methods. Culture refers to the norms and value systems that give rise to the policies and activities, and is associated with qualitative methodologies such as case studies. In a sense, culture is a broader concept that includes climate. As will be seen later, we believe that our methodology, while focused on climate, also measures aspects of the culture of the organization.

The concepts of creativity and innovation have both been studied as organizational attributes. Creativity has been more associated with the effect of the organization on the individual (Pelz and Andrews 1976), and innovation has been more associated with the organization's structure and policies and their impact on its ability to output innovative products and services (Kanter 1983). We believe that the creativity of ideas produced within the organization is largely a function of the internal environment and its effect on stimulating or obstructing the creativity of employees. The organization's innovativeness is related to the structures and policies that affect its ability to implement creative ideas and turn them into innovative products or services. Of course, the two concepts are related: One must have a creative idea before one can implement it, and one must implement it before the creative idea is made real. We believe that our methodology, while focused primarily on assessing organizational creativity, provides knowledge about the organization's innovativeness as well. Our working definition of creativity is "Novel associations (new ideas) that are useful," and innovation is defined as "the successful implementation of new useful ideas."

RATIONALE—RESEARCH METHOD

In 1983 we began our study to answer the question, "What in organizational environments influences creativity?" What makes the difference between high and low levels of creativity? In the first step of developing our methodology, we interviewed 120 research and development scientists (this constitutes our original database). We asked all interviewees to tell us about two events from their work experience, one event that exemplified high creativity and one that exemplified low creativity. Assuming that they were far more expert in their fields than we, we told the interviewees to take as creative whatever *they* judged as creative. We also said that they themselves need not be one of the central characters in the story, as long as they had observed the event closely enough to be able to describe it in detail. Moreover, we asked our interviewees, in telling their stories, to describe as many details as they could remember about both the person(s) *and* the work environment surrounding the event. We did this in an effort to make our information as broad as possible and, thus, as useful as possible.

Nearly all of our 120 scientists did come to the twenty-minute interview prepared to tell the two stories, one exemplifying high creativity and one exemplifying low creativity. We felt that, by using this critical incident technique, we would be more likely to avoid the interjection of personal beliefs about creativity than if we simply asked interviewees what they thought was important for supporting or undermining creativity in organizations.

We then did a detailed content analysis of the typed verbatim transcripts of the tape-recorded interviews. Out of this analysis technique, which will be described in detail later, we developed nine categories of environmental stimulants to creativity, and nine categories of environmental obstacles to creativity. A full report of the research on the original data base can be found in a Technical Report from the Center for Creative Leadership titled *Creativity in the R&D Laboratory* (1987) which was published in Kuhn's *Handbook for Creative and Innovative Managers* (1987).

We then wrote a ninety-three item questionnaire, called the Work Environment Inventory, to capture these eighteen categories. This questionnaire will be described in detail later as well. The methodology as we currently apply it in assessing organizational climates for creativity uses a combination of the questionnaire, for breadth and quantitative measurement, and interviews, for depth and qualitative assessment.

Many other researchers have looked at creativity in organizations. What makes our methodology unique, however, is a combination of three factors. First, most other work examining creativity in organizations has employed questionnaires as the major (or sole) data source. Second, the net we cast in the interviews was essentially without limits, allowing the interviewees to describe whatever came to mind, rather than being based on our preconceptions or a literature review. Third, our concepts are based on data that came directly from individuals working in large organizations in an area traditionally charged with "being creative": the R&D department, rather than only from our own experience.

Ekvall, Arvonen, and Waldenstrom-Lindblad (1983) have developed a climate assessment questionnaire that is most comparable to our current process. They originally did a literature review (Ekvall 1983) to determine factors to include in an assessment questionnaire. Our of this review, four "climate variables" were hypothesized: mutual trust and confidence; challenge and motivation; freedom; and pluralism. As we will see later, some of these same concepts emerged along with others from our research. Ekvall developed and tested a fifty-item questionnaire, which has been used in a number of organizations. Ekvall and his colleagues (1983) report that the instrument is reliable, measures the concepts for which it was intended, differentiates between organizations, and has criterion validity. Factor analysis of data has identified seven factors in the climate: challenge, support for ideas, trust, freedom in the organization, freedom in the job, dynamism, and tension. In practice, the instrument is given out in the organization to be assessed, and data are reported back both by item and factor.

Rickards and Bessant (1980) prepared a climate questionnaire that they call the Creativity Audit. In designing their instrument, they "prepared a checklist of factors linked to creativity and innovation based on our own practical experience." Eventually, a twenty-six-item version was tested on scientists from six different laboratories. In general use of the creativity audit, data are reported back as a mean for each item. Comparisons are provided with the means for a larger group, either the larger organization or all groups studied to date. This difference-of-means method is reported to have high face validity with the participants and to be useful to them in understanding where improvement is needed. Rickards and Bessant express the hope that their questionnaire will be used by others in order to develop standardized norms for different populations. They also acknowledge that further validation efforts are needed.

Siegel and Kaemmerer (1978) developed a sixty-one-item questionnaire that measures the "perceived support for innovation in organizations." Based on their experiences, they thought five dimensions to be characteristic of innovative organizations: certain types of leadership, ownership, norms for diversity, continuous development, and consistency. The questionnaire was developed with a sample of 1,899 students from a variety of school systems that have been independently rated as either innovative or traditional. Factor analysis identified three categories: support for creativity, tolerance of differences, and personal commitment. Data analysis validated that the instrument did differentiate between the innovative and the traditional schools.

Of all instruments available in the public domain, the aforementioned questionnaires appear to be the most similar to our methodology. Of course, other research has been done, such as that by Pelz and Andrews (1976), which has a broader focus on understanding how the organization affects the overall effectiveness of scientists, and by Kanter (1983), who focuses more on organizational innovation than creativity. We chose to review authors who, like us, are focused on assessing internal organizational climates for creativity. A number of commercial firms such as Arthur D. Little are also offering some kind of organizational assessment of creativity, but their methodology is not available in the public domain.

PRELIMINARY DATA SETS

The first use of our combined interview and questionnaire methodology was with the charge card division of an international bank, which we shall call Bank, Inc. Bank, Inc. had requested a training course from the Center for Creative Leadership. The methodology we call Innovation Audit was used to collect data as a needs assessment prior to designing the course. In this very large division, 100 questionnaires were sent to a random sample of which 57 were returned completed, and 16 of these 57 were randomly selected for interviews. The data analysis report was given to the Director of Human Resources for the division. The process occurred in fall 1985.

The second use of the methodology was with the sales and marketing division of a major railroad, which we shall call Railroad, Inc. This division consisted of 1,100 exempt employees, of which about 500 were in a union, and 600 were not. Only the nonunion employees participated in the assessment. Of the 250 questionnaires mailed to randomly selected employees, 220 questionnaires were returned completed, and 25 of those employees were interviewed. The sample consisted of all levels of management from the entry level to the level just below vice-president. Four subunits of the division were analyzed as well as the total. The report was given to the four vice presidents that headed up the four subunits of the division.

The third use of the methodology was with the marketing and medical division of a large pharmaceuticals firm, which we shall call Pharmaceuticals, Inc. Of the total of 82 exempt employees, 69 completed questionnaires, and 13 were interviewed. Two subunits of the division were analyzed in addition to the whole. The report was given to the vice-president of the division and five members of his management team.

The questionnaire alone, without the whole methodology, was administered to a widely scattered lower-to-middle management sample of a large Canadian petrochemical firm, which we shall call Petrochemical, Inc. This sample of 249 employees is included in the overall database for the questionnaire.

Table 12-1. The Innovation Audit Process of the Center for Creative Leadership.

1. *Kick off meeting* with the advisory committee, a client group consisting of the top management of the organization being assessed and the corresponding human resource professionals assigned to that organization.

2. *Select a sample population* for questionnaires and interviews. The selection process is random within targeted areas of the organization unless client introduces reasons for a nonrandom selection.

3. *Mail questionnaires and conduct interviews.*

4. *Analyze data.* Questionnaire data is processed and analyzed, interviews transcribed, and transcripts' content analyzed.

5. *Prepare written report* as "draft," sent to advisory committee one week before presentation.

6. *Present report to advisory committee.* Meet individually with top management before committee meeting if appropriate; at meeting establish if the committee agrees with our interpretation of the data by considering the report a draft until the committee endorses it.

7. *Finalize recommendations* with the advisory committee after an overnight break.

8. *Issue the final report.*

9. *Assist in implementation* of actions as needed, such as feedback to the larger organization.

10. *Follow up to determine results.*

OVERVIEW OF THE METHODOLOGY

Table 12-1 outline of our methodology, the Innovation Audit. The audit process is intended to serve as an organizational intervention with the goal of improving the climate for creativity. Therefore, the clients are constantly involved in the process as coresearchers, the end objective is clearly stated at the start, consideration is given to the emotional impact of feedback on management and on the organization overall, feedback from all participants is encouraged, and heavy emphasis is given to determining recommendations that are actionable and internalized as the client's own desired actions. The balance of this chapter will concentrate on the specific methodology of the critical incident interviews and the questionnaire.

CRITICAL INCIDENT INTERVIEWS

About a week before the interview, the interviewee receives a letter from the Center for Creative Leadership interviewer that asks the interviewee to prepare notes for the interview on two topics. Instructions say, "Come prepared to describe an event that has occurred in your work in the last twelve months that you consider to have been highly creative, and a separate event that you consider to have been low in creativity." (The specified time period is not always twelve months. It may be different depending on what the organization's advisory committee deems appropriate.) The letter states that interviewees can use their own definition of creativity and need not have been personally involved in the event (though they certainly can be); the important point is that they should have observed the event closely enough to describe details. They are encouraged to talk about anything that they feel made the difference between this event and other less creative events, in terms of the persons involved and in terms of the work environment.

The interview is conducted at the client's site by a CCL staff member. Confidentiality is assured, and the tape recording is described as necessary for accuracy. The interviewee is given permission to turn off the tape recorder at any time, though interviewees rarely take advantage of this opportunity. Interviews last twenty to thirty minutes.

After verbatim transcripts are made, their contents are analyzed. The content analysis occurs in two stages. In stage 1, two separate coders read identical copies of the transcript independently and look for comments that they feel should be coded as examples of environmental factors that either stimulate or obstruct creativity. Environmental factors are defined as "factors outside of the problem solver(s), including other people, that served to stimulate or obstruct creativity." Stimulants are coded by highlighting with a green marker, and obstacles are coded by highlighting with a red marker. The comment coded may be a word, phrase, or sentence. When the transcript is completed, the two coders compare their transcripts and note their disagreements. Where disagreements exist, the two coders must come to a decision. Reliability is calculated according to this formula:

$$\text{reliability}_1 = \frac{2(C_1, C_2)}{C_1 + C_2} \times 100\%,$$

where C_1 = total number of comments marked by coder 1; C_2 = total number of comments marked by coder 2; and C_1, C_2 = number of comment assignments both coders agreed on before discussion.

Reliabilities for stage 1 have been acceptable to date, averaging above 70 percent in the agreement level (see Table 12-2).

In stage 2, another team of two coders takes the master set of transcripts from the stage 1 team (with all the final agreed-upon categories), and proceeds to code all stimulants into ten stimulant categories. These subcategories of environmental stimulants and obstacles are a priori categories that were intuitively determined by reading the original 120 transcripts. The subcategories do appear useful for capturing the data. In all data sets using this categorization, less than 8 percent of comments have been assigned to the "Miscellaneous" subcategories. See Table 12-3 for a complete listing of these twenty categories with a brief description of each.

The team 2 coders work from the master set of transcripts marked by team 1. They work independently, passing transcripts back and forth and marking their categorizations of each comment on their separate coding sheets. They work first on the obstacles, coding all comments into the ten subcategories, and then on the stimulants. They first attempt to place each comment into categories 1 to 8, and only then consider the broader categories 9 and 10. When both

Table 12-2. Critical Incident Interviews, Content Analysis Procedure— Stage 1 Interrater reliabilities.

Group	N	Reliability (%)
Original database Interviews	120	79.7
Bank, Inc.	16	64.4
Railroad, Inc.	25	75.8
Pharmaceuticals, Inc.	13	64.0

Table 12-3. Critical Incident Interviews, Content Analysis Procedure—
Environmental Factors.

Subcategory: Environmental Stimulants

1. *Freedom and control.* Freedom to decide what to do or how to do it; a sense of control over one's work or ideas.

2. *Good supervisory management.* Manager communicates effectively, sets clear direction without managing too tightly, supports group.

3. *Challenge.* Challenging work, need for solution, work feels important.

4. *Sufficient resources.* Access to appropriate resources, including people, funds, facilities, information.

5. *Encouragement.* Management enthusiasm for new ideas, nonevaluative atmosphere, risk orientation.

6. *Recognition.* General sense that creative work will receive appropriate feedback, recognition, and reward.

7. *Pressure.* Positive feelings of pressure from high expectations and time deadlines.

8. *Sufficient time.* Enough time for developing creative solutions to problems.

9. *Various organizational characteristics.* Aspects of the overall organization that do not fit the above categories—e.g., cooperative and collaborative atmosphere, good communication, valuing of creativity, open atmosphere.

10. *Miscellaneous other.* Any stimulants in the environment that didn't fit above.

Subcategory: Environmental Obstacles

1. *Constraint.* Lack of freedom to decide what to do or how to do it, lack of control over one's work or ideas.

2. *Poor supervisory management.* Manager with poor planning skills, unclear goals, poor communications and personal skills.

3. *Organizational indifference.* Lack of psychological support in organization for new ideas or creative work; apathy; low expectations.

4. *Insufficient Resources.* Lack of the appropriate resources including people, funds, facilities, and information.

5. *Status quo.* Emphasis on keeping things the same; avoiding risks, avoiding controversy, taking the conservative course.

6. *Inappropriate evaluation.* Too much criticism of new ideas or work; work evaluated on external criteria, not on the value of the work itself; lack of feedback on work.

7. *Competition.* Inappropriate competition within the organization.

8. *Insufficient time.* Too much workload in too little time.

9. *Various organizational characteristics.* Aspects of the overall organization that do not fit the above categories, including inappropriate reward systems, lack of support from other areas, overly formal and bureaucratic procedures, little regard for creativity, overly political atmosphere.

10. *Miscellaneous other.* All other obstacles in the environment that did not fit the above categories.

Table 12-4. Critical Incident Interviews, Content Analysis Procedure—
Stage 2 Interrater Reliabilities.

Group	N	Stimulants (%)	Obstacles (%)
Original database	120	78.8	69.3
Bank, Inc.	16	57.7	57.0
Railroad, Inc.	25	70.1	62.1
Pharmaceuticals, Inc.	13	72.4	69.5
Totals:		73.3	64.9
Grand Total: 70.0%			

coders have completed the same transcript, the codings are compared. After disagreements are resolved, a master subcategorization
coding sheet is prepared. Interrater reliabilities are calculated according to the following formula:

$$\text{reliability}_2 \ = \ \frac{C_1, C_2}{C_t} \ \times \ 100\%,$$

where C_1, C_2 = total number of comment assignments both coders
agree on before discussion, and C_t = total number of comments that
had to be assigned (as designated by the team 1 coders).

Reliabilities to date have averaged in the 705 area (see Table
12-4). Interrater reliabilities have consistently been lower in stage 2
than in stage 1, probably because of the greater number of categories into which each comment can be placed. Also, for whatever reason, comments about stimulants seem consistently easier to code
than comments about obstacles.

Data are compiled from the master data coding sheet by obtaining
frequency counts for each interview on the number of the subcategories of stimulants and obstacles that were mentioned at least once.
Repeated mentions of a subcategory within an interview are not
counted. This conservative approach is taken in order to reduce the
effect of a garrulous person making the same point a number of
times. Interviewees average comments on 4.5 of the 10 stimulant
categories, and 4.0 of the 10 obstacle categories. For each group of
interviews, the categories can be ranked by the total number of mentions over all interviewees. See Table 12-5 for an example of how
categories ranked at Railroad, Inc.

The primary use of the content analysis data in the report to the
client is the use of quotes from the interviews to bring to life, in the
local jargon of employees, what the stimulants and obstacles are in

Table 12-5. Critical Incident Technique, Content Analysis Procedure—
Rankings of Subcategories at Railroad, Inc. (Of the total comments made,
what percentage fell into each subcategory?)

Stimulants		Obstacles	
Subcategories	% of Total	Subcategories	% of Total
1. Freedom and control	14.8	1. Various organizational characteristics	22.8
3. Various organizational characteristics	14.1	2. Status quo	15.4
3. Encouragement	14.1	3. Organizational indifference	13.2
3. Sufficient resources	14.1	4. Constraint	12.5
5. Good supervisory management	12.6	5. Insufficient resources	9.5
6. Challenge	11.9	6.5 Poor supervisory management	7.4
7. Pressure	6.7	6.5 Miscellaneous other	5.9
8.5 Sufficient time	4.4	8.5 Insufficient time	5.9
10. Miscellaneous other	2.9	10. Competition	0.0
	100.0		100.0

that particular environment. For example, at Railroad, Inc., the stimulant category freedom was primarily spoken of as the *lack* of the usual top-down management control, rather than the presence of true freedom. Following is a quote from one of the interviews illustrating this:

> Nobody was in town when the project started. When the initial meeting was held, none of our superiors were here. So we just plunged ahead. That's the thing that helped us most, because we had nobody providing us with "insights" as to the shoulds, couldn'ts, and don'ts.

In addition, the "Miscellaneous other" category may contain an important environmental factor that is not captured in the a priori categories. For example, at Pharmaceuticals, Inc., the environmental obstacle of "medical profession" was mentioned by a number of interviewees. The medical profession's emphasis on not taking risks with human life was considered a climate factor that led to risk aversion. Thus, in the final report, this unique obstacle was reported as its own category. Following is a quote from one of the interviews illustrating this category:

> I have problems with the word *creativity* because when you come through medicine in training there is very little you can be creative in. You can be creative in personal relationships, the way you handle people, the way that you handle situations—you have some movement there—but there are certain lines and certain community medical practices that need to be followed which do not allow for a terrible amount of creativity.

Looking ahead, we will attempt to subdivide the broad "Various organizational characteristics" categories into more focused categories. Our initial review of comments in these categories indicates that the stimulant category may be broken into "Unity and cooperation" and "Creativity supports." The obstacle category may be broken into "Political problems" and "Structures and procedures." On the whole, we are convinced that the content analysis of critical incident interviews plays a crucial role in the assessment of climate, one that is both supplementary and complementary to the questionnaire: It translates general concepts into local language; it provides a place for specific examples of concrete problems to which the client can refer; and it allows capture of important environmental factors that are unique to the organization.

WORK ENVIRONMENT INVENTORY

The Work Environment Inventory (WEI) is a ninety-three-item inventory that was developed from the content analysis categories that we captured from the original 120 interviews. Items were written for each of the nine identified stimulant and obstacle categories, eliminating only the "Miscellaneous other" categories (see Table 12-3 for the list of categories). Wording of the items was kept close to the wording the interviewees used. In the assessment of organizational climate, the WEI enables much larger sampling than the interviews, as well as more sophisticated quantitative analyses.

In the instructions, respondents are told to answer the questions in terms of the feelings or impressions they most often have about their current work environment. Current work environment is defined for them as the day-to-day social and physical environment in which they currently do most or all of their work. A four-point response scale we used: 1 = never or almost never true of your current work environment; 2 = sometimes true of your current work environment; 3 = often true of your current work environment; and 4 = always or almost always true of your current work environment. We developed this frequency response scale from the assumption that most stimulants and obstacles appear at some time in every environment. Our major interest is in the frequency with which each factor appears; this should give an accurate picture of the environment. Moreover, we chose a scale without a midpoint to force respondents away from a neutral default option.

The number of items written for each a priori category varied from a low of one in the obstacle category of "Insufficient time" to a high of thirteen in the stimulant category of "Various organizational characteristics." See Table 12-6 for examples of items written for the categories of "freedom and "Status quo."

The primary data analysis that is returned to the client consists of the calculated means for each item and each category. Categories are ranked by means within stimulants and obstacles from most prevalent to least prevalent. See Table 12-7 for the category rankings at Railroad, Inc.

It is interesting to compare Table 12-7 to Table 12-5. At first one would expect that the rankings of stimulant and obstacle categories would be the same from the content analysis procedure and the WEI. However, they are obviously different. We believe this is due to differences in the techniques. In the critical incident interview, people are asked to tell about an event that stands out in their mind as especially high or low in creativity. By definition, they are describing an unusual event. In the WEI they are being asked to report on the usual—two very different tasks. This helps explain, for example, why encouragement was the third most mentioned stimulant category in the interviews while being ranked the sixth most prevalent stimulant in the WEI. Its very rarity in the usual environment brought it to mind in the interview.

Table 12-6. Work Environment Inventory, Category Item Examples.

Stimulant Category Freedom

I have the freedom to decide how I am going to carry out my project(s).

I feel a sense of control over my own work and my own ideas here.

There is a generally open atmosphere here.

Obstacle Category "Status quo"

There is much emphasis in this organization on doing things the way we have always done them.

Management does not want to take risks in this organization.

This organization generally takes a conservative approach.

Table 12-7. Work Environment Inventory, Category Rankings at Railroad, Inc. (N = 220).

Rank	Category Mean	Stimulant Category	Rank	Category Mean	Obstacle Category
1	3.3	Sufficient resources	1	2.8	Insufficient time
2	3.1	Challenge	2	2.6	Status quo
3	2.9	Freedom and control	3	2.6	Inappropriate evaluation
4	2.9	Good supervisory management	4	2.3	Constraint
5	2.6	Pressure	5	2.3	Various organizational characteristics
6	2.5	Encouragement	6	2.1	Competition
7	2.5	Recognition	7	1.8	Organizational indifference
8	2.3	Various organizational characteristics	8	1.7	Poor supervisory management
9	2.3	Sufficient time	9	1.7	Insufficient resources

Clients are told that the WEI statistics are descriptive and should be considered as most reliable as an indication of the relative presence of the factors within the organization. They are told that they must exercise their own judgment as to how serious the prevalence of the obstacles is. Until the scales have been further developed and independent validation has been completed, no claims are being made about the predictive nature of the data. The WEI data is used in conjunction with the interview data to give a well-rounded description of the climate within the organization.

In the final report, only the top three or four most prevalent obstacles and stimulants are considered, to keep the data digestible. The categories are presented in their WEI category mean order, and each category is "brought to life" with comments from the interviews that illustrate that category. When the report draft is presented to the client's advisory committee, the client is encouraged to challenge the findings. To date, all clients have found the data to have high face validity. The recommendations for action in the report are based on the Center for Creative Leadership staff's experiences with improving organizational climates for creativity in various organizations. The overall process of the climate assessment intervention and its effect on client organizations to date is reported in a Center for Creative Leadership Technical Report.

Now that our WEI sample is large enough (currently an N of 595), we are proceeding with scale development. In order to provide more useful, nonredundant information to clients and to analyze the data in statistically meaningful ways, we combine stimulant and obstacle categories into basic scales where it seems reasonable to do so. For example, we have one time scale called "Sufficient time" consisting of the original "Sufficient time" item (positively scored) and the "Insufficient time" item (reverse scored). As another example, we combined "Freedom" and constraint items into one "Freedom" scale. Using the data from the first three audits, we have found these preliminary scales to have generally good internal consistency (see Table 12-8).

Besides internal consistency analyses on our a priori scales, we are simultaneously conducting several other types of analyses in our scale development effort, including

- Item analyses, examining responses for skewness, kurtosis, and unusual variances

- Factor analyses, comparing the item groupings that emerge with item groupings that emerge with item groupings on the a priori scales

Table 12-8. **Work Environment Inventory, Preliminary Scale Analyses** (N = 390).

	Number of Items	Alpha
Environmental Stimulants		
Freedom and control	5	.72
Challenge	3	.67
Sufficient time	2	.71
Pressure	3	.53
Good supervisory management	14	.91
Overall organizational support	25	.89
Recognition	4	.79
Sufficient resources	4	.60
Environmental Obstacles		
Status quo	9	.82
Inappropriate evaluation	4	.66
Organizational indifference	4	.76

- Discriminant item-total correlations, determining if each item in fact fits best on the scale to which we have assigned it

Items with low correlation to their scale or high correlations with many scales will be dropped. Resulting scales will be reviewed to ensure that all major concepts are covered. If missing, new scales will be written and tested. Factor analysis will be used in parallel with our a priori scales to determine the most effective and understandable scales. Reliabilities will be obtained for internal consistency and consistency over time.

THE NEXT STEP: VALIDATION

Results of our climate assessment methodology still need to be validated. Specifically, we need to determine the extent to which each scale on the WEI differentially predicts *creativity*, as distinct from other aspects of organizational effectiveness, such as *efficiency* or *productivity*, by relating the findings to independent measures of the creativity and productivity of the groups being studied.

As part of our validation efforts in future climate assessments we will collect, along with the WEI and interview data, independent self, peer, and supervisor ratings of the creativity and productivity of the groups being studied. We hope in future work to have outside experts rate these same characteristics of the groups being studied. Finally, we are proceeding to find an organization where the creativity levels of different groups have already been assessed by various methods, and to see whether the WEI findings predict the differences in creativity.

CONCLUSION

This methodological approach (combining content-analyzed critical incident interviews, questionnaires, and a battery of validation techniques) should ultimately prove useful for studying not only creativity and innovation, but a wide variety of content areas. As far as the particular content of creativity and innovation, our creativity interviews and Work Environment Inventory are proving to be useful tools for clients in unearthing particular climate factors that are stimulating or obstructing the creativity of their employees.

Our primary work now is to finish the scale development and the validation efforts so that we may make the process widely available. Our goal is to improve the effectiveness of organizations by releasing the creativity of the individuals working within them.

REFERENCES

Amabile, T.M., and S.S. Gryskiewicz. 1987. *Creativity in the R&D Laboratory.* Greensboro, N.C.: Center for Creative Leadership.

_____. 1987. "Creative Human Resources in the R&D Laboratory: How Environment and Responsibility Impact Innovation." In R.L. Kuhn (Ed.), *Handbook for Creative and Innovative Managers.* New York: McGraw-Hill.

Bennis, W.G. 1969. *Organizational Development.* Reading, Mass.: Addison-Wesley.

Ekvall, G. 1983. *Climate, Structure, and Innovativeness of Organizations* (Report 1). Stockholm: The Swedish Council for Management and Organizational Behavior.

_____, 1983. J. Arvonen, I. Waldenstron-Lindblad. 1983. *Creative Organizational Climate* (Report 2). Stockholm: The Swedish Council for Management and Organizational Behavior.

Kanter, R.M. 1983. *The Change Masters.* New York: Simon and Schuster.

Lawler, E.E., III, D.A. Nadler, and C. Cammann. 1980. *Organizational Assessment.* New York: John Wiley.

Levinson, H. 1972. *Organizational Diagnosis.* Cambridge, Mass.: Harvard University Press.

Peltz, D.C., and F.M. Andrews. 1976. *Scientists in Organizations,* rev. ed. Ann Arbor: Institute for Social Research of the University of Michigan.

Rickards, T., and J. Bessant. 1980. "The Creativity Audit: Introduction of a New Research Measure during Programmes for Facilitating Organizational Change." *R&D Management 10:* 67-75.

Schneider, B. 1985. "Organizational Climate and Culture." *Annual Review of Psychology 36:* 573-611.

Siegel, S.M., and W.F. Kaemmerer. 1978. "Measuring the Perceived Support for Innovation in Organizations." *Journal of Applied Psychology 63:* 553-62.

13 REQUIREMENTS FOR STUDYING INNOVATION PROCESSES

Andrew H. Van de Ven

Little is known about how innovations actually emerge, develop, grow, or terminate over time. Yet an appreciation of temporal processes is fundamental to managing innovations. Basic to developing knowledge about the management of innovation is a methodology for studying the process of innovation in real time while an innovation develops from concept to implemented reality. Four requirements are necessary to undertake research on the process of change in general and innovations in particular.

1. A clear set of concepts about the object being studied
2. Systematic methods for observing change in the object over time
3. Methods for representing raw data to identify process patterns
4. A motor or theory to make sense of the process pattern

While simple to set forth, these requirements are challenging to achieve. As Pettigrew (1985), Nisbet (1970), and Van de Ven and Poole (1987) indicate, they represent basic methodological steps in processual analysis and for building "process theories" as distinct from "variance theories." Since methods for processual analysis have

I gratefully acknowledge stimulating comments and ideas developed in this paper from M. Scott Poole, as well as other colleagues involved in the Minnesota Innovation Research Program. Support for this research program has been provided (in part) by a grant to the Strategic Management Research Center at the University of Minnesota from the Program on Organization Effectiveness, Office of Naval Research (code 4420E), under contract No. N00014-84-K-0016, as well as other sources.

received far less attention and codification than methods for variance analysis (Mohr 1982), this chapter addresses how these four requirements might be achieved to study processes of organizational innovation and change over time. The major example that will be used to illustrate these requirements will be the Minnesota Innovation Research Program. The MIRP research program, which began in 1983, consists of thirteen longitudinal studies that are tracking a wide variety of innovations in real time as they are being developed.

The four requirements for processual analysis derive from definitions of change and processes of change. By definition, *change is an empirical observation of differences in time on one or more dimensions of an entity.* All four elements in this definition are necessary. As Nisbet (1970) describes, a mere array of differences is not change; only differences. Time is also a critical element, for any differences necessarily involve earlier and later points of reference. Mobility, motion, or activity in themselves do not constitute change, although each is to some degree involved in change. Certain dimensions or categories of an entity are the objects being transformed. Change without reference to an object is meaningless.

The process of change adds an additional and more abstract element to the definition of change. Whereas change is an empirical or manifest observation, the *process of change is an inference of a latent pattern of differences noted in time.* Thus, change processes are not directly observed. Instead, they are conceptual inferences about the temporal ordering of relationships among observed changes.

With these definitions, the relationships among the four requirements for processual analysis become apparent. While the first requirement specifies the objects being investigated, the second requirement deals with empirical observations of changes in these objects. The third requirement addresses methods for inferring processes of change, and the fourth requirement is concerned with theories or conceptual motors that can explain these processes of change. The remainder of this chapter elaborates on these four requirements.

A CLEAR SET OF CONCEPTS ABOUT THE OBJECT BEING STUDIED

Implicitly or explicitly, observation of any innovating process entails examination of a set of categories or variables. As should be expected, different categories will produce very different substantive inquiries. For example, the MIRP framework focuses on five key concepts: ideas, people, transactions, context, and outcomes. These concepts derive from the MIRP definition of the innovation process, which is the development and implementation of new ideas by people engaged in transactions with others within an institutional context. Outcomes are perceptions about performance of the process as the innovation develops over time.

Whatever the concepts and organizational settings examined in a study, research on innovation processes requires a clear understanding of how change can be observed. Measurement of change necessarily implies not only a longitudinal study, but also rigorous methods for observing differences over time in the conceptual categories of the innovation being investigated.

SYSTEMATIC METHODS FOR OBSERVING CHANGE OVER TIME

Most studies of innovation or change to date have been retrospective case histories conducted after the outcomes were known (Van de Ven and Associates 1987). However, it is widely recognized that prior knowledge of the success or failure of an innovation invariably biases a study's finding. While historical analysis is necessary for examining many questions and concerted efforts can be undertaken to minimize bias, it is generally better, if possible, to initiate historical study before the outcomes of an strategic change process become known.

Moreover, time itself sets a frame of reference that directly affects our perceptions of change. As Pettigrew (1985) notes, the more we look at present-day events, the easier it is to identify change; the longer we stay with an emergent process and the further back we go to disentangle its origins, the more likely we are to identify continuities. Appreciating this dilemma requires that investigators carefully design their studies in order to observe changes that are relevant to the purposes and uses of their research.

For example, if the purpose of a study is to understand the management of innovation, it is generally necessary for researchers to place themselves into the manager's temporal and contextual frames of reference. Presumably, this initially involves conducting a retrospective case history to understand the context and events leading up to the present innovation being investigated. However, the major focus of the study would entail conducting real-time observations of the innovation effort as it unfolds over time, without knowing a priori the outcomes of the actions taken.

Both regularly scheduled and intermittent field observations are necessary for a processual analysis of how changes occur over time. Repetitive surveys and interviews provide comparative-static observations of the organizational concepts or dimensions being traced over time. As defined above, *difference scores* between time periods on these dimensions determine what *changes* occurred in the organizational unit or program. But to understand how these changes come about, there is a need to supplement regularly scheduled data collection with intermittent real-time data. For example, this involves observing key committee meetings, decision or crisis events, and conducting informal discussions with key participants engaged in an innovation. Both regularly scheduled and occasional observations are necessary in a processual analysis because, while difference scores between regularly scheduled observations will identify *what* changes occurred, real-time observations at key moments are needed to understand *how* these changes occurred.

As Argyris (1968, 1985) has forcefully argued over the years, significant new methods and skills of action science are called for to conduct this kind of longitudinal real-time research. In addition, longitudinal studies require significant commitment on the part of the researcher and long-term organizational access that few researchers have achieved to date. As a consequence, very few processual studies of innovation have been conducted. Our processual research experience (Van de Ven and Associates 1987) suggests that one reason why gaining organizational access has been problematic is that researchers seldom place themselves into the manager's frame of reference to conduct their studies. Without observing the innovating process from a manager's perspective, it becomes difficult (if not impossible) for an investigator to understand the dynamics confronting managers who are involved in an innovation effort and thereby to generate findings that are relevant to the theory and practice of innovation management. If organizational participants perceive little potential use of a study's findings, there is little to motivate their providing access and information to an investigator.

METHODS FOR TABULATING RAW DATA
TO IDENTIFY PROCESSUAL PATTERNS

Obtaining systematic observations of the innovation process over time using multiple methods quickly produces an overwhelming amount of rich raw data about an organizational innovation effort. Drawing inferential links between these data and theory requires methods for organizing and evaluating the raw data in a manner that facilitates identifying processual patterns.

While the task may seem formidable on quantitative data, an extensive methodology has developed over the years to codify procedures for handling longitudinal panels of quantitative data, including procedures for constructing computer data files and for analyzing longitudinal data (Tuma and Hannan 1984). Far less has been written about methods for analyzing longitudinal qualitative data. The following paragraphs outline four basic steps we have found useful to tabulate qualitative data in a manner that helps identify processual change patterns.

Chronological Listing of Qualitative Events. The first step in tabulating qualitative data is developing a chronological listing of events that occur in the development of an organizational innovation being investigated, as illustrated below.

Month/Year	*Event*	*Data Source*
.	.	.
.	.	.
.	.	.

Events require careful definition, and vary with the concepts being investigated. For example, the MIRP defines an *event* as a point in time when a change occurs in either the ideas, people involved, transactions or relationships engaged in, context, or outcomes of the innovation being examined over time. The chronological listing of events would be obtained by combining data collected through multiple methods and sources over time, including surveys interviews, participant observations, archival sources, and published information.

Coding Chronological Events into Conceptual Tracts. The next step in organizing the longitudinal data into a format that facilitates identifying change processes is coding the chronological listing of events into multiple tracks that correspond to the conceptual research categories (see requirement 1, above). Poole's (1983) Multiple Sequence Model provides a useful descriptive system which specifies tracks used for recording process activities. Poole's method avoids the problem of preordaining the existence of stages or phases to the process, yet provides a way to identify cycles or transitions among activity tracks and, in this way, facilitates the development and testing of models or theories about innovation and change processes. Instead of picturing the strategic change process as a unitary sequence of phases or stages, Poole (1983) suggests portraying events as a set of parallel strands or tracks of activities.

Each track represents a different concept or category in one's research framework. For example, following from the MIRP definition of innovation process, a minimal description of innovation requires at least five tracks.

Illustration of General Activity Tracks Used in MIRP

People track	_____
Ideas track	_____
Transactions	_____
Context track	_____
Outcomes track	_____

TIME   └─ └─ └─ └─ └─ └─ └─ └─ └─ └┘

For each track, a coding scheme is applied that enumerates the kinds of activities or issues occurring at each point in time, as follows:

People track is a coding of the people or groups involved in an activity and the role each performs at a given moment.

Ideas track is a coding of the substantive ideas, strategies, or metaphors that the innovation group uses to represent and make sense of the innovation at a given moment.

Transactions track is the informal and formal relationships among innovation group members and other firms and groups involved in the innovation effort.

Context/environmental track is a coding of the exogenous issues and events outside of the innovation unit in the larger organization and industry or community that are perceived by innovation group members to affect the innovation.

Analuzing Process Patterns or Cycles in Activity Tracks. After the chronological data are coded in these conceptual tracks, a search begins to identify processual patterns that may be reflected in the activity tracks. Cycles and breakpoints are useful for identifying processual patterns. A recurrent pattern of behavior is called a *cycle.* Cycles are identified when repetitions occur within tracks over time. *Breakpoints* are of key importance to understanding change processes because they represent transitions between cycles of activities. They indicate the pacing of activities within tracks and possible linkages between tracks of activities. Poole (1983) and Mintzberg (1976) describe four types of breakpoints: normal breakpoints or topical shifts, delays, internal disruptions, and external interrupts.

Poole (1983) points out that when breakpoints interrupt cycles within a track, this suggests that the track is loosely coupled or operating somewhat independently of the other tracks. On the other hand, when breakpoints occur in many tracks, those tracks are likely to be highly interdependent, and the rupture may presage major events or shifts in developmental activity. Thus, when cyclical breaks in multible tracks occur in some coherent fashion, phases or stages similar to those in classical models may be found. However, at other points, there may be no relationship in the cyclical breaks between tracks, and therefore no recognizable phases. In this case, each track is analyzed in its own right, but the entire ensemble of tracks does not yield a coherent analysis.

Vocabulary for Describing Processual Progressions. New concepts about developmental processes are often needed to describe and analyze longitudinal processual patterns in the above activity tracks. Based on mathematical set theory, Van den Daele (1969; 1974) proposes a rich vocabulary of operational concepts for describing and analyzing change processes.

1. Simple, unitary progression. $U, V, W, , ,$

2. Simple, multiple progression. U, V, W may contain subsets; in set theory $[Ui] \rightarrow [Vi] \rightarrow [Wi], , ,$

    Multiple progressions can be of three forms:

Parallel	*Divergent*		*Convergent*	
$U \rightarrow V \rightarrow W$		W	U	
	V			V
$U \rightarrow V \rightarrow W$	U	W	U	W
		W	U	
$U \rightarrow V \rightarrow W$	V			V
		W	U	

3. Cumulative progression (unitary or multiple).

    More than one stage may belong to a unit at a time; in set theory: $U\,a, V$ Abstract, $W\,bc$ (unitary model). For example, a multiple parallel partially cumulative model would look like this:

    $$U\,a \rightarrow V\,a\,b \quad \rightarrow W\,a\,b\,c$$
    $$U\,a \rightarrow V\,b \quad \rightarrow W\,b\,c$$
    $$U\,a \rightarrow V\,a\,b \quad \rightarrow W\,c$$

4. Conjunctive progression (unitary, multiple, or cumulative). The elements of subsets may be related, such that aRb, or $aR'b$

Van den Daele (1969) points out that these forms of progression do not occur independently. Every developmental model makes a commitment (implicitly or explicitly) to some form of invariant sequential order, between unit variation (unitary or multiple sequence), within-unit variance (simple or cumulative structure), and in the relationship of developmental elements (conjunctive or disjunctive). Given modal relations among these dimensions, Van den Daele develops four typical patterns of change processes.

1. Simple, unitary progression include most of the stage models of innovation and change in the literature.

2. Simple, multiple progression patterns provide alternative developmental sequences for different units, but with only one stage belonging to a unit at a time. Binary fission is a good example.

3. Cumulative, unitary progression patterns assume the maintenance of some earlier and later stages of a single sequence. The model implies one "proper" path. Progressive ossification of cartilage is a good example.

4. Cumulative, multiple progression patterns imply the coexistence of earlier and later stages along with the option of developmentally alternative characteristics, accommodating to between-unit as well as within-unit differences. This cumulative pattern of multiple progression is captured in Alexander Gray's adage, "No point of view, once expressed ever seems wholly to die. Our ears are filled with the whisperings of dead men."

Obviously, this processual analysis of longitudinal tracks cannot go far unless it is driven by an explicit motor or theory of change processes.

MOTORS OR THEORIES OF CHANGE PROCESSES

Theories of choice and decision-making processes have perhaps received the greatest attention to date by organizational innovation and change scholars. Indeed, Schroeder et al. (1986) in their review of the literature find that most models of individual, group, and organizational change or innovation in the literature appear to rely uncritically upon choice process models. If knowledge of strategic decision processes is to advance in the future, study of alternative choice processes should be emphasized. Special emphasis should be given to evaluations of the conceptual motors. They are outlined below.

- *Rational.* Logical necessity motor
- *Contingency.* Situational congruency motor
- *Incremental.* Political-negotiative motor
- *Random.* Systemic probabilistic regularity motor
- *Structuration.* Socially constructed sense-making motor

Although very little is known about the conditions under which these different theories of choice processes apply, they are in all likelihood decendents from a few basic theories of change in historical social theory.

As discussed in Van de Ven and Poole (1987), social theorists have historically relied upon one of three basic theories to explain change: evolution (or developmentalism), accumulation (or epigenesis), and punctuated equilibrium theories. While evolution and accumulation theories of change have deep historically opposing roots, their differences can be reconciled with a punctuated equilibrium model of change processes.

Evolutionary or Developmental Models. Evolution is a continuous and gradual change that proceeds endogenously (that is, directly from within the unit that is undergoing change). In an evolutionary or developmental model, the forces for change lie within the system. While external events can and do affect development through deceleration, acceleration, distortion, or even obliteration, the seed or genetic structure for change is contained within the social system. An evolutionary theory of change underlies processes of differentiation in structural-functional social theories, the sequential stages of variation, selection, and retention in Social Darwinism, and of thesis, antithesis, and synthesis in dialectical theories.

Accumulation of Epigenesis Models. There are many social units whose emergence cannot be adequately explained by evolution. Instead, "adult" units often seem to emerge through a process in which parts that carry out new functions are added to (or subtracted from) existing ones, until the entire unit is assembled. Earlier parts do not include the "representation" of later ones. Accumulation theories explain change as externally (exogenously) and discontinuously produced by the addition of totally or radically new components or delegations of other components of a social system.

Etzioni (1963) suggests that periods of initiation, startup, and takeoff are useful for examining accumulation processes. *Initiation* is the time when people decide to form a new unit (if successfully launched, the date will become the unit's birthday) and *takeoff* is the time when the unit can do without the support of its initiators and continue growing "on its own." The period between initiation and takeoff could be called *startup*, when the new unit must draw its funds, staff, and power from the founding leaders and groups in order to accumulate followers and contributors directly committed to developing and sustaining it.

The image here is of an airplane that first starts its engines, then begins rolling, still supported by the runway, until it accumulates enough momentum to take off, and continue in motion "on its own" energy to carry it to higher altitudes and speeds. Thus, while the action at first relies on external support, the necessary condition for autonomous action is produced through a process of accumulation.

Punctuated Equilibrium Models of Change. A punctuated equilibrium model (as described by Tushman and Romanelli 1985) uses time as one avenue to reconcile and incorporate both evolution and accumulation theories of change. In punctuated equilibrium, accumulation best describes the process of occasional discontinuous reorientations in part or all of a social system, while evolution characterizes the periods of continuous convergence and morphogenesis. Accumulation appears to be the basic process underlying discontinuous punctuations because the resulting transformation represents a metamorphic or radical change that no longer includes representations of the earlier organization. Evolution describes morphogenic change, where an organization converges over time toward increasing order, complexity, unity, or operational effectiveness. Thus, change in a given organization may be empirically observed to result from either evolutionary embodiments of old functions or punctuated accumulations of totally new functions.

Accumulation and evolutionary change processes may be observed to occur at different times in the same organization. As Tushman and Romanelli (1985) indicate, most of the time an incremental, continuous, and imminent process of evolution may occur, punctuated by occasional discontinuous periods of externally stimulated epigenesis. Thus, as we argue elsewhere (Van de Ven and Poole 1987), time provides the vehicle for incorporating contradictory change processes in a punctuated equilibrium model to explain both internal and external sources of organizational change.

TOWARD A THEORY OF ORGANIZATIONAL INNOVATION AND CHANGE

In conclusion, we must touch upon a few basic normative questions. Where do we go with this processual analysis and search for process models? Where do we want to end up? While each reader is likely to have different answers to these questions, it seems to me that we not only want to describe observed innovating processes, we also want to explain how and why they occur. Scientifically valid explanation not only requires systematic procedures for observing and tabulating longitudinal data (as proposed with the first three requirements for processual analysis), it also requires the development and evaluation of theories or motors of the change process itself. It is hoped that the destination of this journey will yield some practically useful and theoretically robust theories for the management of innovation and change.

We must therefore ask, "What are the requirements for a good theory of change?" Hernes (1976) and Dahrendorf (1959) have proposed standards for a theory of change which is useful in answering this question. Adapting their criteria to innovation management suggests that our theories should attain the following four requirements for a good theory of innovation.

1. It should explain how structure and individual purposive action are linked at micro and macro levels of analysis. "The dominant paradigm of social science rests on the firm belief that any macro theory of organizational or industrial change must be grounded in the purposive actions and ambitions of individuals" (Coleman 1986).

2. It should explain how innovation and change is produced both by the internal functioning of the structure and by the external purposive actions of individuals. If one concludes that innovation is totally controlled by natural or structural forces imminent to the social system, no room is left for individual purpose, and no theory of action can result. And vice versa, if one concludes that organizational change is totally controlled by purposive individual action unconstrained by natural or structural forces, only a teleological or utopian theory can result.

3. The theory should explain both stability and instability. "In its fundamental structure a theory of organizational innovation or change should not be remarkably different from a theory of ordinary action" (March 1981, p. 564). Without this requirement,

any theory of innovation would explode and be unable to explain the amazing persistence and fixity observed in common organizational life.

4. It should include time as the key historical metric. By definition, change is a difference that can only be noted over time in an entity. *Chronos* (or calendar time) tends to predominate in studies of structural change, while *kiros* (periods of peak experiences, as in the planting and harvesting periods of a growing season) appears to be the most common metric of time in studies of individual creativity and purposive action. A theory of innovation and change that links structure and action must therefore link chronos and kiros time metrics (Van de Ven and Poole 1987).

REFERENCES

Argyris, C. 1968. "Some Unintended Consequences of Rigorous Research." *Psychological Bulletin 70*, no. 3: 185-97.

_____. 1985. *Strategy, Change, and Defensive Routines*. Marshfield, Mass.: Pitman.

Coleman, J.S. 1986. "Social Theory, Social Research, and a Theory of Action." *American Journal of Sociology 16* (May): 1309-35.

Dahrendorf, R. 1959. *Class and Class Conflict in Industrial Society*. Stanford, Calif.: Stanford University Press.

Etzioni, A. 1963. "The Epigenesis of Political Communities at the International Level." *American Journal of Sociology 68*: (407-21).

Hernes, G. 1976. "Structural Change in Social Processes." *American Journal of Sociology 82* (no. 3): 513-45.

March, J.G. 1981. "Footnotes to Organizational Change." *Administrative Science Quarterly 26*: 563-77.

Mintzberg, H., D. Raisinghani, and A. Theoret. 1976. "The Structure of 'Unstructured' Decision Processes." *Administrative Science Quarterly 21* (no. 2, June): 246-75.

Mohr, L.B. 1982. *Explaining Organizational Behavior: The Limits and Possibilities of Theory and Research*. San Francisco: Jossey-Bass.

Nisbet, R.A. 1970. "Developmentalism: A Critical Analysis." In J. McKinney and E. Tiryakin (Eds.), *Theoretical Sociology: Perspectives and Developments*. New York: Meredith, ch. 7, pp. 167-204.

Pettigrew, A. 1985. *The Awakening Giant: Continuity and Change in ICI*. Oxford, England: Basil Blackwell.

Poole, M.S. 1983. "Decision Development in Small Groups, III: A Multiple Sequence Model of Group Decision Development." *Communication Monographs 50*.

Schroeder, R., A. Van de Ven, G. Scudder, and D. Polley. 1986. "Managing Innovation and Change Processes: Findings from the Minnesota Innovation Research Program." *Agribusiness 2*, (no. 4): 501-23.

Tuma, N. B., and M. T. Hannan. 1984. *Social Dynamics*. Orlando, Fla. Academic Press.

Tushman, M. L., and E. Romanelli. 1985. "Organizational Evolution: A Metamorphosis Model of Convergence and Reorientation." In L. L. Cummings and B. Staw (Eds.), *Research in Organizational Behavior*, vol. 7. Greenwich, Conn.: Jai Press, pp. 171-222.

Van de Ven, A. H., and Associates. 1987. "The Minnesota Innovation Research Program." Final Report to the Office of Naval Research Program on Organizational Effectiveness.

Van de Ven, A. H., and M. S. Poole. 1987. "Paradoxical Requirements for a Theory of Organizational Change." In R. Quinn and K. Cameron (Eds.), *Paradox and Transformation: Toward a Theory of Change in Organization and Management*. Cambridge, Mass.: Ballinger.

Van den Daele, L. D. 1969. "Qualitative Models in Developmental Analysis," *Developmental Psychology 1* (no. 4): 303-10.

_____. 1974. "Infrastructure and Transition in Developmental Analysis." *Human Development 17*: 1-23.

14 PARADIGMS LOST AND REGAINED

Stephan L. Chorover

PROLOGUE

I am a scientist. My graduate training was in the hybrid field of neuropsychology and most of my academic and professional work has been carried out in laboratory and clinical settings.

At first I was preoccupied with the old and abiding problem of understanding how the anatomical and physiological organization and development of the human central nervous system (especially the brain) relates to the organization and development of human mental life and behavior. Gradually, however, I began to specialize more and more narrowly (as scientists commonly do), and almost before I knew what was happening, the focus of my research had become pretty much limited to the study of a single aspect of relations between two particular subsystems of the mammalian brain.

To be still more precise, I had become fascinated by the fact that certain naturally occurring odors, pheromones, play a critical role in the reproductive activities of rodents, carnivores, and primates and wanted to understand more about how the limbic and olfactory subsystems of the brain are implicated in sexual behavior and other species-specific activity patterns upon which individual and species survival depend. Eventually, my research horizon had become narrowed to a point at which it encompassed little more than the neuro-electrical activity at the tip of a tiny microelectrode situated in the vicinity of a single cell in a bit of tissue located in a particular part of a specific nucleus (the amygdala) comprising a portion of one of the three principal subsystems of the brain.

Now, the brain, for its part, is an organ, and part, in turn, of the central nervous system, one of the organ systems of which we, as organisms, are composed. And there is more: We, in our turn, are more than merely organisms. We are also "social animals" (in Aristotle's famous phrase) and we live among others of our kind in a world that is spatiotemporally, socioculturally, and ecologically organized.

But it took me many years patiently laboring at a microscopic level of organization before events forced me to think seriously and systematically about the larger sociocultural context in which all neuropsychological events and processes arise and of which they (we!) are a part. It is best that I leave for later a more detailed account of those events. Suffice it for present purposes simply to say that it gradually became inescapably evident to me that the essentially mechanistic and reductionistic approach that I had been taking was insufficient as a basis for neuropsychological understanding. Today my research horizon has expanded and extends some distance beyond the boundaries of the discipline in which I was originally trained.

To be more precise, I am currently preoccupied with the development of a rather more comprehensive approach to the study of human systems. I conceive of the term *human systems* as broadly denotative of a set of conceptually and materially composite unities that includes (among others) human brains, individuals, and social groups. These systems, moreover, appear to me to be principally and irreducibly organized in terms of the essentially interdependent *levels* and *aspects* of organization illustrated in Table 14-1.

With respect to the specific human systems indicated, my aim is to develop this composite conceptual framework to a point at which it is capable of comprehending their "neurobiopsychosocioculturally" interdependent character in terms of relations within and among their respective cognitive, affective, and expressive counterparts. Beyond that, it is also one of my ultimate objectives to find a theoretically and practically sustainable way to describe or depict relations between human systems and the larger natural environment of which we are a part.

I have not recited these particulars of my life and work at the outset merely to indicate the nature and limits of my scientific background. My main purpose in talking about myself in this way is to emphasize that I am, with respect to the field of management, an

Table 14-1. Human Systems: Levels and Aspects of Organization.

	LEVELS:	neurobiological (organism) brains	psychological (individual) persons	sociocultural (community) groups
A	generic	———————————— specific		———————————
S				
P	cognitive	neocortex	thinking	worldview(s)
E				
C	affective	limbic system	feeling	value system(s)
T				
S	expressive	core	acting	practice(s)
	DOMAINS:	—— neuropsychology ——	—— social psychology ——	

Three principal *aspects* of human systems (cognitive, affective, and expressive) as manifested at three successive *levels* of organization (neurobiological, psychological, and sociocultural). Note that aspects are conceived of as having counterpart representations at different levels. The absence of hard and fast boundaries between adjacent "cells" of the table is intentional, since the evidence suggests much overlapping and interpenetration of categories as well as extensive mutual and reciprocal interplay among, between, and within the indicated levels and aspects of organization.

almost perfect stranger. It seems pertinent to say so at the outset, since what I shall try to do in what follows is not only describe my own personal and professional conception of "creative and innovative management," but also to suggest a direction in which I believe it is appropriate for research and development in the field to go.

WHAT IS CREATIVE AND INNOVATIVE MANAGEMENT?

Creative and innovative management is described as "a new discipline of academic research and business practice." A. Charnes and W.W. Cooper (1984, p. xvii) state that, "Making things work successfully is an old and abiding task of management. It is the coupling of this task with new ideas, directions and the like that makes it innovative and creative."

Perhaps it is just because I am a stranger in a strange field, but it does strike me as rather remarkable to find a "new discipline of academic research and business practice" emerging in schools and departments of business or industrial administration who lay claim to the business of "making things work successfully." The fact that one is not an entrepreneur, manager, or administrator does not necessarily make one a stranger to the old and abiding task alluded to. In the course of my own personal and professional life, for example, I have had a fair amount of experience "making things work" more or less successfully. And, in the process, I have also learned a worthwhile thing or two, both about what it takes "to make things work" and what it means to do so "successfully."

I have learned, for example, that making things work is not, without qualification, a good thing. (As the late Professor Donald O. Hebb, a noted neuropsychologist, used to say: "Research that isn't worth doing, isn't worth doing well.") And I've learned that *success* and *failure* (along with *creative* and *innovative*) are relative and value-laden terms. As such, they are open to a variety of different interpretations. Thus, for all serious theoretical and practical intents and purposes, this means that whatever meaning they have is bound to be context dependent.

And this means that such terms are literally meaningless unless defined (in any given instance) not only in relation to the methods or acts or activities to which they are intended to refer but also in relation to the interests and objectives of their users. More to the point, insofar as different persons or parties have different interests and objectives, there is every reason to expect certain kinds and degrees of disagreement to arise, say, around the question of whether or not a given "act of management" (call it creative or innovative or what you will) properly deserves to be denoted "successful."

Although there are, beyond question, many so-called zero-sum contexts in which the success of one person or party depends upon the failure of some other(s), it is neither necessary nor desirable to suppose that all contexts are of this kind. Further to the point, I have at least one contemporary social context in mind in which the task of making things work is plainly so complex and multidimensional that it deserves to be conceived of as everybody's business. And within this context, I would like to point to a problem that is simply too important to be entrusted solely to entrepreneurs, managers, administrators, scientists, engineers, linguists, philosophers, or any other single set of academic experts or corporate specialists, however creative and innovative they (or we) may be.

The context to which I am referring is familiar to everyone. And so is the problem. But the problem takes so many superficially dissimilar forms that it is difficult to single out the best way of defining it. Indeed, I find truth in a passage in T. S. Eliot's "Four Quartets":

Trying to learn to use words, and every attempt
Is a wholly new start, and a different kind of failure
Because one has only learnt to get the better of words
For the thing one no longer has to say, or the way in which
One is no longer disposed to say it. And so each venture
Is a new beginning, a raid on the inarticulate
With shabby equipment always deteriorating
In the general mess of imprecision of feeling,
Undisciplined squads of emotion. And what there is to conquer
By strength and submission, has already been discovered
Once or twice, or several times, by men whom one cannot hope
To emulate—but there is no competition—
There is only the fight to recover what has been lost
And found and lost again and again: and how, under conditions
That seem unpropitious. But perhaps neither gain nor loss.
For us, there is only the trying. The rest is not our business.

Home is where one starts from. As we grow older
The world becomes stranger, the pattern more complicated
Of dead and living. . . .

STARTING FROM HOME

How is this admonition to be understood in this particular context? The contributors and readers of this book include persons with direct management experience as well as research scientists and scholars. Taking this description of the context, and supposing (as I must) that the problem of defining "new directions for research" in this field is one that each person or party is bound to approach from a somewhat different geopolitical as well as ideological and disciplinary perspective, where in the world does it make any "common" sense to begin? Whose home are we to start from? What are we to take as our point of departure?

These questions are not intended to be merely rhetorical. And, after giving them serious and sustained consideration, the conclusion to which I have come is that it is going to be necessary for us to leave home in order to find it. Fortunately for us, and notwithstanding the ties that bind us so closely in all relevant theoretical and practical respects to our own particular geopolitical, ethnic, academic, and professional perspectives, there is a sense in which it is less difficult than it once was to do the sort of distancing I have in mind.

A JOURNEY

Pretend with me, if you will, that we are living in a planetary biosphere beyond whose immediate local and global boundaries it is possible for us to travel and that we are about to embark on journey at mindspeed to a point from which our habitat is visible in its entirety.[1] Our journey starts (from wherever we happen to be) and takes us vertically outward and upward along a path perpendicular to the surface of the earth at a speed that grows exponentially. The area of the earth's surface encompassed within our view expands by a factor of ten every ten seconds. Thus, the sight that starts with a 1-meter square becomes a 10-meter square ten seconds later, a 100-meter square twenty seconds into the journey, and so on. Merely a little over seventy seconds into the journey, our vision covers a 13,000-kilometer square, wide enough to encompass the entire planet earth—our "home." Then, we have reached our destination. Looking down from here the most amazing thing about this home of ours is that it looks alive.

Indeed, the ancients regarded the earth as a living organism, and this idea has recently reappeared as the so-called Gaia hypothesis (Lovelock and Margulis 1974). If we could have been watching from here for a geologically long enough time, we would have been able to see the tectonic plates that are our continents drifting apart, held afloat by the fiery molten magma beneath.

This far-off vantage point is as close as we can get to home if we truly want to attain an international perspective. To be more precise, it is the only *common* vantage point available for our present scientific and managerial intents and purposes. In other words we have to begin from here if we genuinely propose to approach the tasks facing the discipline of creative and innovative management on an international scale.

Indeed, in a world that has been so recursively divided up and broken down along so many separate parochial (national and disciplinary) lines and fragmented into so many materially and conceptually distinct bits and pieces, this global image should be borne in mind in all efforts to define "new directions for research in creative and innovative management."

Coming back down to earth, and taking myself at my word, I propose to devote the remainder of this chapter to a description of what the image arrived at through our journey means to me and what I take to be some of its implications for applied research in the field of creative and innovative management.

WONDERMENT AND ANGUISH

In February 1971 astronaut Edgar D. Mitchell journeyed to the moon as a member of the Apollo 14 lunar expedition. Three years later, he reflected on this experience (Mitchell 1974, pp. 29–30).

When I went to the moon, I was as pragmatic a test pilot, engineer, and scientist as any of my colleagues . . . I knew well that analytical and logical thought, using objective data, could produce a technology that would reveal new secrets of the universe by probing the reaches of space and, at the microscopic level, the structure of atoms. Prior to the lunar exploration, I became as familiar with the spacecraft and its vast support system of people and equipment as a man could be, with confidence in it all. Despite that familiarity and confidence, however, there were moments during the flight when I felt an amazed and profound respect for the rational abilities of the human intellect—that it could find ways to guide a tiny capsule of metal through a half million miles of space with such precision and accuracy. . . .

But there was another aspect to my experience. . . . It began with the breathtaking experience of seeing planet earth floating in the vastness of space.

The first thing that came to mind . . . was its incredible beauty. Even the spectacular photographs do not do it justice. It was a majestic sight—a splendid blue and white jewel suspended against a velvet black sky. How peacefully, how harmoniously, how marvelously it seemed to fit into the evolutionary pattern by which the universe is maintained. . . .

Next I thought of our planet's life-supporting character. That little globe of water, clouds, and land no bigger than my thumb was HOME, the haven our spacecraft would seek at the end of our voyage . . .

Then my thoughts turned to daily life on the planet. With that, my sense of wonderment gradually turned into something close to anguish. . . . I realized that at the very moment when I was so privileged to view the planet from 240,000 miles in space, people on earth were fighting wars; committing murder and other crimes; lying, cheating, and struggling for power and status; abusing the environment by polluting the water and air, wasting natural resources, and ravaging the land, acting out lust and greed; and hurting others through intolerance, bigotry, prejudice, and all the things that add up to man's inhumanity to man. It seemed as through man were totally unconscious of his individual role in—and social responsibility for—the future of life on the planet.

It was also painfully apparent that the millions of people suffering in conditions of poverty, ill health, misery, fear, and near slavery were in that condition from economic exploitation, political domination, religious and ethnic persecution, and a hundred other demons that spring from the human ego. Science, for all its technological feats, had not—more likely could not—deal with these problems. . . .

The magnitude of the overall problem seemed staggering. Our condition seemed to be one of deepening crises on an unprecedented scale, crises that were mounting faster than we could solve them. There appeared to be the immediate possibility that warfare might destroy vast segments of civilization with one searing burst of atomic fury. Only a little further off appeared the possibility of intolerable levels of polluted air and of undrinkable water. A more remote, but no less real, likelihood was the death of large portions of the population from starvation, abetted by improper resources management by an exploding population.

Some two decades earlier, Albert Einstein had recognized the same crisis. "The unleashed power of the atom," he said, "has changed everything save our ways of thinking, and we thus drift toward unparalleled catastrophes." Nor did he stop there. On the contrary, he proceeded to identify a source of the problem and then went on to define what is, at very least, a reasonable research agenda for internationally minded creative and innovative managers in the nuclear age. "By painful experience we have learned that rational thinking does not suffice to solve the problems of our social life. We need a substantially new way of thinking if humanity is to survive."

WHAT IS TO BE DONE?

There is no single answer, but this is the question that all of us must discuss together and decide for ourselves. However, speaking strictly for myself, and from my own present vantage point, I can discern at least one thing that creative and innovative entrepreneurs, managers, and administrators who are faithfully intent upon pursuing the search for substantially new ways of thinking will probably have to do: Start working toward a reconciliation of what have been the mutually irreconcilable values of economic growth and ecological stability. The new direction that needs to be followed in this regard is one that will provide sustainably balanced and harmonious responses to *both* the economic and the ecological imperatives that confront us. Creative and innovative answers are needed to such questions as these: How can the relatively parochial, short-term marketplace objectives customarily pursued by entrepreneurs, managers, and administrators operating to maximize such economic values as organizational growth, industrial competitiveness, agricultural or manufacturing productivity, and financial profitability be reconciled with relatively more catholic, long-term, and generally broader human and ecological objectives? Can a system be devised and made to work in which economic and ecological values are more harmoniously blended? How can creative and innovative managers contribute to the development of more ecologically as well as economically sustainable modes of industrial and agricultural development and the fashioning of neurobiopsychosocioculturally healthier modes of human existence in a generally less violent, hazardous, and toxic, planetary environment?

A PARADIGM FOR OUR TIME

As a scientist who is committed to doing what he can to help bring about the conceptual reorientation that the present crisis demands, I have been concentrating within the domain encompassed by Table 14-1. More to the point, I have thus far been trying both to reevaluate and to revise the scientific paradigm presently prevailing within the realms of inquiry with which I am most familiar. It is my hope thereby to make at least a small contribution to the development of a more sustainable approach to the study of human systems.

Where to begin? The problem, as defined, has something to do with our ways of thinking. But ways of thinking do not arise or exist or change in a conceptual and material vacuum. On the contrary, just as theory is related to practice, so thinking is related to acting. Thinking of the kind that Einstein was talking about is more than or different from a mere matter of personal mental activity. To be more precise, the thinking that we do about the nature of the world and its contents (including ourselves) is everywhere and always conditioned and constrained by influences arising from the particular sociocultural context in which we live. Nor is thinking of the kind that we ordinarily refer to as "scientific" any exception. The point is worth pursuing.

Once upon a time, the old Latin word *scientia* meant, simply 'knowledge'. In our own day, however, *science* is generally understood to mean both knowledge of a rather specific kind, and the rather specialized system of tools and techniques that has been developed to produce it. Indeed, what passes for scientific knowledge in any context (and contemporary Western society is no exception) inevitably tends both to reflect and to reinforce the beliefs, values, and practices of the persons and parties who are in a position to participate most directly in its production.

Another way of saying this would be to assert (as many historians and philosophers of science have done) that all scientific thinking necessarily proceeds (along with all other kinds of scientific activity) within a particular sociocultural system or context (a community, discipline, field, or other functional equivalent thereof) and that it is generally the hallmark of such systems that their members individually and collectively subscribe to the same more or less self-consistent set of scientific beliefs, values, and practices. To denote such composite cognitive or affective and expressive sets (see Table 14-1). Thomas Kuhn (1962) proposed that we use the term *paradigm.*

In traditional usage, the word *paradigm* refers, quite generally, to a pattern or set of forms. In the present context I am using it to refer not only to the consensually shared beliefs, values, and practices prevailing within a given scientific community at a given point in its development, but also to other comparably composed set or patterns held or expressed by given persons or parties in given places and times, including the thoughts, feelings, and actions characteristic of particular individuals and the worldviews, value systems and lifestyles of particular groups or organizations.

FRAGMENTATION AND WHOLENESS

It was as a student at the Bronx High School of Science that I first received formal exposure to the beliefs, values, and practices associated with the modern scientific paradigm. At around the same time, I began trying to learn how to think, feel, and act like a scientist. Through college and into my first years of graduate school I was particularly inspired with a keen longing for the kind of unified, all-embracing knowledge that we are reminded of by the names given to our institutions of higher learning. Indeed, it was my distinct impression of the ideal image of science that it was only the *universal* aspect of knowledge to which full credit was properly due. Nevertheless, as I noted at the outset, it was not long before my own career in science had begun to reflect the limitations of focus and the disciplinary specialization that is so plainly characteristic of the modern scientific enterprise as a whole.

The history of neuropsychology, like the history of the development of modern science as a whole, is largely the story of the proliferation of increasingly specialized fields and subfields of inquiry. Concurrently, the experience generally involves a progressive narrowing of the intellectual horizon. As this happens, the individual usually experiences growing difficulty in understanding more than a small fraction of what is going on beyond the boundaries of his or her particular area of specialization. Thus, in my own case, what began as an area of interest roughly coextensive with the domain of neuropsychology as a whole became gradually more and more limited until it reached a point at which my principal concerns were with a particular class of individual neurons in a specific region of the mammalian brain.

From a recent study of the social division of labor within my own field (Chorover 1985), I concluded that the relatively extreme fragmentation presently existing within it is systematically related to the widespread and generally uncritical acceptance by neuropsychologists of a scientific worldview and value system according to which there is only one wholly respectable epistemological and methodological approach for human beings to take for all significant social as well as scientific intents and purposes.

In neuropsychological contexts, as elsewhere, this approach requires that things and events be systematically broken down or divided up into smaller and smaller (supposedly therefore conceptually and materially more "manageable" units). In the context of science and scientific discourse, this approach is variously referred to as analytical atomism or mechanistic reductionism or the rational scientific method. It also serves as the ostensibly rational basis of what has come to be called scientific management, and as such has also exerted a powerful effect upon the quality of work life in many industrial and business occupations (Braverman 1974). In each case, however, it is fragments that tend to become the wholes of personal and professional experience when productive work is organized in accordance with this model (Neville 1974; Bohm 1976).

In my own case the effort to pursue less fragmented lines of scientific and professional activity has led to the gradual broadening of interests already mentioned. However, moving as it does against the trend toward fragmentation, my effort proceeds in opposition to the prevailing norms and attitudes, which generally discourage the individual member of a scientific or professional community from straying beyond the boundaries of his or her own field of specialization.

However, if I am correct, the fragmentation that I have experienced within my own field is not an isolated phenomenon.

Rather, it is systematically related to the fragmentation of western society as a whole and, as such, is part of a more general sociocultural process; one in which widespread and uncritical adherence to an outmoded worldview and value system is characteristically coupled with heedless participation in a grossly fragmented and destructive lifestyle, with consequences that now threaten the survival of humanity and the sustainability of the biosphere as a whole (Myers 1984; Brown 1986).

What, precisely, are the beliefs and values and practices that I am talking about? And where did they come from? To answer these questions it is necessary to take a closer look at the modern scientific paradigm and its origins. But before there was modern science there was Gaian science.

GAIAN SCIENCE

In the millenia before the deep and wide-ranging reorganization of Western society that took place during the sixteenth and seventeenth centuries, thinking about the world and its contents was done within the context of a classical, or medieval, or scholastic scientific paradigm. What were its characteristics?

Involvement. Adherents to this paradigm differed greatly among themselves about many things, but most of them conceived of humanity and nature as counterparts (microcosm and macrocosm) in an organic and purposeful cosmic whole, fully involved with each other.

Organismic Orientation. Moreover, within this scheme, as in the cosmogonies of those whom we currently call Native Americans the forces and elements of nature were personified in various ways. The earth, with its airs, waters, and places, was not infrequently conceived of as a living organism. Among the predecessors of those whom we call the Ancient Greeks, for example, there was a tradition that identified nature as a whole—in all of its manifestations—with the body of the original pagan mother goddess: Gaia or Ge (as in *geography, geology*; see Sachtouris 1985).

As Merchant (1980, p. 3) has pointed out, this image, "served as a cultural constraint restricting the actions of human beings. . . . As long as the earth was considered to be alive and sensitive, it could be considered a breach of human ethical behavior to carry out destructive acts against it."

With the advent of the Renaissance (or Enlightenment), however, there occurred a decisive paradigm shift (Hanson 1958; Kuhn 1962). And one of its necessary ontological and epistemological corollaries was the emergence of a new (so-called modern) scientific worldview and value system.

MODERN SCIENCE

To do the nature and scope of modern scientific paradigm full justice would require a more thoroughly detailed and comprehensive review than it is possible to undertake here. Accordingly, it will have to suffice merely to mention a few of its principal characteristics.

Detachment. For present purposes, one of the most noteworthy things about the modern scientific paradigm is the fact that it is predicated upon a number of radical distinctions. Not the least significant of these, as far as our present predicament is concerned, is the absolutely categorical stipulation of a thoroughgoing conceptual and material detachment of man from nature.

Domination. With the coming of the modern scientific worldview and value system, science for the first time not only sets itself apart from and above nature but also, and more ominously, defines the subjugaton and domination of nature as its avowed goal (Liess 1977).

Masculinization. This is an important characteristic to consider because of the gender identities ordinarily attached to nature and science in our tradition. What I am referring to will become immediately apparent if we recall some the terms in which a few of its principal early proponents and architects described it.

In Francis Bacon's influential view, for example, "human knowledge and human power meet as one" in the scientific enterprise. As Bacon saw it, there were "laid up in the womb of nature many secrets of excellent use." In order to make these secrets his own, it was necessary for the newly self-conscious scientist to "hound nature in her wanderings" so that she could be "forced out of her natural state and squeezed and molded." Only after being "put in constraint," asserted Bacon, could nature be properly "bound into service," made a "slave." (These and many additional quotations along similar lines may be found, along with pertinent commentary regarding the blend of sexual and violent imagery therein, in Liess 1972; Merchant 1980; Easlea 1981; and Griffin 1980.)

René Descartes was of similar mind. Indeed, what we encounter in Cartesian rationalism is a pure masculinization of thought, with a characteristically individualistic masculine intellect laying claim to worldly omnipotence. In the introduction to Part 4 of his seminal "Discourse," for example, Descartes describes his new "Method" as a means by which we scientists might hope to "render ourselves masters and possessors of nature" (1955).

Mechanistic/Deterministic/Reductionistic Orientation. The ontological and epistemological hallmark of the modern scientific worldview is a rigorously mechanistic and deterministic conception of the universe as a whole. To Descartes, for example, the material world was a machine and nothing but a machine. In his view, which soon became virtually universal within the scientific community, all living organisms are likewise machines operating according to strictly deterministic mechanical laws that are (in principle, at least) completely amenable to discovery through the rigorous application of the epistemological and methodological tools and techniques of mechanistic reductionism and analytical atomism (Lasswitz 1890).

Given the goal of dominating nature and given the reliance on methods of procedure that involve dividing things up, taking them apart, and breaking them down, it should come as no surprise that there is no proper place in the modern scientific paradigm (as there was in its predecessor) for values that might restrict or constrain the abusive exploitation of nature for human ends. Indeed, it is notable in this connection that proponents of the modern scientific world-view ordinarily deal with questions about values by claiming the entire enterprise of scientific inquiry to be morally and ethically neutral, objective, and value-free. In order to understand how this curiously detached posture is justified, it is necessary to consider the ideology of dualism.

Dualism. The distinction that sets human beings apart from nature depends, in turn, on the acceptance of another and more fundamental gesture of separation. indeed, behind the goal of dominating nature and beneath the Cartesian view of the universe "out there" as a vast, insensate clockwork, lay Descartes' fundamental division between spirit (or mind) and matter (*res cogitans* and *res extensa*). This division was supported, in turn, by the demonstrative or categorical (either/or) logic embodied in rational thinking itself.

Once established, the supposedly mutually exclusive categories of Cartesian dualism began to multiply and ramify. To his divorce of mind from matter was soon added not only the separation of mind from nature but also Newon's fundamental distinction between absolute space and absolute time (Capek 1961).

The Archimedean Point. The Sicilian scientist and wonder worker, Archimedes (287–212 B.C.), is famous in part for his ultimately unsuccessful struggle to find a single absolutely fixed, immovable, nonrelative position of rest to serve as the point of departure for his own reasonings about the world and its contents. According to legend, he prayerfully entreated the gods for such a point because he believed that from it he could "move the world."

The Archimedean point upon which Descartes grounded his entire philosophical system was the (to him inconcussible) fact of his own self-conscious existence. This led him to make what remains today his most famous of statements: I think, therefore I am ("Cogito ergo sum"; Discourse, Part 4).

Once rational thinking had thus declared itself the acme of human mental life (*raisonnement* disposing of the reasonableness of sentiment, and cognition denying the cogency of affect, so to say), the "thinking thing" proceeded to define itself also as the sole facultative basis of all knowledge. That having been accomplished, at least to the satisfaction of the faculty of reason itself, it was only a short step further for reason to convince itself that the thinking thing is an entirely insubstantial and ephemeral immateriality altogether separate and distinct from things and events with which it might cognitively deal.

The significance of this confusing conception of mind for the development of the modern scientific worldview cannot be overemphasized. For with it human reason, hoisting itself by its own bootstraps, convinced itself that it occupied a position from which the world out there could be viewed in a completely detached way.

Further to the point, this curiously spiritualistic Cartesian conception of the completely disembodied human mind served for centuries to support the otherwise patently absurd and unsupportable notion of scientific "objectivity" according to which it is supposedly possible for human observers to detach themselves from things and events observed. In other words, when we speak of the "specular ideal" of scientific objectivity, we are talking about a kind and degree of mental detachment that is the Cartesian equivalent of the Archimedean point.

As we shall shortly see, there are realms of scientific inquiry in which this has been shown to be a completely untenable notion. Nevertheless, it continues to flourish within those fields of inquiry that deal most directly with human systems.

MODERN SCIENCE AND THE HUMAN SCIENCES

There can be no doubt that the modern scientific paradigm has been the principal guiding force in the century-long struggle of the human sciences to become "real" sciences (Boring 1950; Peele 1981; Krasner and Houts 1984; Howard 1985; Koch and Leary 1985). Across the spectrum of psychological subfields, for example, from laboratory-based experimental psychology to clinic-based personality studies and psychoanalysis, its influence has been overwhelming. Freud, for example, consistently tried to pattern his descriptions of psychological phenomena after the basic concepts of Newtonian mechanics. With evident pride, he proclaimed himself and his followers to be "at bottom incorrigible mechanists and materialists" (quoted by Capra 1982, p. 180).

A comprehensive and up-to-date picture of the thoroughgoing influence of the modern scientific paradigm upon the development of a particular human science during the past century can be found in the volume edited by Koch and Leary (1985). My aim here is merely to note some respects in which the inherent limitations of this paradigm in modern science are becoming increasingly apparent in my own subfield.

MECHANISTIC REDUCTIONISM IN NEUROPSYCHOLOGY

Throughout my training as a neuropsychologist, I was taught to regard rationalism, along with its epistemological and methodological counterparts (including analytical atomism and mechanistic reductionism), as not merely necessary but ultimately also sufficient for all scientific and technical purposes. However, I gradually came to realize that this approach, when taken by itself, creates a host of problems (Chorover 1980b, 1986). This realization developed with particular force in connection with what has come to be called "the psychosurgery debate" (Valenstein 1980).

PSYCHOSURGERY: THE MODERN SCIENCE OF VIOLENCE OR VICE VERSA?

As many readers may realize, some neuropsychologists have actively (not to say enthusiastically) promoted the idea of using brain surgery as a means of dealing with otherwise allegedly intractable forms of socially disruptive behavior. This idea (an example of mechanistic and reductionistic thinking if there ever was one) made its most recent reappearance in the United States during the 1960s, a period of heightened social turmoil marked by urban rioting, antiwar and civil rights demonstrations and a general intensification of domestic and international violence and conflict among contending social forces. (For historical overviews, see Valenstein 1973, 1980; Chorover 1973, 1974, 1976, 1979, 1980a, b).

After the stormy series of ghetto uprisings that swept the nation during the summer of 1967, for example, the prestigious *Journal of the American Medical Association* published a paper in which three physicians affiliated with a leading medical school and hospital offered it as their professional opinion that a previously undiagnosed form of "brain disease" was responsible for the violent and assaultive behavior of some slum dwellers who participated in the riots (Mark, Sweet, and Ervin 1967).

Having thus reduced the broad-based sociocultural phenomenon of racial violence to a psychological and thence to a neurobiological problem, the authors proceeded to suggest a particular form of psychosurgery (bilateral stereotaxic amygdalotomy) as the treatment of choice in such cases (Mark and Ervin 1968, 1970).

None other than the modern scientific paradigm justifies taking it as a fundamental neuropsychological tenet that all aspects of human psychological existence (all thinking, feeling, and acting) are ultimately reducible to "expressions of the functioning brain" (Sweet 1970). But once that tenet is accepted, it seems simply a matter of inescapable logic to regard human social violence and other comparably problematical forms of human mental activity and behavior as expressions of a malfunctioning brain. And that is the line of reasoning by which some neuropsychologists are led to advocate the use of brain surgery as a means of dealing with social violence.

Of course, that kind of reasoning makes about as much sense as trying to deal with the problem of human malnutrition and starvation by destroying those portions of the brain where activity is related to feelings of hunger and food-seeking behavior. In point of fact, there are no credible scientific grounds for believing in the discrete localizability of brain malfunctions specifically associated with violence (Chorover 1980b). Consequently, blind faith in the sufficiency of rational reductionistic thinking is, in effect, the only basis that exists for attempting to reduce human violence to the status of a localizable brain malfunction amenable to psychosurgical treatment. In other words, the whole idea of bringing socially problematical aspects of human mental life and behavior under control by selectively destroying particular brain regions is supported by nothing but the belief (itself directly contradictory to the point that Einstein was trying to make) that rational thinking is sufficient, in and of itself, to serve as a basis for solving the problems of our social life.

In short, political expediency aside, it is only by way of a logic based on complete confidence in the universal validity of the modern scientific worldview and value system that one can defend the mechanistic and reductionistic approach to human social problems that psychosurgery represents. This helps to explain why the most outspoken advocates of the psychosurgical approach to violence (like promoters of comparably reductionistic approaches to other human problems) are so often to be found unabashedly justifying their positions on the grounds that what they are doing is completely rational, objective, morally and ethically neutral, and value-free. Such efforts at justification notwithstanding, it is increasingly evident that human systems are simply not amenable to understanding in purely mechanistic and reductionistic terms (Chorover 1980b, 1985, 1986; Eccles 1979).

PSYCHOPATHOLOGIZING HUMAN PROBLEMS

But if psychosurgical theory and practice provide a clear example of how easily we can be led astray when we rely solely on rational thinking as a basis for defining and dealing with social problems, it should not be imagined that this is but an isolated or somehow uncommon example. On the contrary, it is important to understand how commonplace it is for human social problems of broad scope to be defined and dealt with by reduction to the status of personal maladjustments. Indeed, in the course of the effort to clarify my own ideas about psychosurgical theory and practice, I came upon many other ostensibly rational and scientific attempts to define and deal with human problems of broad scope in terms of individual psychopathology.

Perhaps the most notorious contemporary case in point is the Soviet practice of labeling political dissidents as mentally ill. An equally instructive case in point was the "discovery," by scientifically oriented clinicians in the antebellum southern United States, of a theretofore unknown "mental illness" that allegedly caused certain black slaves to run away (Cartwright 1851, Chorover 1979).

But these too are but extreme examples of attempts to apply the modern scientific paradigm to the solution of human problems. Indeed, the entire point of my argument here is to suggest that the tendency to approach human problems of broad scope in this narrowly mechanistic and reductionistic way is so deeply ingrained in the thinking of most of us that we are inclined to regard it as not only the most obvious and natural way of approaching such problems, but also as the only truly scientific way of doing so.

This, in short, is the legacy that belongs to those of us who have been brought up to believe in the sufficiency of the mechanistic and reductionistic approach to human problems.

THE EMERGING PARADIGM

Fortunately, however, a substantially new way of thinking about the world and its contents (including ourselves) is beginning to emerge out of the fragmentation that presently prevails. And there are reasons to believe that the emerging paradigm, by pointing toward new directions for research, may provide us with precisely the sort of material and conceptual tools we need if we are to deal more creatively and effectively with the problem of human survival in the nuclear age.

By way of an introduction to the following description of the emerging paradigm, let us first recall some of the salient features of the modern scientific worldview. Its vaunting ambition, as we saw, was to master and possess nature. Toward this end, a number of radical distinctions and separations were invoked. Fundamental was the divorce between humanity and nature. This depended, in turn, upon mind being cut off from matter no less completely than matter was cut off from energy and no less absolutely than space was cut off from time. Coupled with these conceptual and material disconnections was a thoroughgoing epistemological and methodological detachment of the observer from things or events observed. There is, however, a catch to this Cartesian conception of the Archimedeian point and it was identified in 1905 by Albert Einstein.

Relativity. "It is impossible by any experiment whatsoever," he wrote, "to determine absolute rest." This was the founding statement of the theory of relativity. It signaled and helped to initiate the paradigm shift that is presently underway. And as a result of it, "we are now moving into a phase of scientific thinking that differs from the science of the eighteenth and nineteenth centuries quite as significantly as the 'new philosophy' of the seventeenth century differed from the science of pre-Renaissance Europe" (Toulmin 1982, p. 231).

With the advent of relativity, the very idea of an Archimedean point is revealed as absurd. The human observer can no longer pretend to occupy a position radically separate from things or events observed. Rather than being detached from things and events observed, the observer becomes a part of the system(s) about which he or she is concerned, and his or her point of view and frame of reference can no longer be ignored. Indeed, the human observer must now be included as part of a composite observing and observed system.

In essence, therefore, relativity renders untenable both the Cartesian subject-versus-object dichotomy and the kindred notion of a detached observer pursuing the specular ideal of objective knowledge (Wheeler 1982).

Uncertainty. But if the perspective of the emerging paradigm is relativistic, it is also relational and interactive in a deeper sense. That is to say, it recognizes that in the act of observation, the observer is engaged in a mode of active participation.

Perhaps the most dramatic demonstration of this aspect of the new paradigm comes from research at the theoretical and experimental limits of twentieth-century high-energy physics where, for example, the energy required to observe a system has been shown to interact with the energy inherent within the system in ways that make it impossible to describe the system independently of the observation process. Formalized in quite precise mathematical terms in Werner Heisenberg's famous "principle of uncertainty," this constitutes one version of a lesson that all students of living systems have time and again been taught but that, on the whole, we have been slow to learn—namely that systems are affected by the process of probing them. And with the knower thus materially and conceptually implicated in the known, we can no longer claim to know anything as a "Ding an sich." Thus, whereas modern science purported to be capable of producing a picture of nature, we have learned that the most we can hope to do with any confidence is to produce "a picture of our relation to nature" (Heisenberg 1958, pp. 58, 81).

From what has already been said, it should be obvious that the emerging scientific paradigm restores connections between and among the entities and events that its predecessor insisted upon regarding as essentially separate and distinct. It recognizes, for example, the ultimate continuity of spacetime, the fundamental interrelatedness of matter and energy, and the irreducible neuropsychological interdependence of the mental and material (the human mind and the human brain). It also acknowledges the thoroughgoing material and conceptual interpenetration of humanity and nature, and the comparably inescapable epistemological and methodological involvement of the knower with the known.

And, as the illusion of detachment slips away, we begin to rediscover scientific inquiry as the human social enterprise it is and always has been. We also realize that the ways in which we think about the world and its contents, far from being objective, are human social products that have developed and presently exist within the context of a particular paradigm.

We are reminded too that we are "merely" human and have all sorts of neurobiological and sociocultural limitations; that we are prone to error; that "in the naming, classing and knowing of things in general we are notoriously fallible" (James [1890] 1950, vol. 1, pp. 191-2); and that, because "we may go astray. . . . The only safeguard is in the final *consensus* of our farther knowledge . . . later views correcting earlier ones until at last the harmony of a consistent system is reached" (emphasis added) (ibid.).

Complementarity. There is a story that a physicist friend of mine likes to tell about a teacher of his who began his own studies of physics during the first decade of the twentieth century. That was a time when much confusion and controversy swirled around the proper way to conceptualize and define such fundamental entities as the photon (which had then been only recently discovered and named).

The question at issue at the time was whether the photon is a particle or a wave. According to the story, the community of physicists most directly concerned was (and long had been) about equally divided. Indeed, there were only two points on which the parties to the discussion were able to agree: that there were only two alternatives, and that they were mutually exclusive. How did the young physicist deal with this situation? "I did the only reasonable thing," he is supposed to have said, "on Mondays, Wednesdays and Saturdays, I was convinced it was a wave; on Sunday, I went to church and prayed for divine guidance."

The point of this story for present purposes is simple enough. And it has nothing to do with the specific issues with which a physicist might be concerned, such as the position or momentum of an elementary entity in a given experimental situation. Rather, the point of the story is that it is necessary to become aware of the potentially pernicious influence that categorical (either/or) thinking can exert on the problem-posing and problem-solving behavior of scientists who have been brought up to rely solely on rational thinking for all theoretical and practical intents and purposes.

For the fact is that the entire community of early-twentieth-century physicists was so completely committed to the rational mode of thought, with its relentlessly categorical logic, that the vast majority of them were literally neither ready, willing, nor able even to conceive of the possibility of there being more than one right and proper way to conceptualize and describe something as fundamental and universal as the photon.

It is testimony to the hardiness of this way of thinking that it took many long years and a great deal of extremely intense emotional turmoil before most members of the immediately concerned sector of the scientific community were finally ready, willing, and able to accept the resolution of this conflict that is embodied in Neils Bohr's "principle of complementarity" (Wheeler 1982).

THE INESCAPABLE PERSPECTIVE

Relative Uncertainty and Complementarity. With their principles of relativity and uncertainty, Einstein and Heisenberg had shown (albeit in somewhat different ways), that science does not provide us with a picture of the world as it "really is." Rather, it provides us with a picture of relations between ourselves and the aspects of the world we are endeavoring to comprehend.

In showing that it is necessary to include both wavelike and particlelike properties of the photon in the picture of the physicist's relation to the subatomic world, Bohr called into question an even more fundamental proposition of modern science: the proposition that there is (or could be) only a single correct way of conceptualizing and describing relations between observers and things or events observed. Oppenheimer (1950, p. 22) explains:

> The basic finding was that in the atomic world it is not possible to describe the atomic system under investigation, in abstraction from the apparatus used for the investigation, by a single, unique, objective model. Rather a variety of models, each corresponding to a possible experimental arrangement and all required for a complete description of possible physical experience stand in a complementary relation to one another, in that the actual realization of any one model excludes the realization of others, yet each is a necessary part of the complete description of experience in the atomic world.

There is little reason to doubt that this is a proper description of the nature of relations obtaining within the atomic world. But what grounds are there for suggesting (as I am trying to do) that the principle of complementarity applies, mutatis mutandis, to the realm of human affairs as well?

> It is of course not yet fully clear how characteristically or how frequently we shall meet instances of quite close analogy to the complementarity of atomic physics in other fields, above all in the study of biological, psychological and cultural problems. Yet it is clear, as has repeatedly been stressed by Bohr himself, that the discovery of complementarity has provided us with a far wider and more sophisticated framework for the synthesis of varieties of scientific experience. It has refined and extended the pluralism natural to science and added new elements of subtlety to the idea of dialectic. Indeed, it seems to offer a far richer and more adequate general point of view for the comprehension of human experience than the misleadingly rigid and unitary philosophies that flowed so naturally from the experiences of Newtonian mechanics. (ibid)

REVISING THE HUMAN SCIENCES:
A SYSTEMS VIEW

There are myriad perils attendant upon unwarranted kinds of extrapolation. In order to justify abandonment of the modern scientific worldview and value system in favor of the emerging paradigm, grounds for doing so must be found by each of us within the context of our own particular fields of scientific or professional specialization (Edelman 1978).

In neuropsychology, the needed grounds are not hard to find. And the same appears to be true throughout the human sciences. This, at least, is the view to which I have come after reexamining some issues that have long been the subject of rather inconclusive debate in the field of psychology.

Once upon a time, psychology was defined as "the science of mental life" (James [1890], vol. 1, p. 1), and its proper subject matter was taken to be "such things as we call feelings, desires, cognitions, reasonings, and the like" (ibid.).

But it was not long before the objection arose that if psychology was intent upon becoming "a real science" it had better abandon its concern with such inwardly experienced things and events and focus, instead on the study of overtly manifested and directly observable behavior (Pavlov 1927; Watson 1914; Skinner 1938).

Indeed, in the century or so since psychology first became a more of less self-conscious science, the argument has raged back and forth between succeeding generations of mentalists and behaviorists (or rationalists and empiricists) as if their respective definitions of psychology must needs be irreconcilable. Thus, no sooner do we enter the realm if psychological discourse at its most general level than we are confronted with an issue that has long remained unresolvable in the either/or terms in which it has been traditionally posed.

As was the case in the earlier example from physics, what we have here is an instance in which it is necessary to choose between two ways of dealing with conceptual dichotomies. On the one hand, we can continue to regard mentalism and behaviorism as mutually exclusive and irreconcilable alternatives and demand that a choice be made between them. On the other, we can regard them as two different ways of looking at the subject matter of psychology and broaden our conception of the field sufficiently to accommodate both.

Of course, the latter approach is inconsistent with the dictates of the unitary notions that flow from the modern scientific worldview, but it is wholly consistent with what the principles of relativity, uncertainty, and complementarity imply in their deepest and broadest sense, namely that in any given instance, there is bound to be a multiplicity of potentially valid ways of describing things and events.

In a sense, this is precisely the lesson that we are taught, again and again, when we descend a bit more deeply into the domain of substantive psychological research. Take the case of research on the perception of reversible or ambiguous figures such as the Necker cube and Rubin's vase, for example. Here we encounter, in pure culture, a set of situations where there are at least two mutually exclusive ways of perceiving the same stimulus object and in which it makes absolutely no sense to imagine that either one or the other way is inherently more or less correct. Perhaps a fuller awareness of the general significance of this deceptively simple perceptual lesson would help us to avoid becoming enbroiled in other ultimately fruitless and inconclusive either/or arguments essentially equivalent to the one concerning particles and waves.

Moreover, since the overall boundaries of human inquiry are necessarily and unavoidably vague (see the Postscript below), we must be prepared to include in our studies aspects of both underlying and surrounding levels of organization. In the case of psychology, for example, a consideration of any phenomenon must necessarily include an exploration of both its neurobiological roots and its sociocultural branches. Thus, as in many such matters, it behooves us to follow the advice of William James [1890] 1950, p. 6):

> It is better not to be pedantic, but to let the science be as vague as its subject, and include such phenomena as . . . can throw any light on the main business in hand. It will ere long be seen that . . . we gain much more by a broad than by a narrow conception of our subject. At a certain stage in the development of every science a degree of vagueness is what best consists with fertility.

Thus, even if there were no grounds for extrapolating from the realm of physics to the realm of the human sciences, there are ample grounds within the latter for adopting the principles of relativity, uncertainty, and complementarity as a guide to theoretical and experimental work and as a basis for thinking about human things and events in general. And do not the same considerations apply, mutatis mutandis, to the field of creative and innovative management?

MANAGING THE MENTAL HEALTH SYSTEM

One way of coming at the foregoing question is to consider a potential area of application. Let us therefore ask: What is the relevance of this systems view (and the emerging paradigm of which it is a part) for questions relating to the administration of our mental health system?

From the vantage point of the traditional mechanistic and reductionistic perspective patterns of thought, feeling and action are generally conceived of as attributes sui generis of the particular individual(s) in question. And while the influence of this way of thinking may be waning somewhat among clinically oriented psychologists, it continues to reign supreme within those regions where the mental health system interfaces with the financial and administrative apparatus of contemporary American society. Thus, for example, irrespective of what the actual providers of mental health services may believe about the complex interplay of biological, psychological, and sociocultural factors in the production of the mental and behavioral symptoms of a particular "identified patient," the possibility of receiving payment for services rendered is not uncommonly contingent upon the willingness of the practitioner to conceptualize and describe each and every case in diagnostic terms derived from a "medical model" (Chorover 1979).

Thus do prevailing administrative considerations and modes of management reinforce the increasingly untenable modern scientific view that the principal determinants of human problems are reducible to personal and thence to neurobiological influences. As I have argued elsewhere (Chorover 1973, 1979), the interests and objectives of administrators often appear to be better served (at least in the short run) by reliance on clinical approaches capable of making it appear that all or most human problems are traceable to localizable malfunctions situated within identifiable "sick" or "defective" individuals. This way of thinking views the individual in relative neuropsychological isolation from his or her surrounding social context and leads, as a general rule, to the framing of diagnoses and therapeutic interventions in essentially individualistic terms.

To the scientist or manager who adopts the vantage point of the emerging paradigm, by contract, it is no longer sufficient to think solely in such narrowly analytic and atomistic terms. Thus, prevailing administrative regulations notwithstanding, all of us must change our ways of thinking and acting to accommodate the fact that it is no longer scientifically credible to regard the individual as a "Ding an sich," whose mental and behavioral patterns can be adequately defined and dealt with in neuropsychological isolation from the environing sociocultural and ecological context in which he or she happens to live.

RELEVANCE TO THE PRESENT CRISIS

Most people alive today are too young to have any living memory of the moment, early in August 1945, when the first American-made atomic bombs devastated the cities of Hiroshima and Nagasaki. Destruction by such means, with such suddenness and on such a scale was entirely without precedent in human history. By the same token, and for the same reasons, fewer and fewer of us can recall the essentially contemporaneous moment when the world began to learn the full measure of what has come to be called the Nazi holocaust (Chorover 1979, ch. 5). But whether our personal memories contain traces of these events or not, all of us are today living in a world that has been deeply and permanently scarred by them and their sequelae. Is it possible that one aspect of the impact of these events on our lives has been to impair our ability to respond both creatively and innovatively to the crisis that confronts us?

An affirmative answer that makes good sense to me is given in a recent monograph by Macy (1983). In effect, she takes Edgar Mitchell's feelings of anguish about the human predicament as her point of departure and hypothesizes that the knowledge we all have about the present condition and future prospects of humanity engenders natural and normal feelings of distress and anguish in all of us. Moreover, she proceeds to notice that, contrary to conventional psychological wisdom, according to which such feelings are ordinarily supposed to engender adaptive patterns of mental activity and behavior (responses aimed at eliminating their sources), this is not, on the whole, what has happened. On the contrary, the more we know, the worse we feel, and the worse we feel, the less ready we appear to be to think and act in creative and innovative ways that might otherwise be capable of changing the conditions responsible for initiating and maintaining this vicious cycle. Instead of engaging in creative and innovative problem solving, we tend to deny that a problem exists, repress our feelings of fear and anguish and frustration about it, or resort to patterns of addictive behavior in an effort to deal with the pain.

Macy's analysis of what is going on here is both clear and to the point: Because of fear of pain and social taboos against the expression of feelings of anguish, despair, dread, grief, anger, and powerlessness, these feelings are generally denied and repressed. This denial and repression also engenders psychic numbing, apathy, and the many other signs of cognitive and behavioral paralysis that are so common among us today. And this is precisely why every new attempt "to discuss the present crisis on the informational level alone, or . . . to arouse the public to action by delivering ever more terrifying facts and figures" tends to exacerbate, rather than to relieve, our predicament (Macy, 1983, p. xiii).

Indeed, it is both necessary and insufficient to expose ourselves and others to information and argument without more. Taken alone, knowledge of our peril and rational discourse about it only lead to a deepening of our feelings of anguish and despair; only exacerbate our sense of helplessness, hopelessness, and powerlessness.

Moreover, in both economic and ecological terms, and with respect to our legitimate local and global concerns, the long-term human neurobiopsychosociocultural costs of this denial and repression and escapism are beyond reckoning. Likewise impoverishing, in the short run, is the expenditure of enormous personal and social resources in an ultimately self-defeating effort not to notice or deal with what is actually going on. Clearly, the neurobiopsychosocioculturally dear currency in which we all pay for this gross mismanagement of ourselves and our planet is not available for more creative and innovative cognitive, affective, and behavioral purposes.

What is to be done? Macy's prescription is as creative as it is simple. In her view our only and best way out of the present crisis begins with a focus on ourselves and our own attitudes toward the predicament we are in.

Describing her book as "a guide to despair and empowerment work," she suggests some sensible step-by-step ways of managing "the work of dealing with our knowledge and feelings about the present planetary crisis in ways that release energy and vision for creative response" (1983, p. xiii).

And this is a kind of work, she insists, that simply cannot be done solely via rational thinking. Nor can it be done in social isolation. On the contrary, it must begin on the affective level and proceed in a supportive social context. (Here, it will be noticed, is yet another illustration of the wisdom in Einstein's remark about learning from painful experience that rational thinking alone does not suffice to solve the problems of our social life.)

In a sense, then, what Macy offers us is a way of approaching the challenging task of conceptual change that Mitchell and Einstein (among others) have set before us. If we would be creative and innovative in our approaches to the task of making things work in a more sustainable fashion before it is too late, we must begin by learning how to help ourselves and each other recover from the deleterious effects that prevailing ways of thinking and acting have been exerting on our personal and professional lives. Only after this despair and empowerment work has been done will we be in a position to manage human systems more creatively and innovatively; only then will we be able to develop more successfully sustainable cognitive and behavioral responses to the present crisis.

Toward that end, we who are scientists and practitioners, managers, teachers, health care providers, and others must learn to be understanding when confronted (as we are and increasingly will be) by friends and colleagues and students and clients and patients suffering, in myriad ways, from distress of the kind Macy is talking about. And that is not all. We must also try to have something else to offer to ourselves and each other than more of the same mechanistic, reductionistic, individualistically oriented prescriptions we have inherited along with the modern scientific worldview and value system that has thus far been our main and sole guide for all academic and professional intents and purposes.

It is not at all my intention to suggest that the emerging paradigm whose characteristics I have been endeavoring to describe is a panacea. What it offers, however, is a provisional alternative to a paradigm that has proven itself to be largely unworkable in relation to human systems, as the following example will clearly show.

LEARNING FROM BHOPAL

In December 1984 a massive leak of highly toxic methyl isocyanate (MIC) vapors from a pesticide plant operated by the Union Carbide Company killed and injured many thousands of men, women, and children in Bhopal, India. Most of the victims were residents of an industrial shanytown adjacent to the plant. The chemical to which they were exposed is well known as an extremely hazardous and potently neurotoxic substance closely related to, but perhaps five times more deadly than, phosgene, the chemical weapon used with such devastating effect in the First World War.

Shortly after the disaster, I received a telephone call from a friend and colleague, a clinical neuropsychologist who told me that he'd been asked to help design a protocol to be used in assessing the mental and behavioral status of some of the survivors of the disaster. In effect, what had prompted him to call me was his sudden and sobering realization that the modern scientific paradigm is simply incapable of providing a sensible approach to this problem. Why?

There are many reasons. For one thing, it is impossible to determine the amount and duration of MIC exposure experienced in any given case, and hence no rational way of arriving at reliable quantitative estimates of dose-response relations. But that is not the main problem. The main problem is that the symptoms from which the survivors were (and still are) suffering cannot be directly attributed in any simple way to the neurotoxic nature of the substance to which they were exposed.

Please do not misunderstand. MIC is a deadly poison and exposure to it is invariably a neuropsychopharmacological disaster. But it is impossible to make sense of the victims symptoms in isolated neuropsychological terms because the victims' exposure to MIC did not occur in a neuropharmacological vacuum. On the contrary, it occurred in a sociocultural context marked by multifarious kinds and degrees of individual and collective stress and disorganization (Everest 1985; Banik 1986). And the modern scientific paradigm is quite simply incapable of dealing with such a state of affairs.

Let me put it this way: As things now stand, it remains extremely difficult to perform a systematic study of the effects upon human systems of radical multilevel disruptions (Wapner 1983a). Accordingly, research involving the neurobiological, and sociocultural impact of exposure to environmental toxins remains a promising but still woefully underdeveloped area (Fein et al. 1983; Weiss 1983).

Whether or not it may eventually prove possible to develop methods of procedure that permit the credible scientific study of such things as the mental and behavioral effects of exposure to neurotoxic substances under real-world conditions is questionable. Some advances in the study of complex multilevel interactions are presently being made, however, in the closely related domain of neuroimmunology. Recent research findings make it increasingly clear, for example, that there is much mutual and reciprocal interplay and modulation between the immune system and the nervous system. To be more precise, it is now apparent that immunological competence and other factors involved in the mediation of resistance or susceptibility to disease are subject to modulation by neuropsychological processes involved in the mediation of moods and emotions (Shavit et al. 1985; Stein, Keller, and Schleifer 1985).

But this much is already clear: The form and content of human mental life and behavior are conditioned and constrained (both under normal conditions and otherwise) by complex and recurrent bidirectional interplay between internal (neurobiological) and external (sociocultural and ecological) factors. And this is a state of affairs that the modern scientific paradigm, by virtue of its rigidly one-dimensional commitment to the mechanistic and reductionistic approach, is incapable of making comprehensible. By contrast, research based upon the principles of the new paradigm shows promise of making the interplay scientifically comprehensible (Reason and Rowan 1981).

In sum, the paradigm shift that is urgently needed for all scientific as well as social intents and purposes is already getting underway. Psychological specialists of all kinds are in a position to make a significant contribution to its continued advancement.

SUSTAINABILITY

In the summer of 1979, the World Council of Churches held its triennial meeting at the institution where I work. Delegates gathered from around the globe to discuss (among other things) the interplay of science and religion in the present age. As the meeting drew to a close, an important and timely resolution was issued. After taking note of the many ways in which what I have been calling "modern" science and technology have influenced and are continuing to influence the course of human events, the resolution called upon those of us who are in a position to do so to apply ourselves to the task of making science and technology more responsive to human needs by using it to help in the creation of a more just, sustainable, and participatory mode of human life on earth.

This is not the place to enter into a detailed discussion of these notions. I would like to suggest however that, under conditions presently prevailing, the concept of sustainability appears to offer a basis for evaluating the extent to which acts intended to be acts of creative management are "making things work successfully" or not. Further to the point, the term *sustainability* has both material and conceptual entailments that, in the context of the emerging paradigm, may help us to confront our local and global problems while continuing to pursue—as we all must—the old and abiding task of making things work successfully at home. If creative and innovative management is to succeed, it must succeed here.

POSTCRIPT

Regarding Human Systems

As indicated in Table 14-1, psychology is, in my view, a field situated on the disciplinary spectrum midway between the neurobiological and sociocultural domains of inquiry. Further to the point, psychology is centrally concerned with human mental life and behavior and, even more particularly, with relations between and among the cognitive, affective, and expressive aspects of individual existence and experience.

When viewed in this way, the inescapable duplexity of the psychologist's involvement with the subject matter of psychology becomes apparent. Surely no less than our colleagues in physics, we students of human systems are both observers of and participants in the systems we are endeavoring to comprehend (Wheeler 1982).

We, ourselves, are organisms and persons and members (of biologically defined species and socioculturally defined communities or groups) and inhabitants, along with uncountable others, of a particular planetary biosphere. And while there is much detailed complexity in the concrete relations implied by this conception of systems inhabiting systems within systems, there is not necessarily any irreconcilable contradiction involved in the process of seeing ourselves in this way.

For to see ourselves as composite neurobiological/psychological systems arising both transgenerationally and ontogenetically within an environing sociocultural and ecological context is immensely more fertile than to imagine the human mind or human behavior as detached and existing in psychological isolation.

Throughout this chapter I have been trying to make definitions quite explicit. But, until now, I have had nothing explicit to say about the centrally important term: *system*. The aim of this postscript is to make up for that omission.

What Is a System?

The word *system* is a compound derived from the Greek *syn* = 'together' and *stem* = 'to stand'. Here, as in common parlance, the term refers to things and events of a conceptual or material kind that appear to be "standing together" in a manner betokening a composite unity.

My usage of the phrase *human systems* derives from an earlier discussion (Chorover and Chorover 1982) and is closely related to the conception concurrently being developed by Wapner (1986). As illustrated in Table 14-1, the systems of particular interest to me in this connection thus far have been human brains, persons, and groups. In this connection, also, it must be acknowledged that there is substantial vagueness and imprecision inherent in the way I have been using the phrase *human systems*. This state of affairs contrasts so markedly with the emphasis on clarity and precision inherent in the modern scientific paradigm that it obviously warrants an explanation: When viewing human systems from the vantage point of the emerging paradigm, a certain amount of fuzziness is unavoidable. And that which is evident at the boundaries is both necessary and normal.

Central Clarity and Peripheral Fuzziness

Perhaps the best way to elaborate on this point is by considering the following description of a prototypical human system (Oxford 1971, p. x):

> a widely-diffused and highly-cultivated living language is not a fixed quantity circumscribed by definite limits. That vast aggregate of words and phrases which constitutes the Vocabulary (for example) presents to the mind that endeavors to grasp it as a definite whole the aspect of one of those nebulous

masses familiar to the astronomer, in which a clear and unmistakable nucleus shades off on all sides, through zones of decreasing brightness, to a dim marginal film that seems to end nowhere, but to lose itself imperceptibly in the surrounding darkness.

Moreover, the same principle applies to the constituent elements of which a human system is composed. Thus, any one of the cells in the Table 14-1

may be compared to one of those natural groups of the zoologist or botanist, wherein typical species forming the characteristic nucleus of the order, are linked on every side to other species, in which the typical character is less and less distinctly apparent, till it fades away in an outer fringe of aberrant forms, which merge imperceptibly in various surrounding orders, and whose own position is ambiguous and uncertain. For the convenience of classification, the naturalist may draw the line, which bounds a class or order, outside or inside or a particular form; but Nature has drawn it nowhere. (ibid)

The essential idea here is that it ultimately is as impossible to draw definite lines of demarcation or circumscription around human systems as it is to specify a particular point of separation or connection between constituent elements of which such systems are composed. In order to appreciate the generality of the point that these examples are intended to make, the reader is encouraged to reflect upon the applicability of the foregoing description to any human system or aspect thereof with which he or she is already relatively familiar.

How is this interplay of central clarity and peripheral fuzziness to be understood? To view this question from the vantage point of the modern scientific worldview and value system is to understand it as asking whether what is being discussed is a generic attribute of the human systems being observed and described or is due to something inherent in the human systems doing the conceptualizing and describing. But, when the question is approached in this way it is ultimately impossible to answer it for certain one way or the other. On the other hand, to come at the same question from the vantage point of the emerging paradigm is to recognize that what is at work here is yet another example of our inescapably duplex role as both observers of and participants in the systems we are endeavoring to comprehend.

The proposition therefore to consider is that many if not all of our efforts to conceptualize and describe human systems will eventually lead us to a point at which this interplay of central clarity and peripheral fuzziness will appear. Moreover, through a detailed consideration of yet another specific case in point, it can be shown that this state of affairs presents no untoward barrier to comprehension and is not indicative of any shortcoming in the overall approach.

The Triune Brain: A Prototypical Human System

In Paul MacLean's well-known and influential concept of the triune brain we encounter a pertinent neuropsychological instance of the attempt to conceptualize and describe a prototypical human system as a composite unity consisting of three major subsystems. As Mac-Lean has argued, substantial evidence exists to justify an hierarchical or concentric partitioning of the human brain into three more or less separate and distinct "cerebrotypes," each with its own special mode of organization and development. MacLean denotes these, in ascending order (from deepest to outermost and from phylogenetically most ancient to most recent) as "reptilian," "paleomammalian," and "neomammalian" (MacLean 1967, 1969, 1970).[2]

From the description of MacLean's schema, it is easy to be misled into thinking that the boundaries between these three principal subsystems are structurally or functionally definite and clear-cut. But that is not, in fact, the case. And this becomes apparent almost at once to anyone who attempts to use available methods of investigation to precisely characterize or circumscribe the intermediate (paleomammalian or limbic) subsystem.

The term *limbus* means 'border' or 'ring' and, as its name implies, the limbic system is a composite entity consisting of a number of more or less separate and distinct neural nuclei or subsystems (including the amygdala and hippocampus, among others) which collectively form a ring or border around the brainstem. Since it serves both to separate and to connect the underlying and overlying portions of the brain, it might also be described as an interface between them.

Further to the point, a great deal of clinical and experimental neuropsychological evidence is consistent with MacLean's evolutionary view of the triune brain. Thus, from research involving laboratory animals, and from clinical case studies, it has been learned that the limbic system is intimately involved in the mediation of a wide range of mental and behavioral activities upon which individual and species survival depend. It also plays a major role in all affective aspect of human mental life (feelings, moods, emotions).

But this is far from the whole story. Just as our feelings are intimately related to our thoughts and actions, so the limbic subsystem is intimately involved in the mediation of relations between the overlying neocortex and the underlying core brain. In addition, portions of the limbic system are directly involved in the mediation of cognitive and expressive functions as well as affective ones. Further to the point, there is little sharpness in the manner in which the outer and inner boundaries of the limbic system merge into the immediately overlying (neomammalian) and underlying (reptilian) portions of the human brain.

To be more precise, at its upper, outer, more rostral limits, the limbic system includes a ring of tissue that merges imperceptibly into surrounding neocortical regions (including portions of the frontal lobe and cingulate gyrus) that are intimately involved in the mediation of multifarious cognitive processes. And, at its lower, inner, more caudal limits, the limbic system intermingles with numerous core brain regions (including the hypothalamus) involved in the regulation of basic vegetative activities and the integration of fundamental sensorimotor functions.

Here then, is a sense in which what we actually know about the organization of a prototypical human system corresponds quite precisely with what might be expected on the basis of what I have previously said about central clarity and peripheral fuzziness. Indeed, if one were to try to summarize, in a single sentence, the image of the limbic system to which we are led by our most sophisticated and well-informed efforts to be absolutely precise in demarcating its anatomical, physiological, or neuropsychological boundaries, it would be difficult, indeed, to do better than to echo Heisenberg's description of quantum reality, in which "connections of different kinds overlap and alternate and combine and thereby determine the texture of the whole." Nor is this view applicable only to this particular brain subsystem. On the contrary, it appears to be characteristic of neural subsystems in general.

Furthermore, it is not only at the neurobiological level of organization that this fuzziness is encountered. Relations essentially comparable to the ones observed within and between the three principal constituent subsystems of the human brain are apparent at the psychological and sociocultural levels of organization as well.

With respect to the psychological level of organization, it will be noted not only that the indicated cognitive and affective aspects collectively comprise what we inwardly experience as our "mental lives" but also that the boundary between thinking and feeling is notoriously difficult (or rather impossible) precisely to define. Both of these points were made long ago by William James [1890] 1950).

Note also that the table implies the existence of an interplay at the psychological/sociocultural boundary (within the domain of social psychology) between the thoughts and feelings (or attitudes) of the individual, on the one hand, and the beliefs, values, and practices of his or her environing sociocultural context, on the other. One feature of this interplay was referred to earlier in connection with my initial discussion of scientific paradigms. At this point it is the ubiquitousness of this interplay that deserves emphasis, along with the idea that it may operate bidirectionally. Thus, in such commonplace contexts as the family, peer groups, educational institutions, scientific and professional organizations, and so on, cognitive, affective, and expressive aspects of individual and social life mutually interact in such a manner that both levels of organization may be more or less amenable to change. Indeed, it is via this recurrent pattern of interaction that the limits of conformity and deviance are theoretically and practically defined in human society (Chorover and Chorover 1982).

The New Direction

As in any other field, research in creative and innovative management needs new directions indeed. What I have laid out in this chapter is the direction that I believe is needed.

NOTES

1. For the idea behind this imaginary journey, I am deeply indebted to a most remarkable book and motion picture called *Powers of Ten*. That work has an interesting history that is worth summarizing: In the 1950s, a Dutch educator, Kees Boeke, authored and illustrated a children's book called *The Universe in 40 Jumps*. Inspired by it, Charles Eames, a noted American visual designer, began work on its cinematic counterpart, a cosmic-zoom movie. In 1968 he released a preliminary version titled "A Rough Sketch for a Film Dealing With the Relative Sizes of Things in the Universe." The final version took Eames another decade to complete. It was released in 1978, the year of his death. Philip and Phyliss Morrison, in collaboration with The Office of Charles and Ray Eames have since created a book based upon the latter work (*Powers of Ten*, Scientific American Library, San Francisco: W.H. Freeman, 1982). Both the film and the book use exponential notation as the basis for a fantastic, visually seamless straight-line journey through the cosmos, starting from a realm not only beyond the limits of our solar system but also beyond the farthest known galaxies. It next brings us back to the picnic along the same path. But that is not all. After returning to our starting point we continue moving down and into the chaotic inner quarkiness within the deepest imaginable depth of a proton in the nucleus of a carbon atom in a methane group in one of the bases of a nucleic acid molecule within the nucleus of a cell inside the tissue of the skin on the hand of one of the people at the picnic.

2. The paleomammalian counterpart of the human brain corresponds to the limbic system, which is understood to play a central role in affective aspects of mental life and in the mediation of relations between cognition and expression (see also Table 14-1).

REFERENCES

Banik, S.N. 1986. "Psychological Effects of the Bhopal Gas Tragedy and Its Global Implications." Unpublished paper presented at ninety-fourth annual convention of the American Psychological Association, Washington, D.C., August 1986.

Bohm, D. 1976. *Fragmentation and Wholeness.* Jerusalem: Van Leer Jerusalem Foundation.

Boring, E.G. 1950. *A History of Experimental Psychology*, 2nd ed. New York: Appleton-Century-Crofts.

Braverman, H. 1974. *Labor and Monopoly Capital: The Degradation of Work in the Twentieth Century.* New York: Monthly Review Press.

Brown, L.R. 1986. *State of the World—1986.* New York: W.W. Norton.

Capek, M. 1961. *The Philosophical Impact of Contemporary Physics.* Princeton, N.J.: D. Van Nostrand.

Capra, F. 1982. *The Turning Point: Science, Society, and the Rising Culture.* New York: Simon and Schuster.

Cartwright, S.A. 1851. "Report on the Diseases and Physical Peculiarities of the Negro Race." *New Orleans Medical and Surgical Journal*, May 1851, 691-715.

Charnes, A., and W.W. Cooper (Eds.). 1984. Foreword. In *Creative and Innovative Management: Essays in Honor of George Kozmetsky.* Cambridge, Mass.: Ballinger.

Chorover, S.L. 1973. "Big Brother and Psychotechnology." *Psychology Today* 7: 43-54.

_____. 1974. "Psychosurgery: A Neuropsychological Perspective." *Boston University Law Review 54*: 231-248.

_____. 1976. "The Pacification of the Brain: From Phrenology to Psychosurgery." In T.P. Morley (Ed.), *Current Controversies in Neurosurgery.* Philadelphia: W.B. Saunders, pp. 730-767.

_____. 1979. *From Genesis to Genocide: The Meaning of Human Nature and the Power of Behavior Control.* Cambridge, Mass.: MIT Press.

_____. 1980a. "The Psychosurgery Evaluation Studies and Their Impact on the Commission's Report." In E. Valenstein (Ed.), *The Psychosurgery Debate: Scientific, Legal, and Ethical Perspectives.* San Francisco: W.H. Freeman, pp. 145-263.

_____. 1980b. "Violence: A Localizable Problem? In E. Valenstein (Ed.), *The Psychosurgery Debate: Scientific, Legal and Ethical Perspectives.* San Francisco: W.H. Freeman, pp. 334-47.

_____. 1985. "Psychology in Cultural Context: The Division of Labor and the Fragmentation of Experience." In S. Koch and D.E. Leary (Eds.), *A Century of Psychology as Science.* New York: McGraw-Hill, pp. 870-79.

_____. 1986. "Reductionism/Holism and Human Systems: Thesis/Antithesis or Synthesis?" Unpublished paper presented at the International Conference on Perspectives and Applications of the Holistic Approach to the Human Sciences, Catania, Italy, November-December 1986.

_____, and B. Chorover. 1982. "Towards a Theory of Human Systems." In S.P.R. Rose (Ed.), *Towards a Liberatory Biology: Proceedings of the Bressa-*

none Conference on the Dialectics of Biology and Society in the Production of Mind, vol. 2. London: Allison and Busby, pp. xxx–xxx.

Descartes, R. 1955. *Philosophical Works*, vol. 1, edited by E.S. Haldane and G.R.T. Hall. New York: Dover.

Easlea, B. 1981. *Science and Sexual Oppression*. London: Weidenfeld and Nicolson.

Eccles, J.C. 1979. *The Human Mystery*. Heidelberg: Springer.

Edelman, P.D. 1978. *Physics and Psychology: From the Newtonian to the Modern Worldview*. Unpublished, S.B. thesis Massachusetts Institute of Technology, Cambridge, Mass.

Einstein, A. 1905. "Ueber einen die Erzeugung und Verwandlung des Lichtes betroffenden heuristischen Gesichtspunkt. *Annelen Der Physik*. Ser. 4, 117: 132–148.

Everest, L. 1985. *Behind the Poison Cloud: Union Carbide's Bhopal Massacre*. Chicago: Banner Press.

Fein, G.G., P.M. Schwartz, S.W. Jacobson, and J.L. Jacobson. 1983. "Environmental Toxins and Behavioral Development: A New Role for Psychological Research." *American Psychologist 38*: 1188–97.

Griffin, S. 1980. *Woman and Nature*. New York: Harper/Colophon Books.

Hanson, N.R. 1958. *Patterns of Discovery*. Cambridge, England: Cambridge University Press.

Heisenberg, W. 1958. *Physics and Philosophy*. New York: Harper Torchbooks.

_____. 1972. "The Representation of Nature in Contemporary Physics." In S. Sears and G. Lord (Eds.), *The Discontinuous Universe*. New York: Basic Books, pp. 122–35.

Howard, G.S. 1985. "The Role of Values in the Science of Psychology." *American Psychologist 40*: 255–65.

James, W. [1890]/1950. *Principles of Psychology*, 2 vols. New York: Dover.

Koch, S., and D.E. Leary (Eds.). 1985. *A Century of Psychology as Science*. New York: McGraw-Hill.

Krasner, L., and A.C. Houts. 1984. "A Study of the "Value" Systems of Behavioral Scientists." *American Psychology 39*: 840–50.

Kuhn, T.S. 1962. *The Structure of Scientific Revolutions*. Chicago: University of Chicago Press.

Lasswitz, K. 1890. *Geschichte der atomistik von Mittelalter bis Newton*, 2 vols. Hamburg: Voss.

Liess, W. 1977. *The Domination of Nature*. New York: Braziller.

Lovelock, J.E., and L. Margulis. 1974. "Atmospheric Homeostasis by and for the Biosphere: The Gaia Hypothesis." *Tellus 26*: 1–10.

MacLean, P.D. 1967. "The Brain in Relation to Empathy and Medical Education." *Journal of Nervous and Mental Disease 144*: 374–82.

_____. 1969. *A Triune Concept of the Brain and Behavior*. Toronto: Toronto University Press.

_____. 1970. "The Triune Brain, Emotion, and Scientific Bias." In F.O. Schmitt (Ed.), *The Neurosciences: Second Study Program*. New York: Rockefeller University Press, pp. 336–49.

Macy, J.R. 1983. *Despair and Personal Power in the Nuclear Age*. Philadelphia: New Society.

Mark, V.H., W.H. Sweet, and F.R. Ervin. 1967. "Brain Disease and Urban Riots." *Journal of American Medical Association 201*: 895.

Mark, V.H., and F.R. Ervin. 1968. "Is There a Need to Evaluate the Individuals Producing Human Violence?" *Psychiatric Opinion 8*: 32–34.

_____. 1970. *Violence and the Brain*. New York: Harper & Row.

Merchant, C. 1980. *The Death of Nature: Women, Ecology, and the Scientific Revolution*. San Francisco: Harper & Row.

Mitchell, E.D. 1974. "Introduction: From Outer Space to Inner Space." In E.D. Mitchell (Ed.), *Psychic Exploration: A Challenge for Science*. New York: G.P. Putnam's Sons, pp. 25–49.

Myers, N. 1984. *GAIA: An Atlas of Planet Management*. Garden City, N.Y.: Anchor Press/Doubleday.

Neville, R. 1974. "Specialties and Worlds." *Hastings Center Studies 2*: 53–64.

Oppenheimer, J.R. 1950. "The Age of Science: 1900–1950." *Scientific American 183*: 20–23.

Oxford. 1971. *The Compact Edition of the Oxford English Dictionary*, 2 vols. New York: Oxford University Press.

Pavlov, I.P. 1927. *Conditioned Reflexes*, translated by G.W. Anrep. New York: Oxford University Press.

Peele, S. 1981. "Reductionism in the Psychology of the Eighties." *American Psychologist 36*: 807–18.

Reason, P., and J. Rowan. 1981. *Human Inquiry: A Sourcebook of New Paradigm Research*. Chichester, John Wiley & Sons.

Sachtouris, G. 1985. *Gaia's Dance*. Unpublished paper.

Shavit, Y., G.W. Terman, F.C. Martin, J.W. Lewis, J.C. Liebeskind, and R.P. Gale. 1985. "Stress, Opioid Peptides, the Immune System and Cancer." *Journal of Immunology 135*: 834s–37s.

Skinner, B.F. 1938. *The Behavior of Organisms*. New York: Appleton-Century.

Stein, M., S.E. Keller, and S.J. Schleifer. 1985. "Stress and Immunomodulation: The Role of Depression and Neuroendocrine Function." *Journal of Immunology 135*: 827s–33s.

Sweet, W.H. 1970. Foreword. In V.H. Mark and F.R. Ervin, *Violence and the Brain*. New York: Harper & Row.

Toulmin, S. 1982. *The Return to Cosmology: Postmodern Science and the Theology of Nature*. Berkeley: University of California Press.

Valenstein, E. 1973. *Brain Control: A Critical Examination of Brain Stimulation and Psychosurgery*. New York: John Wiley and Sons.

_____. 1980. *The Psychosurgery Debate: Scientific, Legal, and Ethical Perspectives*. San Francisco: W.H. Freeman.

Wapner, S. 1983a. "Living with Radical Disruptions of Person-in-Environment Systems." *International Association of Traffic and Safety Science Review 2*: 133–48 (Japan).

_____. 1986. "A Holistic, Developmental, System-Oriented Environmental Psychology: Some Beginnings." Unpublished paper.

Watson, J. 1914. *Behavior. An Introduction to Comparative Psychology*. New York: Hotl.

Weiss, B. 1983. "Behavioral Toxicology and Environmental Health Science: Opportunity and Challenge for Psychology." *American Psychologist 38*: 1174-87.

Wheeler, J. A. 1982. "Bohr, Einstein and the Strange Lesson of the Quantum." In R. Q. Elvee (Ed.), *Mind in Nature*. San Francisco: Harper & Row, pp. 1-30.

Discussion

Moderator: Karl Weick

Weick: Do we need new methods or more conscientious adaptation of old methods? If you think of the world from the top down from Stephen Chorover's global perspective or Scott Isaksen's starting with one set of thoughts, you have a pretty good range in which to find some comfortable turf.

Cooper: I think one way of bringing everything that we have into focus is the issue of raising the right question. I am reminded of the fact that when we were putting the first conference together, I called Paul Lawrence at Harvard to be a participant. I called Paul, the contingency theorist who is very famous in organization theory, because I knew that for a number of years he had been retained to help redesign the functioning of the National Institutes of Health (NIH). I had heard his very interesting reports. He was surprised by the title of the conference, "Creative and Innovative Management." I said that we would like to have his discuss what he did at NIH. He said that he didn't know anything about creative and innovative management and that he had not given it any thought. I tried to rephrase it by saying, "All we are talking about is the management of creative and innovative activity." NIH, remember, is the organization that is in charge of a large segment of U.S. research activities in the health field. Apparently, in terms of the instructions that were given to him, "creative and innovative management" was left out. The objective was to get the organization functioning better. The word "better" was left open. Somehow or another, it seems to me that we have an opportunity to bring this kind of question into focus. Where in all of our research activity do we have an opportunity to sponsor and encourage the introduction of the creative process itself in the research rather than studying how other people do it?

Lewin: If we don't have any good theories about the innovation process but we know that some organizations are doing it (or if we are as lucky as Bob Kaplan to identify companies that are on the frontier of doing the change) then one way to get started is by observing the natural setting. Hopefully, we can do what Andrew Van de Ven talked about, which will essentially allow us to develop first explanations and out of that data will come theories and implications for the practice of the management of organizations. Where does this creative process come in? To study organizations that are more creative about what they are doing than other organizations, given the complexity of [creativity], you are going to have to cover a whole range of organizations. One of the problems is that in our training we tend to study central tendencies. The way to make real progress is to find those outliers who define the best practice, the best success, and see if we can learn from those top performers in order to motivate and inform the remaining population. But we do not have technologies for identifying the best? That is part of advancing the creative research methodology.

Isaksen: Can we be creative about creativity research and can we use some of the things we gleen about the creative process in examining the creative process? I am intrigued by the questions that Andrew Van de Ven has raised. One of the notions that we see in group processes is managing the collaborative nature of the process itself and trying to bring to bear the differences in perspective that create chaos in the first place, trying to find mechanisms, structures, systems, and common language to overcome those differences, to get at true collaboration. One of our research challenges is how to get true interdisciplinary participation. How do we get real interdisciplinary research going when, in fact, we have vastly different jargons to describe the same thing? And even when we agree on terminology, we still have very different methodologies to understand it. One way to be more creative about creativity research is to be deliberate and systematic about the collaboration. This immediately suggests that we have to develop a common language. That is, what do we mean by this thing that we call the creative process? What are the models that we would choose to use? Maybe we need some convergence. Common language also includes the assumptions necessary to set definitions and make progress. The researcher can say, "Here is my definition of innovation and creativity." The *common process language* and *managing the collaboration* are two of my initial stabs at being creative about creativity research.

Burnside: Asking whether we are raising the right questions is indeed the right question! After doing three innovation audits, I found myself backing up from the original question—which I thought was "How do we assess the climate for stimulants and obstacles to creativity?." Now the first thing that we help a client do (at the point when they decide whether or not to permit an Innovation Audit) is answer the question "Why does the client really want to increase the creativity?." We have learned from the first three audits that this question is the best one you can ask up front. If the client doesn't know why he or she wants to increase creativity, then we need to slow down and clarify. We may, in fact, find out that the organization doesn't really want more creativity. Maybe they just heard about it. Participants have discussed diverse reasons and motivations for people wanting increased creativity—all the way from the survival of planet earth to generating better ideas in an individual's mind. I think raising the right questions is very much what we are all trying to do. It feels like fumbling in the dark. But our question in these audits is "Why do they really want more creativity?." If you spend some time on basic motivation, you begin to find answers about the role you expect creativity to play in your organization.

Chorover: Are we asking or raising the right questions? Within that question lies a phenomenon that a friend of mine calls the politics of pronouns. There is a presupposition that a consensus exists that all reasonable people would necessarily and inevitably share. I think the same thing applies precisely because the setting of agendas and the defining of terms is something that carries a very perspective quality. There is a wonderful passage in *Through the Looking Glass* where Alice meets Humpty Dumpty and has a discussion about how she objects to the way that he is using a word. The question is whether you can make words mean so many things. He says that the only question is who is to be the master. Thomas Hobbes once said that the greatest power in any society is the power to give names and to enforce definitions. The real question is from what perspective or on behalf of whom are we asking the question. Who are we, so to speak? What, in our frame of reference, does the question mean?

Within the context of paradigms, the way things are defined is conditioned and constrained by the perspective of the person or the discipline that is doing the defining. The very idea that there must be a single solitary, unitary, correct definition is a gratuitous assumption. What flies in the face of it is the fact that questions about the rightness or the wrongness of questions or the rightness or wrongness of behavior are confronted by all of us in a social context where there is often a good deal of conflict between different interests. I think it is one of the legacies of an outmoded scientific paradigm that we adhere to the idea of this monadic, single, correct explanation. Physics, at one time, was the model after which all the social sciences tried to pattern itself. Once upon a time, the notion of a unitary explanation prevailed in physics. It hasn't for at least sixty years. Those of us who are interested in being truly scientific about the systems we investigate should realize that we are *involved* in those systems. It took the physicists a very long time to discover that they were *involved* in what they were doing. They are not looking at the world through a plate of glass. Every observation is an act of participation. You affect the system by observing it. The system is different at different moments in time and different ways of observing it yield different views. I think that we have to accept the multiplicity of right questions. The only way to qualify the question is by specifying that it be right in relation to something—innovative in relation to what objectives, creative in relation to what intentions. Then I think that some of the confusion will drop away.

Isaksen: You have to do what you have to do. You invent and adopt those methods and concepts that will help you solve your problem. Problems present themselves in different ways. Some of us are engaged in understanding creativity and innovativeness and, hence, undertake innovation or creativity audits. Others are interested in understanding the process by which we can answer the question "How do things grow?," which is what I was addressing. Then, you have to become engaged in real-time studies. We have to develop some systematic way for thinking about methods for observing what we hope to gain to know.

Kuhn: We have seen much diversity in the papers. I would like all of you to project ten years into the future. We are sitting here again a decade from now, a little grayer and with a little less hair. Looking backward, what sequence of events or what types of results would you be satisfied with in your own research? I'm not interested in the generality of knowing more about creativity. But very specifically, I would like to know where you, in your own research, would feel that you have achieved a decade's worth of work. What understanding would you like to have contributed?

Van de Ven: A decade isn't enought for me. The innovation research program in Minnesota presently includes an investment of about 127 person-years of work by 30 investigators over a four-and-a-half year period tracking just 13 innovations. Most of innovating and creating are not manageable, but I can tell you what small proportions are. If I could also tell you the settings in which things are not manageable or controllable, then I think we would learn a lot. Will we understand "the management of innovation or creativity"? I don't think so—at least not a large proportion of it. Perhaps the management of innovation and creativity will turn out to be similar a professional grand slalom downhill race. The skiers all compete, practice, and accumulate as much competence as possible in order to race, but when they are in the race, they concede victory to the one who is lucky enough not to have a mishap as they are all hurtling out of control down the hill.

Lewin: I don't think that is a very good analogy. These downhill skiers are a very, very select group. They are already at their peak performance. At that level, all are world-class, and a slight difference decides the outcome. If our systems could perform at the level of those downhill skiers, we would have made an enormous jump forward indeed. The problem is that if at any ski mountain where the general population goes skiing, there is an enormous difference between the very good skiers and the not-so-good skiers. There is a lot that the not-so-good skiers could do to attain the level of the very good skiers. Our problem, from a global system management point of view, is to raise the level of the system's performance to the so-called frontier performance.

I think that the area in which we will see the most progress in the next ten years is from the mental research that underlies the problem of creativity—that is, progress at the individual, psychological level on how people learn from experience. I think this relates directly to understanding how organizations can learn from experience. We are close to having a breakthrough in understanding. If we understand that pehnomenon, then we will have a better basis to extrapolate how organizations in which innovation is important learn from experience and adapt. Within ten years we will see something like that.

Chorover: In looking ten years down the road, I think it is helpful to acknowledge and accept the notion that creativity is at once a definable concept and also an undefinable one because it will only reach some limited understanding and we won't find that unitary, perfect understanding. I think in ten years we will be less paranoid about the fact that we don't have the singular, complete definition of creativity. I hope that we will be much more intelligent about targeting our technology from a human systems perspective. In ten years I'd like to see the fusion of those of us concerned with the development of specific methods and techniques for use by individuals and groups. I'd like to know more about the personal orientations that people hold, the assets and liabilities they bring to various problem-solving situations. Part of the manager's responsibility would be to know more about how to choose and facilitate both environmental conditions and process technology. In the next ten years we should be able to have some more intelligent answers to questions about what works for whom under what circumstances.

Burnside: Ten years from now, I would like to see our audit technology (or aspects of it) in common usage. It is expensive and consumes tremendous amounts of energy, both on our part and the part of the client. I think this is characteristic whenever you are trying to bring innovation to bear. At first, it takes high energy and cost. I would like to see it become a simple, cheap, broadly available, predictive instrument that managers at different levels of organizations could use to do two things: 1) to raise their awareness of why they need to increase creativity in their people and 2) to know how to go about implementing creative ideas.

Comment: There is a saying, "To prophesy is extermely difficult, especially with respect to the future." Einstein once said that the unleashed power of the atom has changed everything except our ways of thinking and so we drift toward unparalleled catastrophes. He went on to say that we have learned by painful experience that rational thinking does not suffice to solve the problems of our social life. We need substantially new ways of thinking if humanity is to survive. I think we can begin to see that the new ways of thinking are emerging from science in a number of areas, including what is being called creative and innovative management, which means an emergence of the ideas, the concepts, the ways of doing business, the openness to changing ways of thinking. They will have advanced a quantum, sufficient for us to agree that we are living in a somewhat safer environment, notwithstanding all of the competitiveness and problems we face. We will be less likely to crash going down the slope.

Lewin: There is another evolution that is causing us to feel already behind in studying organizations, the impact of information technology on the way organizations mutate. As this technology takes holds in an organization (think about Sara Keisler's talk), it allows organizations and the people within the organizations to accommodate user-driven phenomena and in fact, to alter the processes and the way organizations think and make their decisions. It is going to be totally different from what we currently think the structure is. The benefit of this is that because it will be relatively easy to do and will be user-driven and a natural phenomenon, it will allow organizations to feel more comfortable with change and more change. That is the positive. The negative is that it becomes much more difficult to study rapidly mutating organizations. It is technology that endangers the transformation.

V NEW DIRECTIONS FOR INSTITUTIONAL CREATIVITY

15 AREA INTRODUCTION AND OVERVIEW

Elizabeth Bailey

An idea that connects this part with the previous parts of this book is that we are trying to learn how to be successful *change agents*. How do we identify and overcome rigidities and dysfunctional behaviors in organizations? It seems to me that there are two necessities. First, somebody has to recognize the need for change either within the firm or to address some external need. The second necessity has to do with the desire of people inside the organization to effect change and their ability to effect change.

There are at least three situations. One involves recognizing the need for change. There is a desire for change inside the organization and the organization has the ability within itself to effect that change. Chapter 2, by Jean-Jacque Servan-Schreiber, provides one example, the desire for change after the Second World War between France and Germany. The ability to effect that change from within their political systems arose because someone worried the problem enough to get a clever idea and figure out an implementation path for that idea. This is what we have been calling the creative and the innovative.

Another example of a desire for change inside the organization and the ability to effect was demonstrated at Carnegie-Mellon University when Richard Cyert became president. At the time, Carnegie-Mellon was in the third tier of schools in terms of the competitive rankings you might find if you were a high school student selecting a college. Dick Cyert aspired to make it a first-rate institution. He had a clever idea, which was to leverage computer science, beginning it a little sooner and with a little more depth than other schools. He found an implementation path through various funding sources.

A second situation occurs where the need for change is noted but there is no desire for change inside. There are not many of these examples in this book, but they have certainly played a part in my own life. When I was brought to the Civil Aeronautics Board to deregulate the airlines, that was a political appointment to effect a certain type of change that was enormously resisted within the organization. But this is an example of a situation in which it is possible to effect change even in a very uncooperative atmosphere. In fact, we did effect the change, but we had to do a number of tough and unpleasant things. We had to cut out the people in the organization who were dedicated regulators—chop heads or isolate them. We had to put in all kinds of incentives to permit some of the people in the organization who had been suppressed and disenfranchised to make themselves known and active. A group of four or five people in different positions in the organization effected significant change. What amazed me was that in a group of 900 people, all you really needed was about four or five prime movers if you had a clear notion of where you wanted to go and how you wanted to effect that change.

A situation where there isn't very much motivation for change, but there is at least a perception of the need to effect change is exemplified in Yuji Ijiri's description of management compensation schemes (Chapter 5)—namely, trying to separate out the momentum of other people's activities and focus on the impulse of the current management and try to measure performance based on that. Such a system strikes me as rather hard to implement in most organizations because there is a big component of momentum. Whether present management caused it or not, they like to benefit from it. Perhaps a way to move this innovation from a clever idea to an organizational reality is to look for a company where the momentum is all wrong. Then a new management team coming in would have an incentive to figure out how to separate the momentum that is all wrong from the impulses that they are creating.

By and large the bulk of the chapters in this book, academic and practice, fall in this last category. That is, there is a recognized need for change either from inside or outside, but the current management is unable to effect the change. They look outside the organization for help. The help comes from consulting companies, by and large, several examples of which follow. I really like these chapters. They are helpful and quite concrete. They give a number of step-by-step procedures for how to systematically generate ideas for new products and how to follow through in an organization.

A good example is the case study presented in Chapter 16, by R. Donald Gamache. The company involved in the freight transportation business, putting in strapping to put packages on large pellets, now makes a snow fence product that uses the same straps but in a radically different industry. The case study describes the procedures used to combine the company's knowledge and expertise with a broader perspective of the outside world. The consulting company accomplished something beneficial.

Let me draw an analogy between what is going on here and what we have been doing at the Carnegie-Mellon's Graduate School of Industrial Administration. We have been going through a process inside of ourselves to look at the future of business education. We are trying to be successful change agents with our own product, business education. Our assessment is that, for the last ten or twenty years, business schools have tended to produce the kind of change agent who perfects and improves within an existing frame of reference, within existing product lines, within an existing mission plan or business plan. In George Kozmetsky's terms, we have been focusing on doing things right. But as both Dick Cyert and George Kozmetsky said—and their message resonages strongly within our own process—we should learn how to teach people how to look for *new* frames of reference, taking into account the kind of cultural and technological changes occurring in the current period. Society will demand changes in the future. We need to teach people how to cope better with this new reality. Dick Cyert called it leadership, which is knowing how to motivate people and get them committed. The direction needed is indicated both in the assessment profiles that follow and in what George Kozmetsky was saying about how to be more systematic about teaching and how to pick out the right things to do. I think we probably need one step more. We need to integrate both concepts: We want to teach students how to do the right things right. That way, we don't have to give up what we have. We just need to augment it in some imaginative ways.

16

PLANNED GROWTH
An Experience-Based Methodology
for Helping Organizations Identify
and Exploit New Opportunities

R. Donald Gamache

IDEAS THAT SUCCEED

I write from nearly twenty years of experience in stimulating creativity and innovation in industry. What we at Innotech have learned comes directly from working with companies to help them create new business opportunities. Innotech's business mission is "helping companies grow into new areas . . . or revitalize existing businesses." Our primary tools are creativity and information gathering, and our efforts often lead to innovations embodied in new products, technical solutions, or new uses for existing manufacturing or other resources.

One premise that emerges is: If management is perceived as operationally distant from creativity and innovation, then the organization will not be effective in doing the truly new but will limit its efforts to the closely related. On the other hand, if workers and managers perceive commitment of top management's genuine support, evidenced by some degree of their personal involvement, the climate for the truly new will flourish.

Another premise is: To do something truly new, companies need to develop the skills to acquire and aggressively pursue information that is new to them. Without such fresh inputs, they are condemned to repeat their successful solutions of the past, incrementally generating minor improvements and variations that typically have little impact in the marketplace. Suffice it to say, we meet many companies destined to eventual extinction because management keeps itself distant from creativity and innovation because of the risks of the truly new. The result of all the company's efforts is a series of minor variations of less and less relevance to their served market. Eventually this lack of relevance is rewarded by the company's demise.

For the purpose of better communication, I would like to define the two key words: creativity and innovation. *Creativity* is getting the idea, and *innovation* is making it happen. Innotech began with a heavy emphasis on creativity; over the years we have moved toward innovation because we found that creativity in itself was not enough. We started with what I would characterize as brainstorming. If you'll forgive me the irreverence, today we say that brainstorming is excellent "executive entertainment." It's fun, it generates a lot of laughs—but it seldom produces significant, tangible business results. I do not denigrate the need for the unbridled creativity that classical brainstorming strives to produce. However, creativity remains a long distance from innovation. We tell people very openly that in our early days of working with creativity inside companies we had a perfect record—we failed all the time, failed to produce tangible results.

Since this inauspicious beginning, Innotech has conducted over 300 growth-related assignments and tested and refined the process worldwide. So far Planned Growth programs have been run in eleven countries. *Our* criterion for success is met if the client moves forward toward commercialization by the end of the program (typically seven to nine months long). Today this happens about 90 percent of the time (on projects with that objective). Clearly, somewhere along the way something changed.

This change was our arriving at what we now refer to as our cornerstone insight: "There's no such thing as a *good* idea." What we mean is that an idea intrinsically is neither good nor bad. It's just an idea. What makes an idea good or bad whether it succeeds or fails." And in business the bottom line is: "Did it make money?" This led us to the after-the-fact definition that a good idea in business is one that succeeds and makes money.

The challenge then became to figure out why certain ideas succeed and others fail. Our first answer was a half truth. We said *companies* make ideas succeed or fail. But we then learned that in reality it is that handful of people who *own* the growth or survival problem who make the idea succeed or fail, usually top management. What we ultimately concluded is that the *fit* of the particular idea-opportunity with this handful of people is the sine qua non in its utlimate success. *Fit* means the idea's relevance to the company's capabilities, resources, goals, and culture. The technical or intellectual brilliance of the idea is almost irrelevant. To be successful the idea has to fit the problem owners as well as fit the trends and changes going on in our dynamic world. This intersect of company fit and world fit is what creates outstanding commercial successes, while lack of fit is what causes "brilliant" ideas to fail.

Because the raw material for an idea exists in many places, it frequently happens that two companies may come upon the same idea at essentially the same instant in time. In one company the idea is implemented with dedication and results in a commercial success. In the other company the same idea fails to see the light of day or, if it does, fails in the marketplace. Clearly then, it is not the idea but its fit with the problem owners that helps lead to the commitment to implement.

This insight led us away from what we call today "the search for the magic idea." A magic idea is one that requires little or no change, little or minimal investment, and has the equivalent of a written guarantee that the idea when implemented will be a huge commercial success and make far more money in a shorter period of time than anything the company has ever experienced in its history. While this may sound facetious, we often see this mind-set at the top management levels. We believe that this "curse" is a major reason why significant companies find themselves in great difficulty and ultimately go out of business.

Companies go out of business because their products or services become noncompetitive or irrelevant in the marketplace. While management *talks* about change, it subconsciously (at least) resists attempts to bring it to pass. Why? Most companies are designed for the steady state rather than the always threatening uncertainty of the truly new. In reality most companies usually repeat the "successful solution" of their founding idea, now their core business, rather than doing something truly new that will move them away from their comfort zone.

Experience has led me to the conclusion that creativity in an organization is a consequence of top management leadership. A sincere and visible commitment to creativity or doing new things fosters it down below. Yet we find that top management often shirks the personal responsibility for doing new things by pushing new business development, innovation, and creativity down into a staff function and then waiting for the magic idea.

METHODOLOGY FOR PROMOTING CREATIVITY AND INNOVATION

I'd now like to get into our Planned Growth methodology for promoting both creativity and innovation in companies, because the process has evolved and been developed to deal with these realities. But before I do I'm reminded of an advertising campaign that appeared many years ago on the theme of the power of an idea. One dramatic picture showed a brick wall with a common yellow wood pencil driven right through one of the bricks. Our view is that exact opposite. Almost anything can stop an idea. Just think about some of the words and phrases we commonly associate with ideas: Giving "birth" to an idea; an idea is somebody's "baby,"; an idea is a "seed" that needs time to germinate. In one of the exercises we use to get hard-boiled executives to suspend judgment long enough to consider an idea, we show them pictures of a speeding express train and an infant. We then ask them which one best characterizes an idea. They invariably choose the baby. Babies and young plants are not very strong. They need tender loving care and nurturing to reach their potential. Perhaps, most important, they need the right ambiance in which to thrive. And this leads us to the first step of the Planned Growth process: predefining success by characterizing the exactly right idea for this particularly problem-owning group.

It is absolutely critical to assemble the key decision makers and implementers, the problem owners, at the right level. (These problem owners become the client team who work with us throughout the program.) This means that a search for a new business opportunity must involve the top management; the search for a technical solution must involve the technical management, and the like. Managers are very busy dealing with their own problems and functional areas. Seldom, if ever, do they actually get together for an honest sharing of views on creative growth opportunities and to what kind of an opportunity they would be willing to commit resources.

The dynamics of a typical business meeting are as hostile to fragile new ideas the Dead Sea would be to a budding plant. Vested interests predominate. So having this group set common criteria for success has many benefits. Because contributions are elicited in a round-robin fashion, everyone's view is heard and, essentially, each participant gets roughly equivalent air time, regardless of title or position. This in itself is a major departure from most business meetings, where two or three people do all the talking and the rest go along or tune out. When this collective input is distilled and fed back to the group (typically on one or two sheets of paper numbering 18 to 23 criteria), it triggers a refinement process we call fine-tuning. Negotiation is involved, but ultimately the group arrives at unanimity. The resulting criteria are tested by asking: "If an opportunity surfaced that you felt had the potential to meet these criteria, would you move forward with it?" By definition, the answer must be yes.

Realizing that there will be some degree of pain in making the changes and taking the risks necessary, we imprint the positive benefits on the group. (We've even developed a Pain Index based on the degree of newness.) We do this by asking each participant to write down five reasons why achieving the objectives embodied in the criteria will benefit the company. This normally results in a collective listing of twelve to fifteen very specific points. We then tell the participants that when the going gets tough (meaning, results are uncertain) they should reread this list to remind themselves of why it's worth their effort and energy. What ultimately results is a common goal for the group to strive toward that, in turn, results in some degree of team building. I should add the postscript that the evening before the criteria-setting event we have a social evening. The consultant and client groups get to know each other prior to getting down to hard business the next morning. We find that getting this "nose rubbing" out of the way in a social setting enables us to move quickly and efficiently into the business discussions. Without it, getting acquainted gets in the way of the discussions, especially the listening functions.

Another benefit of criteria-setting is that it focuses the project's efforts. Our experience internationally leads us to conclude that an estimated 85 percent of the effort, energy, and monies spent in looking for new opportunities is wasted due to the lack of a clear focus. We also refer to this focus as a "domain." To paraphrase Lewis Carroll: "If you don't know where you're going, any road will get you there." Many companies pursue *interesting* and often expensive roads that lead nowhere. After these criteria describe the domain of actionable interest, the next step is to identify trends, changes, discontinuities, technologies, and other factors within the domain that could lead to areas of opportunity with the potential to meet the agreed-upon criteria. We are still deferring creativity until we can come up with a more precise focus.

The primary tool for generating these areas of opportunity is an outside expert session. Companies are designed and staffed for *today's* business. (Many executives disagree and point out that in reality they're designed for *yesterday's* business.) Their staffing and knowledge makes them highly qualified to generate improvements and variations on what they are already doing. However, if the business areas in which they find themselves forecast zero or negative growth, they are forced to stretch themselves into new areas, and this requires new inputs of information. Another of our core tenets is that the client team knows its business better than anyone else. Even though the company has competitors, it is unique in its history, culture, and position in the marketplace.

The objective of bringing together outside experts is to complement the client team's knowledge (more broadly, the company's) and extend it into new relevant areas. The criteria and the domain that flow from it establish the areas of relevance.

The Briefing Document is a tool that Innotech has developed to bring the subconscious mind into play. Because the subconscious mind plays a major role in an individual's productivity and creativity in a session, we strive to get this subconscious mind working on the problem about a week ahead of the event. The Briefing Document, a tailored workbook, does this. In it, the session task is discussed. However, this may not be an accurate or even truthful description. In some cases we find it may be far more productive to disguise the true mission of the session event to create a different perspective. Also, the client company is not identified to the participants. There are two reasons behind this: An obvious one is to preserve as confidential the company's area of interest; another, perhaps more important reason, is to preclude stereotyped reactions that would arise from knowing the company's identity. For example, simply mentioning the name Gillette conjures up visions of razors and shaving. Parallels to these stereotypes are part of what stands in the way of internal people taking truly fresh perspectives on their problem. Here is where the benefit of creative techniques embodied in Synectics come in (see Chapter 17).

Another point we often make is that a company's knowledge base is like an erector set (a child's toy I was fortunate enough to receive for Christmas when I was young). The limited number of parts allowed one to build a limited number of constructions. Having done this, one was forced to go back to some favorites or buy a bigger erector set that had more and different parts. It's a given that most companies have already put all their knowledge-parts together in all the permutations they can think of and need *new* knowledge-parts to come up with truly new ideas and opportunities.

After having generated criteria, identified opportunity areas based on trends and changes, and selected one of these as the focus for the program, the next step (finally) is to get creative. In our early days we would begin with idea generation, and most companies still do. We had yet to recognize that much psychological ground had to be carefully prepared if our infant ideas were to take root and grow to fruition.

The way we approach idea generation is, again, to assemble a group of targeted outside experts who have relevant knowledge in the area selected as the target. A new briefing document is written that incorporates creative techniques that will enhance the production of insights and ideas. The session is prestrategized in terms of its objectives (the areas to be covered) and the creative techniques that will be used.

I should point out that we view the output of a session as white noise, which means that it must be processed, shaped, augmented, and amplified to result in meaningful information. This process entails database and literature searches, as well as phone calls and meetings with appropriate consultants or outside sources. Without the substance that these activities lend to the usually fragile ideas, they have minimal chances of survival. A significant point is that we view the carefully prepared output of a session merely as raw material, more knowledge-pieces with which to expand our client's usually limited knowledge base in the new area. Our hope is that combined with the existing internal knowledge base (because we've been focused at a relevant area) the client team can produce insightful combinations resulting in their own new relevant ideas. These ideas are relevant because they are created in an opportunity area selected based on criteria generated by the decision-making group that owns the growth problem. At this point another benefit of the criteria generated in the first step of the process is that it can be used as a screen through which to sift the large number of ideas. Without a mechanism for quickly screening the ideas, the work involved can become exponential and the fit of the ideas never be objectively evaluated.

At this point there may be, in the view of the client team, a sufficient number of promising ideas to move toward implementation, creating an innovation. If not, another outside expert session is convened with totally new experts relevant to the refined and refocused area of interest. In any event, at some point it is agreed that the objective is no longer to *generate* ideas but to qualify, refine, and test them against the needs and interests of the market. Also, at this time it may be relevant to assemble a technology-dominated group to concern themselves with development or production.

Before discussing some quantitative factors of the productivity of a session, I'd like to point out that we run different types of sessions covering the orientation spectrum from heavy creativity to heavy information. A creative session may produce an estimated 150 to 200 ideas. Of this we may feel that 12 to 20 are worth bringing into a meeting with the client team for active building. Out of this event we may net 8 to 12 (some totally new) worthy of further exploration.

A program is usually ready to move beyond idea generation and into the final qualification phase when we have 6 to 10 opportunities that we mutually feel have the potential to meet the criteria. And serious commercialization efforts are seldom applied to more than 2 or 3.

Given that in the course of a program we may be dealing with up to 500 raw ideas, the bottom-line productivity is less than 1 percent. But this is a highly researched and qualified 1 percent already supported by the management group that owns the problem. (In a primarily information-oriented session, we typically generate 100 to 200 "bits" of information relevant to our focus; subsequent research would at least double this number.)

The final phase of the Planned Growth process is to generate the information required to make what we call an investment-level decision. The needed commitments and investments will not be made without satisfying many informational needs. So in essence the process moves beyond creativity into generation of hard information. It is at this point that we often see the group abandon its earlier courageous words and move as close as possible to their comfort zone. If we can characterize companies' existing business activities as being on home plate, we find that it is *harder* to be truly creative when close to home but easier to innovate. The reciprocal is that it is *easier* to be creative farther away from home plate, where one is not tied up with stereotypes and convention, but far more difficult to innovate.

A CASE STUDY EXAMPLE

To help make all this more tangible, I'd like to use a single example of a Planned Growth program that illustrates some of the points made. The client company is Signode Corporation of Chicago, the leader in strapping systems, best known for their application in securing large pallet loads for shipping.

The maturity of this market and increasing competitive pressures led management to look for new growth opportunities. But rather than merely giving this goal lip service, the top management team actively participated in generating the guiding criteria and establishing the "macro" strategic opportunity area. One of these was plastic products for nonpackaging applications. This focus itself expresses an understanding of, and commitment to, the need to move outside of their core business in pallet and product strapping.

Of great significance was that they visibly supported this commitment by assigning some of their best and brightest people to venture teams and charged them with bringing new opportunities to fruition. This project was led by the executive vice president, giving it a strong, highly visible champion. So we had the critical elements of top management's tangible support and involvement.

Some of the criteria, selected from the twenty-four specific statements written to guide this effort, are as follows:

1.	Must	Leverages Signode's expertise and/or assets in plastics formulating, processing and after-treatment.
8.	Must	Embodies a means of achieving competitive advantage through cost position and/or product differentiation.
15.	Desirable	Has the potential to be marketed within a one-year period.
16.	Desirable	Has the potential to achieve $50 million in annualized sales revenue within five years of commercialization (first commercial sale).
19.	Desirable	Is targeted toward a growing rather than a mature market/segment.
23.	Desirable	Leverages Signode's position as a major large-volume converter of plastics resin.
24.	Desirable	Has the possibility of achieving dominant market share within specific market niches.

These criteria created the "domain" that, in essence, told us we were looking for nonconsumer opportunities based on large volume applications for simple thermoplastic products directed to areas other than packaging. We also identified as "world class" and highly exploitable a unique Signode capability to produce very high tensile strengths (up to 100,000 psi).

The outside expert team, prepared by a tailored Briefing Document, was brought together to surround this domain and creatively search for and create opportunity areas (see Figure 16–1).

The trends, changes, information, ideas, insights resulting from this three-and-one-half hour session were processed into six opportunity areas. Some of these were oriented plastic webbing/netting, conductive plastic sheet materials for the electronic industry, and sheet materials with programmable frictional properties.

The area oriented plastic webbing/netting was selected for further exploration. The combined efforts of the Signode venture team and Innotech teams ultimately identified a number of specific "actionable" opportunities.

Figure 16-1. Signode Opportunity "Domain."

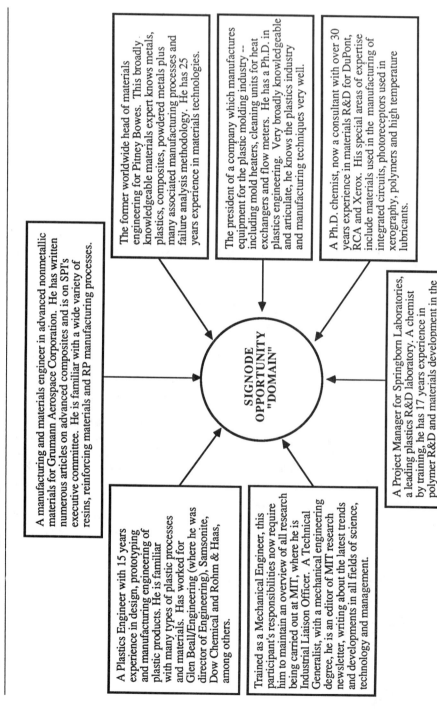

I'll touch on two. Signode's high-tensile-strength plastic strap could be formed into a lattice for use as a geogrid, an emerging soil stabilization technology. These are coming into usage for road building, shoring along highway and watercourse banks, and developing swampy or other marginal land. Tests proved the high-strength Signode material clearly superior.

Another new and growing area identified, which was especially suited for a wider, unslit version of Signode's strapping material, was snow control fencing. New levels of understanding gained about wind driven snow had led to new theoretical designs that needed high-tensile-strength strip to reduce wind loading.

Both of these opportunities—geogrids and snow fencing—elicited immediate market interest, and orders were in hand before the formal nine-month program was even completed.

Based on early encouraging results with both products, management created a new division named High Performance Plastics to fully exploit these and other opportunities that had emerged during the program.

Actual sales results, market receptivity, and forecasts lead us mutually to believe that these new business opportunities can attain significant sales contributing to or reaching the overall project goal of $50 million in annual sales.

We believe that the early success of this effort is largely attributable to the executive vice president's personal support and sponsorship of the venture team and to top management's receptivity to the specific product ideas, because they clearly fit the opportunity area and specific criteria *they* had been intimately involved in establishing. With this support, the venture team members worked with a high level of commitment and enthusiasm to "make it happen."

CONCLUSION

I'm frequently asked the question, "How do you know if someone is creative?" I like to answer that creativity *is* as creativity *does*. If Michelangelo just *talked* about painting and sculpture we would have no evidence of his creativity. Creativity without innovation is of little worth. Experience has revealed some core elements:

1. The success of an idea that ultimately reaches implementation is dominated by its fit with the decision makers who control the organization's resources and funds.

2. Organizations, in spite of great lip service, view changes as at least unsettling, if not downright threatening, and therefore strive to avoid it.

3. Because an organization is designed and staffed to undertake its current businesses, to be innovative and creative outside of its core area requires new inputs of information.

4. Any ideas, no matter how brilliant, must be supported by solid information if commitments and actions are to result.

The quote "Genius is one part inspiration and ninety-nine parts perspiration" has been attributed to at least a half-dozen people. I would like to paraphrase it and say that "Innovation is one part creativity and ninety-nine parts productivity." My objective has not been to denigrate the very great value of creativity but to put it into perspective. Finally, as a practitioner, I'd like to suggest that one area for research might be to study the intimacy of involvement of top management in a creative undertaking and see the effect this has on the ultimate success—the profitable innovation.

17 REVISITING IDEAS

Richard A. Harriman

FIVE APPROACHES TO CREATIVE
AND INNOVATIVE MANAGEMENT

Picture Archimedes jumping out of his bathtub yelling "Eureka!" (I have found it!) Picture a light bulb going off over someone's head.

These two images endure as symbols of new ideas. They endure because they embody the mystery of new ideas that appear suddenly. However, people knowledgeable about the fundamentals of creativity recognize that new ideas are not sudden occurrences, that the subconscious was actively working in incubation prior to the "Aha!" They can surmise, in fact, that a great deal of work was done prior to giving up on the problem and allowing it to go underground into incubation.

What is often not recognized, however, is that the image of the light bulb has shaped the way managers view ideas and, in so doing, has impaired effective management of innovation. Two adverse consequences result from the belief that novel ideas come as an epiphany. The first is that managers are too passive at a critical stage in the innovation process—at the time when novel ideas are needed. Managers often feel that they must wait and not push it. How often have we heard you cannot rush the creative act? Creativity is enshrouded in a feeling of little or no control. Thus we must wait for the idea, which does not show up. Managing creativity this way may feel like "Waiting for Godot," and as you know, Godot never appears.

The second consequence is that managers do not see a role for creativity after the first inspirational idea. The prevailing view is that after we get the flash the creative part is over—and then it is time to do the hard, uncreative work. Innovation does not work this way. In fact, novel solutions involve creative thinking from preparation through implementation. A new idea is only the beginning.

The first part of this chapter is devoted to some methods we at Synetics have developed for generating novel ideas (so we do not have to wait for them to arrive). The second part discusses the need for and methods of incorporating creativity throughout the entire innovation process.

A context for those concepts is a simple framework outlining five approaches to creative and innovative management. It takes the form of an acronym—FACES, or the FACES of Innovation. They are

> F for FIND
> A for ALLOW
> C for CREATE
> E for ENCOURAGE
> S for STIR UP

Each represents a management approach to fostering innovation; each is important; each serves a different need; and each has its own methods.

F for FIND. Management finds novel ideas that already exist but may be unknown to those who make decisions. To find and handle ideas that exist inside the organization, for example, management can designate certain people as lightning rods for employee ideas. They received the "flash" and in turn connect the idea with the people who may need it. Kodak's Office of Innovation is an example of this approach to finding ideas. Some quality circle programs fall into this category. For finding ideas that exist outside the organization, management can create programs that use competitive intelligence systems and staff as technical gatekeepers.

A for ALLOW. Management allows ideas and new directions to be pursued by staff who are excited about them. Commonly, corporations erect obstacles to innovation, many unintended. There are simple things managers can do to overcome some of them—for example, know when to turn a blind eye. To do this well, managers must appreciate the value of experimental behavior. Buckminster Fuller captured this in saying, "There are no failures, only unexpected consequences." This view allows us to treat the unexpected as a learning opportunity. Therefore, as managers, our role changes from the one who stops everything that does not fit preconceived plans to the one

who enables experimentation to occur. Another alternative in allowing innovative behavior is to identify financial resources to support
ideas and experiments that do not fit established budgets.

C for CREATE. This is the most proactive approach of the five.
Managers do not wait for innovations to occur; they *create* them.
They recognize a challenge and bring to bear techniques that create
original ideas, then employ strategies to modify and transform the
ideas into solutions that are both new and feasible. I will expand on
this approach when I speak about new product development.

E for ENCOURAGE. Examples of programs that encourage creativity and innovation are institutionalizing of innovation time (for example, providing staff with the opportunity to spend 10 percent of
their time working on an idea of their own choosing); training sponsors of idea champions to provide breathing room for budding ideas
and internal entrepreneurs; publicly recognizing groups (not just
individuals) who are working in new areas; establishing innovative
reward systems such as pseudo stock that enables staff to put part of
their salary at risk for the opportunity of significant upside potential.

S for STIR UP. Here the manager intentionally stirs things up in
order to create change and ambiguity. As things get shaken up, the
unexpected will happen, and many of these unexpected events will
represent opportunities to the trained eye. An example might be a
corporate reorganization into centers of technology excellence versus
business lines.

ANALOGY–THE FIRST IDEA-GETTING STRATEGY

My company, Synectics®, Inc., has devoted the last twenty-seven
years to working with organizations, primarily Fortune 100 companies, to inject innovation into management decisions. Because novel
ideas are building blocks of innovation, we periodically undertake
new research into the generation of new ideas.

Synectics began its studies of idea generation in the 1950s when
its founders were still part of the invention design group at Arthur
D. Little. The charter of this group was to create inventions, to
develop them from ideas to "breadboard" models that worked or
at least showed promise of working with more engineering and
development.

Brainstorming, a social invention by Alex Osborn, was sometimes
useful in producing initial ideas. However, we needed a process that

would do more—give us better quality ideas and help us to carry these ideas to fruition. Some of our early work is covered in an article in *The Harvard Business Review* published in 1956 titled "Operational Approach to Creativity." In it, W.J.J. Gordon, an early partner in research, notes that certain psychological states are essential to creativity: involvement/detachment, speculation, deferment, purposiveness, and use of the commonplace. The theory was useful in that it focused on some of the frames of mind that were desirable for creativity, but it was not really as operational as the title implied since the theory gave few clues as to how to induce those states.

In 1958 we began to tape record our "invention sessions" in order to analyze what went on whenever we got an idea. Our intention was to replicate that successful process whenever we needed an idea.

The first idea-getting strategy that emerged was the mining of a familiar process for seeing a problem differently: analogy. Many successful problem solvers automatically search for situations parallel to their problem, where similarities exist along with differences and both can give clues to solving the present problem. We found that if we selected analogies from a dissimilar context we would get more fresh and unusual ideas. In general, the more distant the analogy the more original the solution.

As an example of an analogy from our early work in the fishing industry, we used "hunting" to suggest that if the boats cooperated and fished in a U-shaped formation, they would all catch more fish.

As we were working on the problem of making the fishing industry more efficient someone in the group said, "You know, when we use boats like that we are herding the fish. What if we used cowboys instead of boats. We'd save a lot on fuel and boats."

This half-joking, nonrational comment created a surge of energy in the group. One member responded "Who would we use for cowboys?"

"Porpoises" said another. "They are not unionized, get low pay scale, and they can snack on the fish they are herding."

Another said, "Let's make the ocean a prairie—fence in George's Bank, and we can have range wars with the Russians and Canadians!"

Another said, "Let's dredge big areas of swamp and flood them for fish ranches."

The connecting of the idea of cooperative fishing with herding and with cowboys brought out fresh, energetic thinking.

Synectics began to examine two methods for creating innovative solutions:

1. The logical search for ideas
2. The use of analogies

When we analyzed tapes of each method we began to see differences that were puzzling. For example, in the logical strategy there was not much play. Ideas were proposed seriously and considered seriously. They were analyzed as presented. With analogies, play was a recurring element. The ideas and their ramifications were listened to more like jokes, and this appeared to be what made them grow into more useful ideas.

We now know that this playful listening and response is significantly different from the judgmental listening that serious proposals receive. With serious proposals, even though I may have agreed to withhold judgment, critical comments flash into my mind and blunt the lightning-fast imaginative development of the proposal. By contrast, the ideas proposed as we work with the analogy are listened to like jokes: avidly and with the intent to have them stimulate me into thinking of another one. My mental set is not to spot flaws, but to be open to stimulation and building.

Synectics did not know then what it knows now—that this different listening and building has a high impact on creativity. At the time we merely *felt* the difference and cultivated the play. Now we are able to teach managers what we call third-level listening.

For example, imagine a sales manager listening to a new idea to set up a separate sales force. She might respond on one of three levels. The third is most powerful.

First Level (Judgmental)	Listening for flaws and pointing them out; e.g., "That's too expensive."
Second Level (Directional)	Listening for flaws in a way that invites resolving them; e.g., "Intriguing idea. How can we make it less expensive?"
Third Level (Developmental)	Listening to the idea and its implications as stimuli for new thoughts that build on the original and strengthen it; e.g., "When you said 'separate,' it made me think of cream separating at the top of the milk bottle. You know we might take our top markets only, the crème de la crème, and create a separate sales force there. And, these people could possibly also take on the new product distribution in John's division, which would lower our costs." (Note: The listener interpreted "separate" in a different context that enabled her to build on the idea and generate an enhancement that also addressed the apparent flaw.)

Synectics further systemized the process of idea generation by developing a method called Personal Analogy. For example, to return to the fishing industry problem, we might ask a group member to turn himself into a fish and tell us how he felt. Personal Analogies produced results similar to common analogies except that the group felt more cohesive after everyone had described a Personal Analogy. This was one of the early (unremarked at the time) hints that the relationships between members of the team would greatly influence its productivity and creativity. Subsequently, we have invented a series of guidelines and role definitions that enhance relationships and increase team unity during the wrenching anxiety, change, and exhilaration that accompanies innovation.

From 1958 to 1960, Synectics identified what we called the Operational Mechanisms: Direct Analogy, Personal Analogy, and Symbolic Analogy. These are more fully described in our first book: *Synectics* by W.J.J. Gordon, published in 1961.

In 1960 four of the eight members of the Invention Design Group of Arthur D. Little left to form Synectics. We envisioned ourselves to be in the invention-to-order business. We believed that we knew how to manipulate the creative process at will and had demonstrated that we could build rough models of our creations.

Two difficulties immediately became evident. Without the respectable mantle of ADL we had trouble getting prospective clients to believe we could do what we claimed. The few clients we managed to persuade, accepted and liked the results we delivered. But they were usually top people who were not really involved in the implementation of the concept. The people who were involved took the crude models from these "Cambridge nuts" as an affront to their own creative abilities and had no motivation to solve the many problems standing between a beginning idea and real product. We were going out of business unless . . .

We reinvented Synectics. We asked prospective clients to send their new product people, and we would utilize our new process for idea-getting, but it would be *their* idea-getting. They would invent new products that fit their desires and that claimed their energy for implementation. This service saved us from extinction in 1964 and supplied us with a steady stream of bright people with whom we could try diverse methods of moving the innovation process into unknown areas in order to improve the quality of ideas and solutions.

We continue to use analogies in the management of innovation and find them powerful in helping our clients break out of mental ruts. Today, in addition, we use a process called Connection-Making to increase the fluency of original thinking.

THE CONNECTION-MAKING PROCESS

Analogies themselves *suggest* ideas or directions of exploration. The more distant the analogy, the more likely the suggestions or directions will be novel. In Connection-Making Thinking we *manufacture* ideas. We deliberately take apparently irrelevant material and jam it up beside the problem to fabricate a new idea.

As a Connection-Making exercise, imagine you have the problem that new competitors are entering the commodity end of your business. Put the problem itself out of mind, and in this case select an object at random: say, the dictaphone on your desk. Observe things about it:

> It is black.
> Operates on batteries.
> It can store time.
> Unbiased observer.
> Preserves reality.

Then make connections between these observations and the problem at hand. The step of making the connections is the most difficult to do, in part because we are imbued with prejudices against using irrelevance. It may seem silly or unproductive. Connection-Making requires two simultaneous activities: 1) I have the problem in mind, while I attempt to connect my observation, "black," to it in any way I can. As I make tentative connections, 2) I let my mind go forward in the generation of new Connection-Making material for trial. I discard (without prejudice!) the ones that do not fit. Figure 17–1 is a diagram that illustrates this example.

I connect "black" to the problem and ask, "How can I make 'black' connect to my problem to give me the beginning or the promise of an idea?" Then I make myself available to what my mind gives me.

"Black" brings the thought of a dark night and so I wish customers and competition would only meet at night when they could not see each other: Maybe I can keep them from meeting through a long-term contract. Maybe something's there; put it aside. "See" brings to mind sea change. I think of tidal wave and a massive one-time change: Maybe for six months tie all commodity contracts to high-end contracts at a loss, and thus lock out other competition until the next technology is available. Possible, yet expensive; note it. "Lock out" makes me think of union: Maybe a new type of "union" with employees—we set them up as entrepreneurs to compete at the

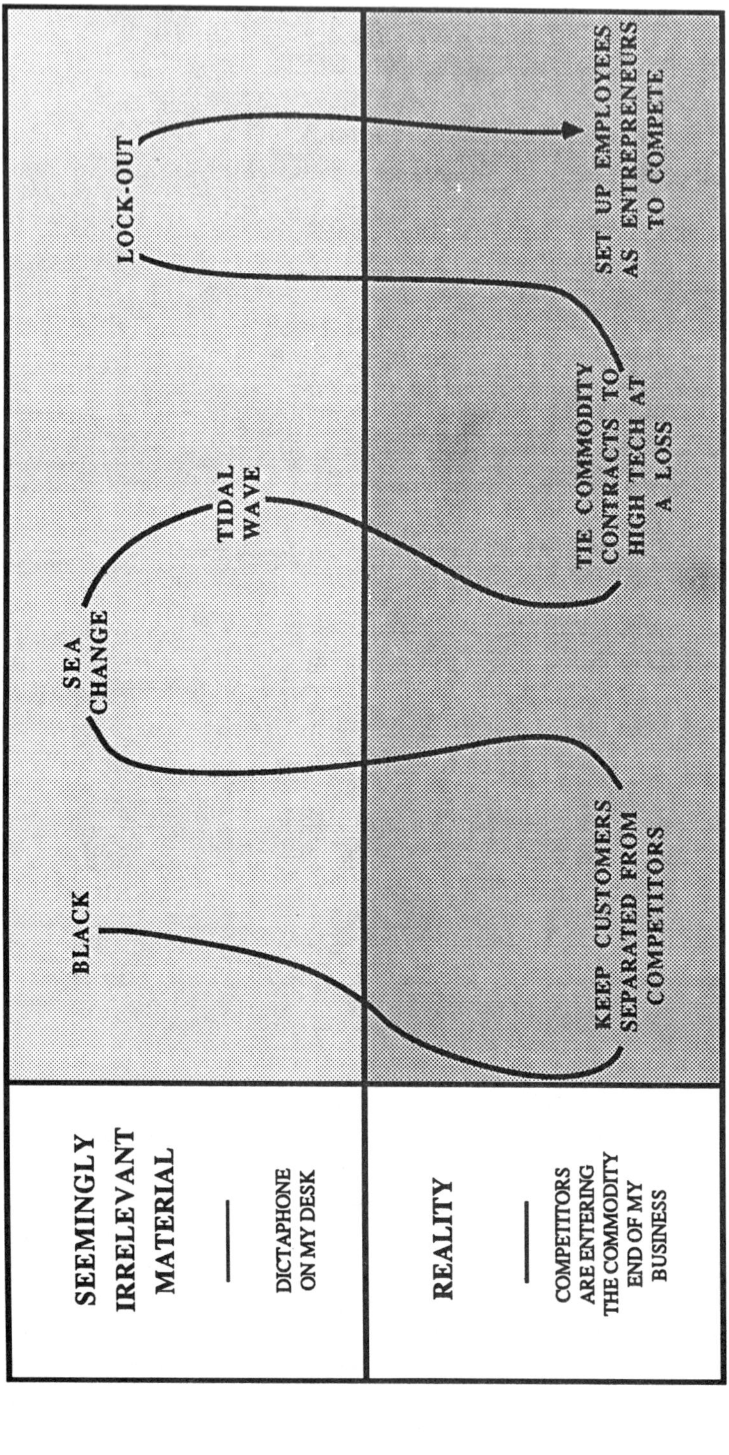

Figure 17-1.   Connection-Making Thinking Path.

SEEMINGLY IRRELEVANT MATERIAL
———
DICTAPHONE ON MY DESK

REALITY
———
COMPETITORS ARE ENTERING THE COMMODITY END OF MY BUSINESS

BLACK

SEA CHANGE

TIDAL WAVE

LOCK-OUT

KEEP CUSTOMERS SEPARATED FROM COMPETITORS

TIE COMMODITY CONTRACTS TO HIGH TECH AT A LOSS

SET UP EMPLOYEES AS ENTREPRENEURS TO COMPETE

low end, and we keep part ownership with a buy-back option. This is an idea I might want to experiment with.

Let me put the exercise aside.

Managers and employees have an enormous wealth of experience, a fraction of which they draw upon when facing a tough problem. Connection-Making Thinking enables them to consciously tap into this experience by removing the filter of apparent relevance. It produces original connections between past experiences and present problems. Training in Connection-Making Thinking accelerates the creative process. It gives the manager skills with which to direct and improve innovative efforts.

In using apparent irrelevance to solve problems creatively, be sure to involve those who can actually decide upon and implement solutions. Our experience is that only those who are responsible for resolving the problem and who understand the attendant constraints can develop feasible solutions to the problem. Skills in manufacturing ideas get them started and draw on their knowledge and experience in new ways. Irrelevance is a key to getting ultimately relevant and truly novel ideas. When the techniques are used by someone outside the problem, the results might be intellectually interesting, but by and large they are not really usable—and, hence, remain ultimately irrelevant.

CREATIVITY AT EVERY STEP

At the beginning of this chapter, I mentioned that two problems are created by the belief that really new ideas just happen, that they come into being, out of our control, accidentally or in a flash. The first arises because managers do not actively manage the creation of novel ideas when they can or should. As discussed, effective methodologies for both suggesting new ideas and for manufacturing them exist.

The second problem comes from the belief that after the flash the creative part of the process is over, and only uncreative work follows. This orientation keeps managers from insisting on creativity in every step; thus, they lose opportunities. Promising initiatives are compromised, innovative actions are impeded, brilliance is diluted.

The ultimate novel solution to a problem results from the unique union of many ideas from a continuously creative process. Edison's remark "Genius is 1 percent inspiration and 99 percent perspiration" is not to be interpreted as a chronological concept; it does not mean "First you get the idea, *then* you work hard at making it reality." Rather, throughout the process of innovation from preparation

Figure 17-2. New Product Commitment Program Flowchart.

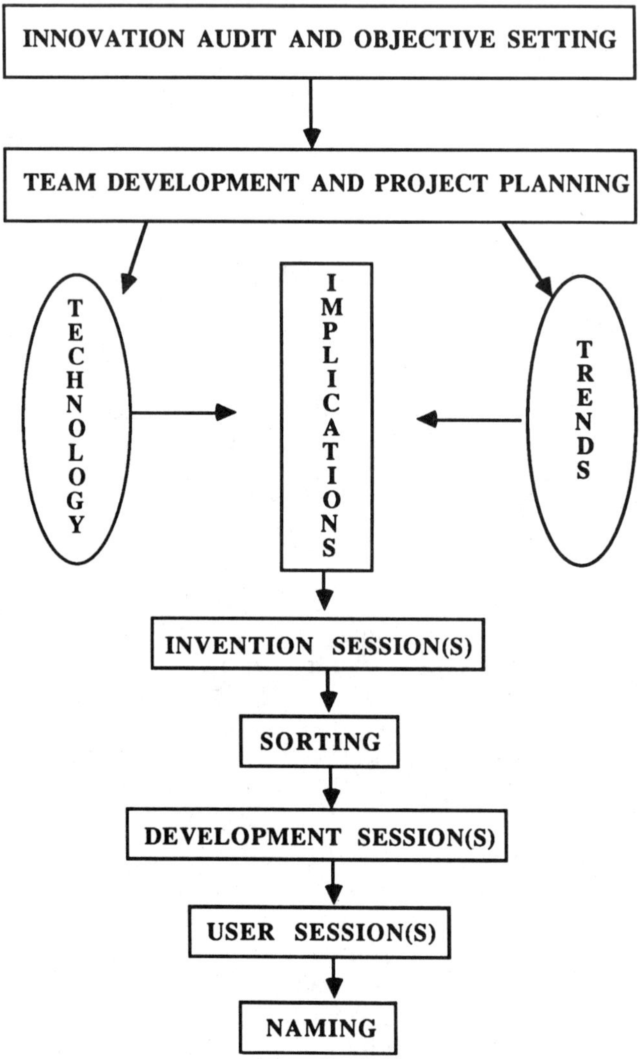

Flowchart Box	Description
INNOVATION AUDIT AND OBJECTIVE SETTING	• Establish direction after assessing strengths and weaknesses in innovative management
TEAM DEVELOPMENT AND PROJECT PLANNING	• Identify a diverse team, train in skills of creative problem-solving and plan for impact of innovation process.
TECHNOLOGY → IMPLICATIONS ← TRENDS	• Interactive review of relevant technologies and socio-economic trends.
INVENTION SESSION(S)	• Generate a wide range of original new concepts and modify them to overcome initial concerns.
SORTING	• Focus efforts on most compelling concerns.
DEVELOPMENT SESSION(S)	• Resolve outstanding concerns and increase corporate involvement in addressing these issues.
USER SESSION(S)	• Tap consumer needs and creativity to refine concepts
NAMING	• Develop unique product name.

through implementation, frequent doses of both hard work and sparking genius are required.

Figure 17-2 is flowchart outlining a program that Synectics uses with clients in new product development. It is a program that calls for creativity at every step.

As an overview of the progression of this program, we first determine a direction to pursue, then put together a multidiscipline core team. We train this team in creative thinking and behaving skills, and conduct interactive review sessions of relevant technologies and trends. We then help them create a wide range of original ideas, and develop these further by overcoming flaws. When the concept is mature, we run it through the implementation process with engineering, manufacturing, packaging, sales, and so on. (These final steps are not illustrated.) Each of these steps needs creative thinking and innovative action.

For example, we were working with a heavy machinery manufacturer that had lost all of its recent bids for a made-to-order product. During objective setting (step 1) it became clear that the company's high cost of equipment delivery was a major problem. In a series of innovative actions that were sparked by this recognition, the shipping manager first meticulously imaged how this huge machinery would be shipped to the customer in New Zealand. He then traveled the exact route that the new product would take. He visited each rail yard, shipping company, and dock facility. He uncovered a variety of unexpected obstacles and costs that he reported back to the core group. Using the creative problem-solving process they redesigned the product saving over $1 million in costs.

As another example, a client who was involved in a review of industry trends (step 3) recognized that they would gain market momentum in redefining their business from "baby products" to "child care." This new view of their business helped them identify new needs that changed the thrust of subsequent invention work to include entry into the service field.

In a recent user session (step 7) with another group, consumers wanted to see the product in its raw form. We carried the material into the room in a small vat that had been used to conveniently carry the product to the session. Surprisingly, the group responded to the vat. Seizing on this accident (the unexpected is critical in innovation management), the client was compelled to change the packaging and positioning of the product to reflect these consumer preferences.

RESEARCH PRIORITIES

Stepping back from the specific examples, let me summarize. We find a compelling need for innovative action at all stages of solution development. This is as true in our programs for cost containment and strategy development as it is in new product development and research.

The programs and methodologies, about which I spoke, highlight areas for additional research. Synectics, has four main research priorities:

Getting Managers to Experiment. Managers often feel they are supporting innovation, and they genuinely want it. Yet they discourage and are fearful of experimentation. Somehow experimenting seems riskier than innovation. Yet, experimentation is the lifeblood of innovation. We need to help managers, particularly outside of R&D, to reframe their understanding of experimentation.

Richer Sources of Originality. Our techniques have pushed us farther to the right of the spectrum in Figure 17–3, from logical search to the direct application of seemingly irrelevant material in order to stimulate greater originality. In exploring what is farther to the right of the graph we hope to discover new methodologies. See Figure 17–3.

Anxiety Reduction. Anxiety accompanies change. It also hampers innovation. Synectics uses numerous techniques that reduce anxiety. We still believe there is much more to be learned. Current investigations include psychological aspects (how to reduce self-punishment), physiological aspects (kinesthetic exercise), and managerial aspects (how failures are treated).

The Relationship Between Learning and Creativity. We have always been interested in the relationship of these two. Synectics is in the process of several experiments with secondary schools to develop a learning model.

SUMMARY

My message is that innovation can be more deliberately managed. Managers can actively promote the creation of new ideas. They can use analogies to suggest them: they can use Connection-Making

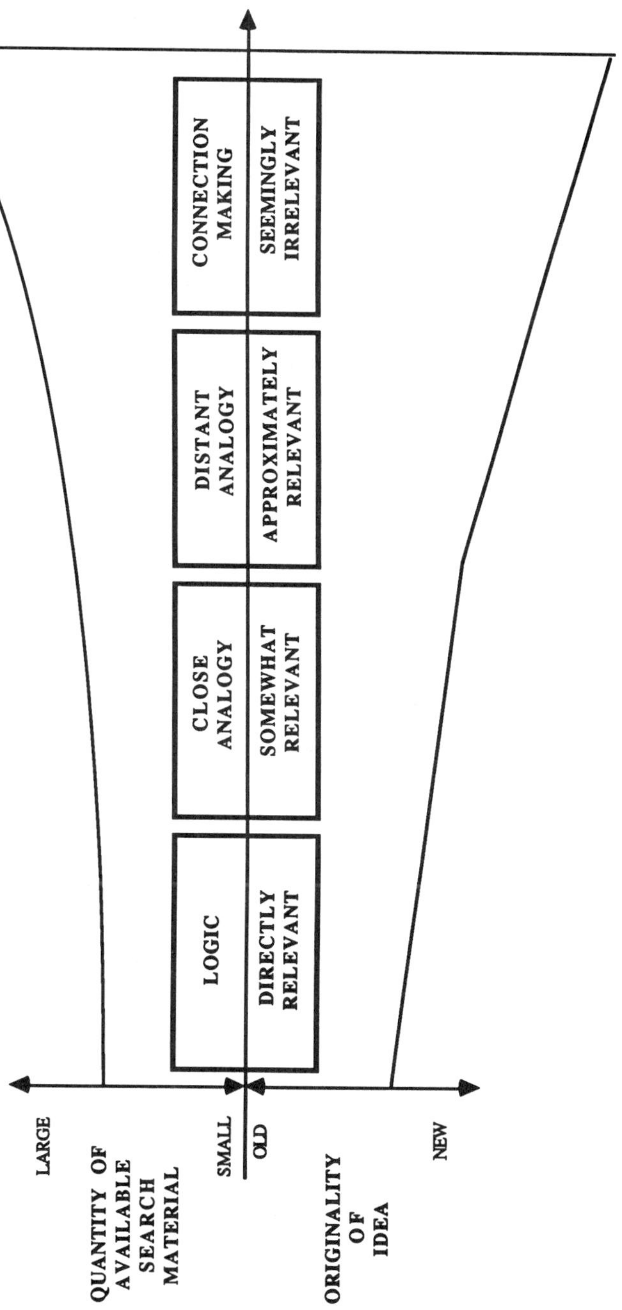

Figure 17-3. Idea Generation Methodologies.

QUANTITY OF
AVAILABLE
SEARCH
MATERIAL

LARGE

SMALL

OLD

ORIGINALITY
OF
IDEA

NEW

LOGIC

DIRECTLY
RELEVANT

CLOSE
ANALOGY

SOMEWHAT
RELEVANT

DISTANT
ANALOGY

APPROXIMATELY
RELEVANT

CONNECTION
MAKING

SEEMINGLY
IRRELEVANT

Thinking to manufacture them. They do not have to wait for them. These methodologies can be used to create original concepts, and to address the issues that stand between the original concept and its successful implementation. And, these methodologies are useful for the full spectrum on management decisions and goals.

REFERENCES

Gordon, Williams J.J. 1956. "Operational Approach to Creativity." *Harvard Business Review*: 41–51.
_____. 1961. *Synectics.* New York: Harper & Row.
Prince, Georhe M. 1970. *The Practice of Creativity.* New York: Harper & Row.
Rosenfeld, Robert, and Jenny C. Servo. 1984. "Business and Creativity: Making Ideas Connect." *The Futurist*: 21–26.

18 TOWARD AN EFFECTIVE METHODOLOGY FOR UNIFYING THEORY AND PRACTICE

Robert Lawrence Kuhn

Both practitioners and theorists are fascinated by creative and innovative management. Though they like looking at the same issues, they do so from the perspective of different cultures. It is vital that each group understand the world of the other.

The iteration between theory and practice is a key paradigm of academic business. After all, management is an applied science designed to work. Elegance in journals is a fine place to start, but impact in markets is where we all must end up.

Motivations, a critical element of academic researchers and business professionals, differ sharply, although both have common interests in the subject matter and in furthering our understanding of it. Business professionals seek to build their companies and to enhance their professional standard. They must serve their customers or clients and make a profit in the process. Academic researchers seek to learn the truth about a matter, discerning why things that do happen happen, and why things that don't happen don't. They, too, seek to improve their professional standing. And the criteria by which they are judged is dramatically different.

Creative and innovative management is a compelling field in which to articulate theorists with practitioners and to iterate conceptual theory with practical approaches. Theory in creative and innovative management, however, has seemed to lag behind the output of those in the trenches, those who have been pioneering these efforts. Yet nowhere in business is the need for guiding theory greater. Theory without practice is sterile and irrelevant, while practice without theory can be wild and directionless. Theory needs the validity and relevance of practice, while practice needs the focus and direction of theory. Each is vital to sustain and support the other.

How can theorists and practitioners of creative and innovative management help one another? One analogy could be the excellent partnership that has developed in this century between theoretical and experimental physicists. Einstein could not have postulated his theory of relativity without the prior Michaelson-Morley experiment showing the constancy of the speed of light. Similarly, many of the experimental results in particle physics and recently in cosmology have been derived from Einstein's theoretical postulates and could not have been imagined otherwise. Without theory, experimentalists, both in particle physics and cosmology, just wouldn't have known where to look. And if by chance they had been looking in the right place, they perhaps wouldn't have been able to understand what they saw. There are many examples. One might be gravitational lenses in the universe, where some extremely faraway object would actually appear in two places. Because of an intervening large body of matter (which might even be invisible) that focuses light, one object appears as if it were two. Such a phenomenon would be a complete mystery if it were not for theory.

What does this mean for our inquiry? We have represented in this book three kinds of groups. We have three for-profit institutions—Innotech, Synectics, SRI International—focusing on creativity in companies. We have representatives from the academic business community, scholars at the forefront of fundamental research of these complex phenomena. Then there is an intermediary group that has elements of both; these are the research institutes—the Center for Creative Leadership in Greensboro, North Carolina and the Center for Studies of Creativity in Buffalo, New York. So we have three different kinds of groups: 1) *practitioners,* who are working with companies to make a profit; 2) *theorists,* who are trying to understand and develop descriptive and explanatory theory; 3) *interfacers,* who use state-of-the-art thinking to intervene actively in corporate situations.

The purpose of this brief chapter is to explore the relationship between theory and practice. To accomplish this, I asked others to participate with me at the conference on which this book is based. I wanted to play facilitator more than instructor. I wanted the contributors to this book to be actively involved in the exploration. Consequently, I said to the distinguished audience:

> I'm going over to the blackboard. I give you fair warning, because although I do have my own ideas, I am not going to use them. I am going to call on you.

Some of you who are sitting there passively need to take heed because I may decide to point my finger and put you on the spot. In fact, I look forward to seeing you squirm.

This will be a brainstorming session. There are no wrong ideas. I am not going to judge you. Picture yourself as either an academic researcher or business practitioner. All of you would fall into either category (some into both). How would you help the other side to work together with you? If you are a researcher, what would you want the practitioner to do? If a practitioner, how can the researcher enhance your objectives? How can you relate together to that person? What can you do differently to reach out to the other culture?

The audience's comments and my replies follow:

Comment: I would like to suggest an analogy of a marriage between truth and goods. Think of researchers as being primarily concerned with the generation of truth and going about generating it in a scientific manner. Researchers must suspend personal opinions so that they can see objectively what is there. Think about practitioners as primarily being concerned with creating value of some kind. Coming from a practitioner's side, I saw a lot of good intentions but very little grasp of the truth. It wasted time. Now being on the research side, I see us also wasting time and energy in producing much knowledge that is not necessarily going to create some value. So, my idea for getting these two cultures to work together effectively is to keep in mind that we need both—knowledge and truth combined with goods and values. Without the marriage, we become inefficient.

Kuhn: Fine, this is a conceptual approach. I am looking for all types—frameworks and specific suggestions as well.

Comment: First, identify some common important questions that both the academic and the practitioners have. Then identify the methodology to answer those questions.

Kuhn: Regarding common questions, we have to recognize that while the questions can be the same the motivations of each culture has to be different. The practitioner is going to think about making a buck and the academic will be concerned about publishing a paper. One has to establish the relationships between the two. Both sides will be thinking of their own careers. The subject will be the same, the career enhancement will be the same, but the way that personal progress is achieved will differ dramatically. We have to find interests in common, but the diverse motivations must be respected.

Comment: Job swap, with the academic person working in private industry for one week and vice versa.

Kuhn: Good. Can we explore this with some specific examples?

Comment: How do we construct this arrangement? There is ambiguity here. Our practitioners that contribute here are more the exception than the rule. What about the practitioner in an industry who, in fact, is successful in doing precisely what these creativity-stimulators are trying to help other companies do? What is it about the characteristics of these organizations and what are these practitioners doing that they are able to be creative internally themselves without outside help? They seem to be applying truth and theory.

Kuhn: Without offending our friends, we call these success stories "real" practitioners.

Comment: The trick is to design organizations to be more creative without incurring various pathologies.

Comment: In talking about formulas, Einstein's formula for success and happiness is A + B + C. "A" is working hard. "B" is having fun. "C" is knowing when to keep your mouth shut. Maybe some of the successful companies really don't talk about their successes but yet they are experiencing these same optimal situations that the academics and the practitioners are talking about.

Kuhn: What is the logical conclusion?

Comment: Perhaps the companies that are successful do it without the outside consultants. They just don't talk about it. They are too busy doing it.

Kuhn: The other side of the argument is that it is not necessarily a pathology if managers and organizations can't be creative by themselves. It may be a natural characteristic of the nature of the creative process that an independent view of things helps facilitate it. It is not a pathology not to be creative without some outside intervention and consulting.

Comment: We should recognize that companies have a larger mission when fostering more creativity and innovation. There is substantial motivation, even with companies that are very innovative, not to share that. That is a competitive, proprietary advantage *not* to share what they do.

Kuhn: This is the great conflict between the commercial and academic worlds. As an example, there is high tension in university-business relationships over the competitive interest of companies and the publishing desire of researchers.

Now, we are getting some good philosophy here, but philosophy is for the nighttime. I want to hear hard, practical things. The job swap is one suggestion. You might not agree, but for one week you could switch jobs. I want to hear from you—specifically, what you could do Monday morning.

Comment: I totally support your position. Theory profits from practice and practice profits from theory. Therefore, I think one approach is to study the practitioners. In our particular case, we have developed some tools that we think are efficacious. We would cordially invite people to study the efficacy of those tools.

Kuhn: Let's explore. You want to study the practitioners. Then you said that we should study the tools. Those are two quite separate things. It would be good if the practitioners you work with would feel special rather than burdened if we brought in one or more academics. Rather than being intruded upon, it should be like the Hawthorne effect: the active intervention of being studied may make managers more dynamic. In the process, you could have theorists and in-field researchers work with the practitioners and, in a separate agenda, study the tools and the processes and the methodologies. In essence, it is a second-order approach; as you use your intervention techniques on the company, you will have theorists studying your methods.

Harriman: Synectics has conducted an experiment at the Graduate School of Business at the University of Chicago where outside clients were brought into the program. The courses were oriented around new product development work. We work with them in providing both the concepts and the clients.

Kuhn: Please describe the program further. It has been operating for ten years. What results have you had?

Harriman: The primary focus has been learning for the students as opposed to research for the faculty. However, such research could be built into the courses in the next generation. The program has given students a better feeling for the process within the client organizations. The practical value has been generally rated as being very high because students are working directly with the clients. The clients participate because they gain fresh thinking from the idea stage through the various market research phases. It is a program that can be carried much further.

Bailey: We at Carnegie-Mellon have several project courses like that, too. In fact, we have a new product development course that feeds into an entrepreneurship course. A student who has a new product idea can learn how to write a business plan for it. We also have project courses where a student might go out to a company in Pittsburgh and solve a particular problem the firm has, such as congestion in some aspect of production. Students may come away with a set of suggestions that can save the company a substantial amount of money.

Comment: There are some things that seem to be essential for success. One is a shared vision between the practitioner and the researcher. That comes out of communications. I think frequent interaction would enhance mutual interests. Personal relationships are important; there must be some respect and trust in the process. If a researcher does a paper or the practitioner has a product, each must gain value from the perspective of the other. There must be something in it for each individually.

Kuhn: In the traditional motivation, the researcher is getting good data and a good paper and the practitioner is getting a new product or facilitating client work. What about switching those motivations? What about designing the reward system so that the practitioner will enhance his or her career by coauthoring a publishable paper and the academic theorist will participate financially to a greater degree than a normal consulting fee. In this manner, each can get a taste of the other side's motivation to feel what the whole process is about.

Comment: That might work if there are perceived values on the part of the players. If they perceive value, then it could work. If they don't, then forget it.

Kuhn: Sure, its a high-risk strategy, but that's what this game is all about.

Comment: Publications on the part of the researchers is a problem that has to be addressed. I am coming from the industry's side. Nobody has a sustainable competitive advantage in technology. Nobody has a significant competitive advantage in capital. The only real competitive advantage that you have today is people and ideas how to optimize their talents. Why would we want to bring researchers in to publish, for the world to see what our competitive advantages are?

Kuhn: That is a important question. There are answers and we will see if they work.

Comment: I think the answer is simple. Even good systems have problems without good answers. Theory needs to be developed to produce better answers. The advantage of practitioners is they have rich experiential knowledge. The advantage of theorists is that they think in terms of generalized concepts and ideas that can stimulate thinking in multiple situations. We are not going to advance our understanding of organizations if we don't participate one another's interests.

Kuhn: One must be sensitive to the special issues. Academics should be sensitive to the commercial concerns of proprietory data—by disguising information, changing the industry and the numbers, keeping the concept but protecting competitive knowledge. Unless a company would feel totally confident that its rights would be protected, it would probably withhold information—which in turn would ruin the research process.

Comment: From the practitioner's side, I find that every time you bring in a researcher, there is delay. They want to study and study and study. They don't want to be the implementer. Theorists should learn to work along with the practitioner through implementation, and not be satisfied just with the research part.

Kuhn: As I said, if you somehow tie part of the consulting remuneration to some end result (other than a paper), that might energize the process and give the academic a taste of the commercial.

Comment: Particularly if they absorb some of the risks.

Kuhn: What might some of those risks be?

Comment: Instead of being paid on a straight consulting basis, agree to be paid on the basis of the project's success.

Kuhn: If it works, it works, and both sides win. If it doesn't, both sides lose.

Comment: Information is competitive advantage. Whenever we work a particular company, they tend to achieve a certain time-period advantage. It's generally something like three years. It has been as long as seven. That is a real incentive for companies. The argument is that we will improve the firm by augmenting their capacity to learn faster. And speed is money in competitive situations.

Kuhn: This goes to the heart of the process. As a practitioner, you must feel that your competitive advantage over the middle term is enhanced by having the theorist along with you. That can happen because your competitive advantage is improved in the process. If you feel you are only doing social work, for the university or for the country, it is a disaster. You'll do it once for the common good, but no more. You must believe that you are benefiting yourself in the process; you must believe that you and your people are better off at the next stage of your competitive effort. When that word gets around, then other business people will want to join with researchers. The need for this "positive area" puts a tremendous burden on the academic researcher. Such sensitivity is vital. The researcher is not there because he or she is fulfilling some higher mission of general society, but rather because he or she is helping that specific company in a particular task. Then the symbiosis can really work. There is a great responsibility on both sides to make that happen. You can have common interest, you can have good personal rapport, but because you start out with different motivations, practitioners and researchers really have to work to achieve sustainable mutual benefit.

Chorover: I think what is needed is a context—a time and a place in which these two contrasting perspectives can have an opportunity to explore each other in depth. . . . What you have raised is a fundamental question, not just of creative and innovative management, but of our general ways of doing business. The extent to which the division of labor in business and science has created barriers and differences in objective, requires that, mutually to advance, we must periodically find an appropriate context for coming together. That is the function of special institutions and forums.

Kuhn: Perhaps we have catalyzed the creation of such new contexts.

19

THE STRATEGIC INNOVATION MANAGEMENT ASSESSMENT PROFILE

William C. Miller

THE CONTEXT FOR NEW RESEARCH ON FOSTERING INNOVATION

Creativity and innovation certainly has become a hot topic in the 1980s! In this decade, literature has abounded with research, experiences, and advice on "creativity management" (Ginn 1986), "innovation management (Quinn 1985), "intrapreneurship" (Lawler and Drexler 1981), and "skunkworks" innovation (Peters 1983a, b). Popular books by Ouchi, Pascale and Athos, Peters and Waterman, Kanter, and Pinchot have sounded the call for how to stimulate innovation. Consulting groups such as SRI International (the Managing Innovation Change program), Arthur Young (the Institute for Innovation), Innovation Associates, Foresight, Synectics, and Innotech have developed strong corporate following for developing innovation in new products, new production methods, and such.

Various reasons have been given for this emergence (or renaissance, in some people's opinions) of strong interest in how to promote "strategically appropriate" creativity and innovation. For example, Kanter (1983) cites the global economy, competitive market pressures, new technology, the politics of raw materials, government regulation, demographics and consumer preferences, and labor force trends.

Research by the Nomura Research Institute (NRI) in Kamakura, Japan, in 1984–86 cites four basic management problems facing U.S.

and European companies: 1) going from maturity to new business growth (reviving of corporate growth); 2) retrenching of the swollen corporate organization (going to greater emphasis on decentralized management, organizational flexibility, and smaller headquarters); 3) revival of entrepreneurship (within the corporate structure); and 4) strengthening of international competitiveness (aimed at gaining an edge over Japanese and other foreign competition.[1]

In response to the U.S. and European needs, NRI also found seven key factors affecting management renovation in the United States and Europe, all of which could incorporate some element of creativity as a means or innovation as an output: 1) clear-cut strategic objectives, renovation, and execution; 2) profit-minded management—pulling out of poorly performing operations and investment for business growth; 3) corporate rehabilitation through rationalization and marketing of higher value-added products; 4) management with emphasis on human factors, which helps raise employees' morale; 5) promotion of entrepreneurship and development of venture operations within the company; 6) renovation and revitalization in research and development; and 7) entry into promising area and shift to different lines.

In light of these needs for innovation and these approaches to revitalizing business, people such as Lewin and Minton (1986) call for a general management perspective on innovation, rather than a functional manager's perspective, based on key business issues management faces. From research he conducted in 1982 Van de Ven (1986) found that the management of innovation was reported by CEOs he surveyed as "their most central concern in managing their enterprises in the 1980s. He cited three questions: 1) How can a large organization develop and maintain a positive climate for innovation? 2) What are the critical factors for launching business ventures or projects targeted for leading-edge innovation? 3) How can a manager achieve balance between specialization and collaboration?

A plethora of insights, understandings, and motivations for fostering more and better innovation has emerged for identifying both the individuals who can champion the cause of specific innovations or innovation in general and the organizational climates that can encourage and sustain such heroes. For example, Shapero (1985) says individuals should be provided with abundant freedom of action, yet with deadlines and multiproject responsibilities. Greenwald (1985) suggests that the environment should be neither too rigid nor too bureaucratic. This suggestion is similar to that of Johne (1984), who found that the looseness can help during initiation stages while the tight structures can help during prototype stages.

As one other example, Gryskiewicz, Amabile, and Sensabaugh (1986) identified the following factors as major influencers on creativity in R&D.

- Environmental stimulants provided:
    Freedom to choose what to do, given a clear goal
    Access to appropriate resources: money, equipment, people, information
- Environmental obstacles removed:
    Structural issues: communications, rewards, reporting, career progression, etc.
    Great personal interest: beyond defensive mentality
    Proper project planning, including time frames and other details
- Personal characteristics developed
    Self-motivation, high cognitive abilities, willingness to take risks
- Unfavorable personal characteristics transcended:
    Poor motivation, inflexibility

Applying the wealth of information and insights already generated has not been a simple task for the academic, the consultant, the manager, or the professional. For many people I have met in the course of my career—and for me—the "advice" can sometimes seem conflicting, impractical, or simply too complex to master in the day-to-day course of doing one's job. Furthermore, there seems to be little if any reliable information about how to identify and "leverage" the innovation climate factors most pertinent to a particular industry environment—that is, to answer the question "What are the most important factors for *this particular industry* compared to other industries?"

My own experience in this field, primarily at SRI International (formerly Stanford Research Institute) and now with SAI Associates (SAI is an abbreviation for Strategic Approaches to Innovation), has encompassed assignments with Fortune 500 and foreign multinational corporations on two kinds of projects: 1) the development of innovative products, services, processes, or business strategies, and 2) the development of a climate conducive to ongoing creativity and innovation. I have summarized many techniques and perspectives on fostering creativity with individuals, workgroups, and larger organizations in *The Creative Edge: Fostering Innovation Where You Work* (Miller 1987). Also contributing to the viewpoints and methods I find most helpful to managers and professionals was my re-

search with over twenty corporations on "maintaining and enhanc-
ing the innovation climate of entrepreneurial acquisitions (results
unpublished).

My approach to research on the innovation climate, therefore, is
colored by the question, "How can I most ably help a manager or a
work team to resolve specific strategic and operational issues—where
creativity is most often a means, and innovation an output, for resolving the issues?" I am currently conducting research on how to
improve the climate for innovation based on the following understanding of roles and impact, goals, structures, and process for assessing the innovation climate.

THE ROLES AND IMPACT OF INNOVATION
IN ORGANIZATIONS

Creativity and innovation plays at least four key roles in helping
our organizations to grow and prosper.

- *Operations:* to develop leading-edge approaches to individual
  functions within an organization
- *Strategic:* to exercise leadership in chosen markets and industries
- *Organizations:* to manage transitions at the brink of change
- *Personal:* to nurture personal needs for spirited, rich work lives

While the personal issue may often seem the most remote to executive business concerns, it may actually serve as the key to the
inspired, peak performance that accomplishes the other roles. Garfield's (1986) work on peak performers and IBM's own internal studies on the need for self-selected product champions (Peters 1983b)
all point toward this supposition. The personal role is also the arena
where creativity ceases to be a means to an end and may become an
expressive, motivational goal in itself.

Within an organization the impact of creativity and innovation
may appear in numerous ways:

- More awareness and discussion of "being creative"
- Greater flow of ideas (evidenced by more patent applications,
  for example)
- Meeting goals that call for specific innovations (a new chemical, a
  new software system, a new marketing idea)
- Working on challenging goals that require creativity to meet them
  (such as "Grow this business at 1.5 times the industry growth

rate," or "Match this year's production with 10 percent fewer staff.")

- Indirect internal impact (for example, where upfront collaboration on a new auto design between design staff and manufacturing might result in better manufacturing "down the road")
- Indirect external impact (for example, a company with a reputation for innovation might attract better talent, and customers might see more value in their products—both of which might contribute to bottom-line results)

All of these potential impacts on the organization's people and performance should be considered when designing new assessment tools and processes. Social, political, and other impacts external to the organization are also worthy of consideration, depending on the goals of the research.

THE GOALS OF RESEARCH ON FOSTERING INNOVATION

As a consultant the goals I must accomplish in the course of conducting research, both within a single organization and across many organizations, are threefold.

1. Identify "leverage points" for developing organization transition (OT) strategies for a single organization, for an industry, and for organizations in general.
2. Determine the "return on transition investment" (ROTI)—the gains for having invested people, time, information, money, and materials into improving the innovation climate.
3. Improve the organization climate by the very process of conducting the research itself.

The last goal may seem to bely the notion of objective, verifiable research. Yet *any* survey, interview, or other assessment process is by nature an intervention into the organization (the quantum theory nature of measurement). There is no neutral process of research. As a consultant, I want to intentionally take advantage of this unavoidable alteration of the system to benefit the organization.

ONE MODEL FOR RESEARCH

The research model I employ involves the linkage of management practices, innovation styles, and business performance measures relative to fostering innovation. Together they comprise the model and assessment for Strategic Innovation Management Assessment Profile (SI-MAP).℗

Management Practices. The impact of management practices on *people* individually and in groups is the central issue regarding the quality of an organization's climate for innovation. As people, we tend to consciously or unconsciously ask the following questions about where we work (see Figure 19-1). What do I know and expect of myself and others as individuals? What do we intend together? (What are our purpose and goals?) How do we communicate and collaborate? How do we prepare and plan to achieve our purpose and goals? How do we implement those plans? What is our relationship to the external environment? (What difference, or impact, do we make?)

Based on research and experience from SRI and others, including the "entrepreneurial acquisition" study, innovation management practices, as they affect the experience and performance of people regarding creativity and innovation, can be organized into eighteen categories:

- Talent base
- Reporting structure
- Individual values and rewards
- Alignment with purpose and vision
- Alignment with strategy and goals
- Balance of intuition and logic
- Attunement of values
- Leadership
- Balance of internal collaboration and competition
- Resource allocation
- Administration of budget, information, and innovation systems
- Evaluation methods
- Functional operation
- Transition management
- Technology management
- Environmental monitoring and scanning
- Relation to critical success factors
- Performance feedback

For example, the general issue of "reporting structure" is that "The reporting structure, with its levels of delegation and decision making, enhances a business unit's ability to be innovative and re-

Figure 19-1.   An Individual's Experience of Organizational Life: Six Questions.

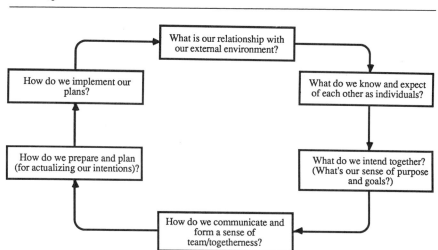

sponsive." Similarly, the general issue of "collaboration/competition" is that "While there is a healthy competition in the business unit for achieving goals, collaboration among people and across departments is more evident than any turf battles." Within each of eighteen such general issues are the myriad subquestions to be asked, which depend in part on the perspectives and goals of the researcher(s).

Each of these eighteen seems to have a more direct impact on one of the questions stated above, as shown in Figure 19-2. Within each of the eighteen, the answers to a host of specific questions can be assessed and profiled, as illustrated generically in Figure 19-3.

Innovation Styles. Building upon research by Kirton (1984) and the Myers-Briggs Type Indicator (MBTI), these seem to be four distinctly different *approaches* to innovation and change, determined by the way people gather information (preferring facts or insights) and what they do with information (preferring to make decisions or to perceive and understand more). People with very different mixtures of these approaches may all have equal *levels* of creativity and innovation, yet differ in the fundamental ways they approach gathering information, generating ideas, solving problems, and implementing change.

Figure 19-2.   Strategic Innovation Management Practices.

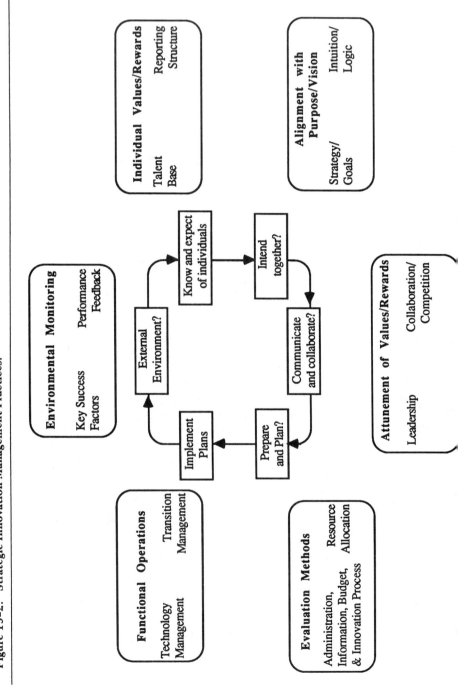

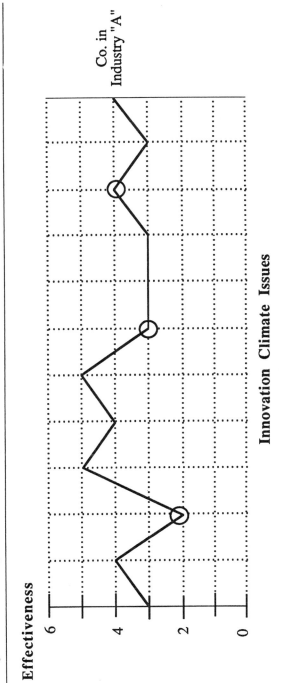

Figure 19–3.   Strategic Innovation Management Assessment Profile (SI-Map).

Individuals and groups each display some combination of all four styles:

- The *modifier* style, based on a preference for facts and decision making. Modifiers innovate by emphasizing incremental change. Modifiers are apt to say, "Lets build on what we already have and make improvements where necessary."

- The *vision-driver* style, based on a preference for insights (or "visions") and decision making. Vision-drivers emphasize power and knowledge. They characteristically say, "Let's develop a clear sense of purpose and goals to focus and drive our creative energy."

- The *explorer* style, based on a preference for insights and perceiving. Explorers innovate by emphasizing adventure and holistic perspectives. They approach an innovation task saying, "Let's explore unknown territory, without any set direction, and see where we end up."

- The *experimenter* style, based on a preference for facts and perceiving. Experimenters emphasize action, characteristically saying, "Let's test one thing at a time, with a clear methodology, and assess the results before going on."

Based on subjective interviews with various client groups, these innovation styles seem to have significance in how all (or most) of the eighteen issues are formulated and "resolved" among the people in an organization. For example, some recent applications of this notion of innovation styles have included defining the composition of new product development teams in an industrial products company, restrategizing how to present new ideas to management in a consumer products firm, and understanding more clearly why an innovation task force in a manufacturing division has trouble coming to closure in making specific project recommendations to management, and maintaining credibility among the general population of managers and professionals.

These differences might also typify entire climates for innovation and help align the climate with the style and pace required for competitive success within a particular industry. (In other words, innovation styles may help answer the question, "Is the way of fostering innovation within a company compatible with the competitive needs within its industry?.")

Business Performance Measures. To determine "leverage points" for improving the climate and performance for innovation, and to measure some return on transition investment, it would be most helpful, and significant, to link management practices and innovation styles either directly or indirectly to various organizational performance measures beyond themselves, such as: financial, competitive positions, production, and human resources. These measures can be formulated in terms that allow comparisons across various types of business units (banking versus toys). For example, productivity can be defined as "value-added per number of employees" where value-added is the cost of output minus cost of input.

A sampling of the performance measures I am employing includes:

- Financial
  Rate of growth
  Return on assets managed
- Competitive position
  Share of market served
  Relative market share
  Relative product quality
  R&D/total sales
- Production
  Value-added per total sales
  Value-added per number of employees
  Quality-defect ratio
- Human resources
  Staff retention
  Percent unionization

Either a direct or an indirect relationship between some of these measures and some innovation management practices would be very valuable knowledge. If direct correlations are found between particular management practices, or factored clusters of factors, and some performance measure(s), a significant leverage point for improvement might be indicated. Indirectly, the composite climate profile for business units with recognized high performance according to these performance measures might also indicate leverage points (see Figure 19-4). This latter, indirect method might help a company compare its practices and style with that of the most successful firms in its industry. Another possibility is to compare the profiles of successful firms in one industry with the profiles of successful firms in a totally different industry—leading to knowledge of industry-specific leverage points for improving innovation (see Figure 19-5). This, I believe, is an important goal to accomplish in the next phase of research on innovation management.

Figure 19-4. Practices Comparing a Company with Top Performers in Its Industry.

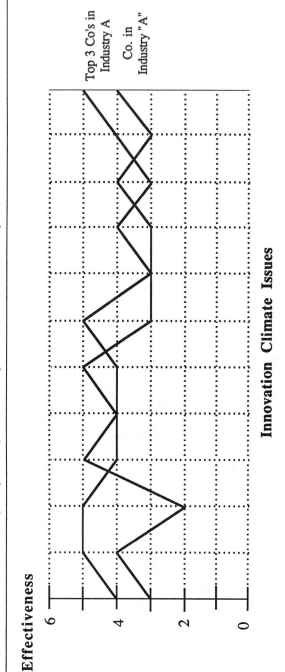

O = Leverage points for change

Figure 19-5. Practices Comparing Top Performers in Two Different Industries.

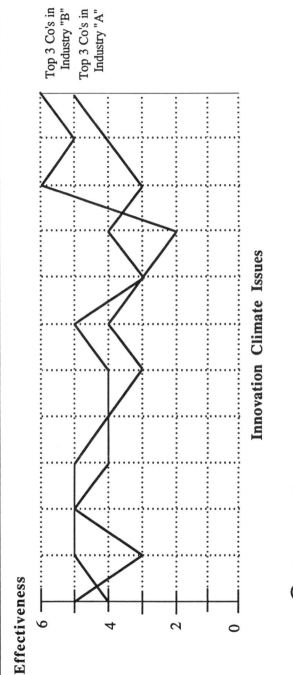

O = Leverage points for change

AN IMPORTANT "PROCESS" CONSIDERATION

As mentioned earlier, the assessment process itself can have a very significant impact on the people and performance of an organization (or an individual work group). A "conscious and supportive" approach to assessing the innovation climate can, it is hoped, complete the assessment process, having already introduced a perceived, positive affect on the climate.

An additional concern in designing an appropriate process occurs when a goal is to make comparisons across different business units or industries. With some important practices, comparisons from one firm to another are difficult, such as whether the business strategy is appropriate to the competitive environment. However, what *can* be compared in such a case is whether the stated strategy of the business unit is understood at different levels of the unit, and supported with committed action.

Therefore, a useful part of a supportive, interactive process might be to have an appropriate executive "fill in" various sections of the assessment tools with statements of strategy key success factors and values that are important to have widely shared in the business unit. The assessment then not only tests for the extent to which they *had been* understood and supported but also accomplishes some of the understanding just by being on the survey. The process of assessment, however, must be capable of following up this communication of potentially new information, to support possible debate with the contents and process of this communication. The results of the assessment may be somewhat "out of date" and inaccurate by the time the results are compiled and delivered. And that could be the good news, rather than a flaw in research methodology.

A FINAL WORD

We as researchers have the opportunity to make a particularly poignant contribution to the lives and prosperity of people everywhere. The issue of creativity and innovation profoundly affects all of us spiritually, mentally, emotionally, and materially. The quality and relevance of our research, therefore, can best be measured by the impact we have on people's *hearts*, not just their heads.

As individuals, we have personally chosen, for whatever reason, to do work in this field. Our personal values and motivations are an important asset in designing research that touches our own deepest selves as well as the deepest parts of others. Unless we personally grow from the type and quality of work, including research, that we do, it is likely that the results of what we do will be equally barren for others. In that sense we have the opportunity, perhaps the need, to create new directions in research on creativity and innovation that are an inspiration for our own spirits and for those around us—to benefit us all.

NOTE

1. Interestingly, NRI identified a complementary set of problems facing Japanese businesses, including 1) adapting to rapid changes in technology and social systems; 2) the need for a new type of international strategy that outgrows the past export-oriented policy; 3) altering the emphasis on harmony and consensus within companies that inhibits innovation.

REFERENCES

Garfield, Charles. 1986. *Peak Performers*. New York: Avon.

Ginn, Martin E. 1986. "Creativity Management: Systems and Contingencies from a Literature Review." *IEEE Transactions on Engineering Management EM-33* (no. 2, May).

Greenwald, R. 1985. "Companies Need to Establish a Climate That Fosters Innovation." *Industrial Engineering 17* (no. 4, April): 10–12.

Gryskiewicz, Stanley S., Teresa M. Amabile, and S. Sensabaugh. 1986. "What Are the Key Ingredients in Creativity?" *Technology Strategies* (July).

Johne, F.A. 1984. "The Organization of High Technology Product Innovation." *European Journal of Marketing 18* (no. 6-7): 55–71.

Kanter, Rosabeth Moss. 1983. *The Change Masters*. New York: Simon and Schuster.

Kirton, M.J. 1984. "Adaptors and Innovators: Why New Initiatives Get Blocked." *Long Range Planning*: 137–43.

Lawler, Edward, and John Drexler. 1986. "Entrepreneurship in the Large Corporation: Is It Possible?" *Management Review* (February).

Lewin, Arie Y. and John W. Minton. 1986. "Organizational Effectiveness: Another Look, and an Agenda for Research." *Management Science 32* (no. 5, May).

Miller, William C. 1987. *The Creative Edge: Fostering Innovation Where You Work*. Reading, Mass.: Addison-Wesley.

Nomura Research Institute. 1985. "Corporate Management Toward the 1990s— Issues and the Need for Innovation." Management Consulting Department, NRI, Institute, May.

Peters, Thomas. 1983a. "The Mythology of Innovation, or a Small Skunkworks Tale—Part I." *Stanford Magazine* (Summer).

———. 1983b. "The Mythology of Innovation, or a Small Skunkworks Tale— Part II." *Stanford Magazine* (Fall).

Quinn, James Brian. 1985. "Managing Innovation: Controlled Chaos." *Harvard Business Review 3* (May–June).

Shapero, A. 1985. "Managing Creative Professionals." *Research Management 28* (no. 2, March–April): 23-28.

Van de Ven, Andrew H. 1982. "Strategic Management Concerns among CEO's: A Preliminary Research Agenda." Strategic Management Research Center, University of Minnesota, Minneapolis.

_____. 1986. "Central Problems in the Management of Innovation." *Management Science 32*, (no. 5, May).

20 A CROSS-ORGANIZATIONAL METHODOLOGY FOR ASSESSING CREATIVITY AND COMMITMENT

Robert Lawrence Kuhn
George Thomas Geis

Creativity as an efficacious mechanism for organizational change is as much dependent on the social psychology of organizations as it is on the individual psychology of personality. There are numerous techniques for studying such organizational psychology, from quantitative questionnaires to focused case studies. Human systems are so complex that it is difficult to isolate and investigate any particular characteristic, and any such technique has assets and liabilities.

We have used a "cross-organizational" methodology for studying organizational characteristics, examining one particular type of organization in order to understand one particular organizational characteristic. Maintaining real-world viability is an important criterion for us.[1] Real organizations in the real world are out only substrate.

Regarding content, we have had considerable interest in the relationship between creativity and commitment in organizational environments. The underlying motivations for our interests are both process and content.

From a *process* point of view, we believe that critical organizational factors can best be studied when seen in relative isolation. This is the general methodology we hope to develop for use in organizational studies. We seek to develop this methodology to facilitate a new view of complex organizations.

From a *content* point of view, we believe that there is an intimate relationship between creativity and commitment in organizational situations. This is the specific organizational result we seek to establish. We seek to understand the essence of commitment and its relationship to creativity.

THE SPECIAL LENS

Our methodology has an organizing principle, a particular way of viewing the world.[2] We believe that organizational characteristics in general, and commitment in particular, can best be studied in their "purest form." This is our operating paradigm, our conceptual prism. It is the heart of our cross-organizational methodology.

Pure form is the crux of our orientation. We define it as those organizational environments where the characteristic we seek to study is most apparent, where its manifestation is overt and its presence powerful. In such settings the target characteristic stands out and, though exaggerated, can be massaged and manipulated. It is one way to examine an intangible in highly complex human systems.

The kind of organizations we require are ones where the desired attribute appears in the strongest and most dominant mode, where the signal of the target trait is highest relative to the noise of all other traits. Once this pure form is isolated and analyzed, then the emerging understanding can be applied. Manifestations of the characteristic in other environments, though not as overt, can then be investigated. Organizations exemplifying the pure form of the characteristic are the special lens, and it is through them that we look.

ORGANIZATIONAL KINDS AND TYPES

Classification is an imaginative task. The process of grouping and splitting may trigger some insights. The structural scheme is both exhaustive and terse:

1. Ideological
2. Collegial
3. Bureaucratic
4. Social
5. Creative

There are five categories of organizations. With them we subsume all kinds of organizations from all sectors and for all purposes. No attempt is made to justify the precision or rightness of the categories, since such precision or rightness does not exist. The categories are presented for simplicity. Our object is to select a prototypical organization, the pure form for each primary characteristic. The point is to understand the essence of "pure form" organizations.

In *ideological* organizations, missions and goals dominate. They are associations founded on philosophical, theological, and conceptual ideas, often a search for the ideal and the ultimate. Classic examples are religious and political movements.

In *collegial* organizations, members are peers and partners. Such groupings of associates and equals include professional organizations (law firms, accounting firms, medical group practices), trade and job associations, academic faculties, government bodies.

Bureaucratic organizations have strict systems of reporting and controls. Lines of authority and formal structures of communication dominate in these hierarchial or pyramidal structures. Examples are traditional corporations and government agencies.

Social organizations have personal, fraternal, or societal objectives. Clubs and community endeavors, civic and charitable organizations, special interest groups all have fulfillment of personal and social needs as their purpose.

Creative organizations have an artistic or intellectual focus. In this category are groups concerned with music, art, writing, advertising, media (television, motion pictures) as well as intellectual institutions (universities, think tanks, research departments, scientific laboratories). The inherent independence of creative and innovative personnel is characteristic.

PURE FORM CHARACTERISTICS

The next list takes a conceptual leap. In it we select the dominant characteristics of each category of organization. The selection is intuitive; the foundation is experience and insight; the evaluation belongs to the reader.

1. Ideological   Personal commitment
2. Collegial   Peer interaction
3. Bureaucratic   Group structure
4. Social   Common community
5. Creative   Personal expression

We seek the pure form. This is our quest. According to our paradigm, finding the pure form would ease the analysis of any organizational factor since we could study the chosen trait in relative isolation, with minimum interference from other organizational factors.

What we learn from investigating the pure form, where the target characteristics are most cleanly exposed, we can then apply to all organizations. The pure form, in this context, becomes our dissecting scalpel, the instrument we use to delineate structure and highlight detail.

Accordingly, if we were to study peer interaction, we might choose law firms, accounting, or group medical practices as the pure form substrate for our analysis. If we were interested in personal expression, we might choose opera and ballet companies, creative departments of advertising agencies, new product research and development laboratories, or think tanks.

What we would learn in these collegial and creative organizations, we could then apply to all organizations, from profit-making corporations to not-for-profit government agencies. The same procedure, studying a chosen characteristic in pure form first, can be applied to all group characteristics. This is our framework.

COMMITMENT AND CREATIVITY

Creativity is the explosive mental energy erupting from individual initiative (see Kuhn and Geis 1988). Commitment is the psychic knot tying together individuals and institutions. It is our thesis that individual creativity must be linked with institutional commitment in order to generate novel thinking and productivity in organizational environments (see Kuhn and Geis 1986).

We suggest that there is a direct connection between the level of employee commitment and the extent to which an employee is willing and able to engage in creative efforts on behalf of the organization. Commitment is the crux of "the firm bond," the effective bridge between individuals and organizations. What exactly is commitment? We define it as the link between personal meaning and company mission. Mission is the heart of company existence just as meaning is the soul of employee dedication. Each is driving energy and directing force. Businesses seek to achieve objectives; employees strive to fulfill purposes. Personal meaning and company mission are the two poles of our axis, and around them this firm bond revolves.

How does personal creativity develop within companies? What makes individual innovation productive for businesses? We believe that personal creativity must be linked with company commitment for beneficial innovation to work well in corporate environments. Personal creativity erupts from individual initiative. Commitment is the firm bond between individuals and organizations. The linkage is key: Only by joining personal creativity with company commitment can novel thinking promote corporate welfare.

Commitment is a primal force impelling employees to achieve company goals, and such commitment is tied closely to company creativity. This coupling is critical. We suggest that there is a direct relationship between the level of employee commitment and the extent to which that employee engages in creative efforts on behalf of the company.

Creative acts demand a level of energy expenditure that is not commonly exhibited persons who are only "routinely" attached to an organization. Personal creativity, we say, is proportional to company commitment. Furthermore, building and maintaining the commitment of people almost always involves a creative, even artistic, effort by leadership. To build commitment, managers must not only understand the needs and goals of employees but also must be sensitive to how their particular organizational society (culture) influences individual level of commitment. Commitment is both vital and delicate, and care must be taken in its development.

Our focus is on deriving a theoretical procedure to aid the managerial process—to assist those managers who are creative themselves and those who manage the creativity of others. Both must understand the commitment-creativity connection. We explore it in a novel way.

Commitment is the emotional lines of force that attract individuals to institutions, the mental might that empowers goal-directed work. Commitment is "purpose with action," an internal desire of employees to achieve an external objective of companies. Metaphors come easy: Commitment is the "glue" that cements the group together. It is the "knot" that ties together independent individuals. ("Knot," not "glue," seems a better metaphor for the firm bond, since ideally one should be "tied," not "stuck," to an organization.) Commitment signals emotional attachment, and it runs the gamut from self-sacrifice to adversarial attack. One way to examine commitment is to watch where it works best. This is our novelty. What we present about commitment is rooted in religion.

THE PURE FORM OF COMMITMENT

Where is commitment best exemplified? In what kinds of organizations is commitment most easily isolated and analyzed? Although a critical component of all organizations, commitment appears most prominently and vigorously in *ideological* organizations, environments of religious and political passion. Here attitudes of mind are more singular, more linear, more focused.

Furthermore, to enhance the effect, we look toward the far end of the spectrum, toward those religious and political settings where collective mission subjugates individual meaning, where party fidelity swamps private desire, where sect purpose crushes personal freedom.

Here, at the extreme outposts of ideological organizations, we dig for concepts and cases. These situations, tailor-made for examining commitment, we label "total organizations."[3]

Why are total organizations ripest for examining commitment? For one, they are both closed and ideological. Closed organizations are impermeable and often this intended and enforced. Commitment, therefore, is both cause and effect, cause at the beginning, effect after a time. (Being both "closed" and "ideological" is required for full impact. Many political movements are ideological but not closed; commitment to them need not be potent. Prisons, on the other hand, are closed but not ideological; few inmates evidence commitment to their institution.)

We utilize total organizations, arenas of powerful religious fervor, as the analytical framework within which to examine commitment. The objective, remember, is not to study these organizations per se; rather, we use these groups to elucidate the essence of commitment, which we then can apply to companies and institutions of common kin. The methodology here is the key: using the pure form to study the normal occurrence.

Religious organizations, therefore, become our special lens and *religious attachment* our magnifying glass. What we see is an enlarged picture of the membergroup bond, a pulsating portrait in three dimensions, one that gives theorists new tools to understand the foundations of employee dedication and company productivity.

RELIGION AND BUSINESS

Religious belief inflames human emotions. With ultimate things at stake, unusual things are done. Religious belief generates mankind's strongest, most soul-stirring feelings. For better or for worse, for good or for evil, religion promotes the pinnacle of human achievement and evokes the height of human emotion.

What might we see under the magnifying glass of religious organizations? For example, can the attitudes of a minister in a sect shed light on the effectiveness of a manager in a company? Can understanding the devotion of church members in a crisis affecting their church improve the dedication of factory workers facing layoffs?

The psychic processes involved in the two situations are very much the same. Religion and business run parallel universes. Just because commitment is more obvious in the former does not mean that it is less important in the latter. The nature of religious commitment is merely a cleaner, more overt form of the same phenomenon, the same magical mental force that binds individuals to institutions and energizes goal-directed action. Understanding what commitment means in extreme religious organizations helps us understand what it means in all organizations. Whatever makes adherence in religion so potent should make allegiance in business more meaningful.

We combine ecclesia and commerce in an unusual brew.[4] Our concern is understanding the motivations of people and the management of companies. We seek meaning and fulfillment for the former, mission and performance for the latter. Finding transcendence—a prime motivator in religion—is relevant, applicable, and necessary for corporate creativity. Vision is vital: Moving hearts and minds is more important than fattening wallets and pocketbooks; generating visceral support for policies and programs is what firm fortune is all about.

How to make employees more committed and creative? How to make companies more productive and successful? Commercial demands parallel spiritual desires. Betty in her bible school parallels Carl in his computer company. What each seeks is personal fulfillment. Life within any organization has spiritual overtones. People and organizations are surprisingly similar whether pushed by profits and position or pulled by eternity and morality. The same mental processes are involved in business and religion. They run equivalent races, occupy parallel universes.

Parallels between business and religion are stunning. Founders of firms are similar in character and style to founders of churches. When "truth" must change, the organization is shaken. Truth to a church is "doctrine," to a company "strategy." Strategic change in the latter echoes doctrinal change in the former. In each the break is traumatic. Liberals strive against conservatives, young radicals against old guard, the infighting often putting politics to shame.

Another example is hype: dated doomsday prophecies in a religion; unachievable earnings projections in a business. When doomsday fails to arrive on schedule, or when earnings fall short of forecasts, faith is shaken and commitment eroded. This is a shame. Biblical belief far transcends misinterpreted prophecies, just as company confidence should well exceed inflated projections.

A fascinating example of religion-business counterparts is the so-called double standard, when leaders enjoy privilege, power, honor, wealth, and license that their followers do not. What the clergy (professional) can do, the laity (amateur) cannot. One reads with regularity reports of religious leaders involved in personal activities hardly religious. This morality gap is severely criticized by outsiders, yet the faithful do not complain.

Such support of superiors, even when discovered in sin, mystifies observers and bewilders critics. Yet there is logic here, and the same social contract, believe it or not, binds executives and employees in companies. Differentiation in personal behavior, privilege of position, power to control subordinates, license to supersede rules, organizational honor, and degree of reward are all present. What executives are permitted, workers are not. The double standard is a two-edged sword. Cutting one way, it legitimizes the social position of workers. Not everyone can be a member of the ruling hierarchy, and the double standard justifies each end of the axis.

How does religion highlight commitment? With ultimate things at stake unusual things are done. How much sacrifice to preach the word! How much inspiration in music, art, literature, law! Religious belief inflames human emotions; so to view commitment, religious organizations become a powerful "magnifying glass." Thus we use this "organizational lens" to focus on commitment, to understand how creativity is generated in companies. What will follow are conclusions about commitment in business; they are derived from examining commitment in religion. But first, a personal perspective.

HOW WE STUDIED COMMITMENT: ORGANIZATIONAL METHODOLOGY

Our work is derived from personal experience as well as from disinterested analysis. We have evinced emotions within the organizations about which we write. Though not commonly considered a virtue for scientific analysis, we do not equate feelings with failure. On the contrary, we believe that personal experience and private emotions are *essential* for understanding the complex phenomenon of human psyches embroiled in organizations.

Our experience is dual, our backgrounds diverse. Each of us, at different times in different groups, has been either participant or observer, each caught in compulsion, each dispassionate in analysis. Sometimes we were hot, burning with organizational fervency. Sometimes we were cool, inquiring with professional precision. At all times, we were committed.

Trained as a scientist and strategist (Kuhn) and as a mathematician and psychologist (Geis), both of us turned to the academic study of management later in our careers, after having experienced the fever of various organizational memberships, after having held managerial roles in various high-tension organizations. Thus, having felt the pulse of various groups, we note the presence of a repetitive beat. A striking signal emerges from clutter and noise. Each organization, when viewed from within, considers itself at least somewhat unique. But these same organizations, when observed from without, suddenly manifest remarkable similarity.

Corporations, foundations, universities, hospitals, government agencies, churches and synagogues—though cultures may differ, issues do not. Fundamentals affect them all: goals, strategy, structure, resource allocation, politics, succession, change—the list is long and the commonality strong. In every case, from company to congregation, *management* plaus the crucial role.

We believe that our cross-organizational methodology can help management theorists understand common concerns by cutting across divergent groups. The process can help enlighten problems too common to appreciate by seeing them reflected in a strange but parallel environment. Thus a political struggle among subsidiaries for resource allocations in a large conglomerate is viewed in a new light when transformed into a doctrinal battle among factions in a large religious denomination. In both cases, ultimate control is a primary issue.

The objective of a cross-organizational methodology is to help clarify problems and suggest solutions. What issues, for example, are shared by both business and religion? A dominant theme, developed with many variations, is the *commitment connection* between individuals and institutions, and the vital role of commitment for creativity.

HOW WE STUDIED COMMITMENT: STRUCTURAL METHODOLOGY

Our structural methodology combines induction and deduction. First, we *induce* the Commitment Model by empirically analyzing the data from individuals and institutions. We examine the disaggregated components of commitment, the pillars that form its foundation: personal factors of individuals (primarily "meaning" oriented); organizational factors of institutions (primarily "mission" oriented); and experience factors between individuals and institutions (primarily the interaction of "meaning and mission"). These elements are combined to induce a Commitment Model (Kuhn and Geis 1986).

Then the Commitment Model is used to describe how commitment can be built and broken, how the bond between individuals and institutions can be formed and severed. Specific techniques are so *deduced* and derived. These techniques can be applied in various personal and organizational situations (Kuhn and Geis 1984, chs. 6-8).

COMMITMENT STYLES AND TYPES

From our work with both business and religious groups we categorize various styles of commitment:

- *Core.* Fervent group belief dominates ("Partisans").
- *Calculative.* Personal benefit rules ("Adherents").
- *Cog.* Status quo dominates ("Routiners").

Commitment also has its dark side, a nether world populated with "Disengageds" (Cog negative), "Disaffecteds" (Calculative negative), and "Adversaries" (Core negative).

Core commitment fuses personal belief with organizational creed. It involves profound private devotion to publicly recognized goals and the melding of these group aspirations into one's own identity. It means that an employee wholly accepts company ideals and values and has internalized them. Such a person will adopt and reflect the style of the organization, the culture of the company, the attitude of the group. An individual with core commitment keeps the organization's specific action. Individual creativity is motivated here, at least in part, by seeking collective benefit. This is the arena where, for normal needs, personal creativity is most productive.

Calculative commitment starts with the individual, not the organization. The prime consideration is personal gain. How effectively are one's total needs being satisfied? How does the employee benefit from the company or from personal creative achievement? How much is he or she "making" in the broadest sense of the term? Calculations, measurements, benchmarks, and yardsticks—these are important. What is one's total net income—financial and psychic, now and in the future? Comparisons are part of the equation measuring current company versus other opportunities. Creativity happens here, but only when the person perceives strong direct benefits.

Cog commitment is present when work is seen only as necessary routine. Little meaning is present, little emotion is felt. The job gets done, but just barely. External pressures and constant controls are necessary for motivation. As for real creativity, forget it for Cogs.

Aspects of Core, Calculative, and Cog commitment can be found in most people. One style, however, usually dominates. This is especially true in response to organizational mission. At different moments in one's business career, commitment style may shift. To cross such a boundary is not without trauma. (Different commitment styles may be expressed in different situations. For example, a person may be Core as a political volunteer in an election campaign,

Calculative as a part-time MBA student, and Cog as a salesman pitching accounts.)

COMMITMENT TYPES

We can use commitment strength types to assess creative contribution on the job. Relationships, however, are complex. Standard journeyman creativity, such as incremental innovations extending current products, is likely to be strongest at both ends of the scale (Core +/- and weakest in the middle (Cog +/-). (Compare, from the New testament, the similar creative efforts put forth by the Partisan Paul and the Adversary Saul. Routiners and Disengageds, Cog +/-, will not likely expend the physical effort or psychic energy necessary for creative development). Dynamic breakthrough creativity, however, is a different story. Generating ideas that challenge tradition and upset the established way, such as devising radically new products that make current products obsolete, often requires peculiar personal traits. Such creativity may be strongest when commitment is calculative, when corporate and personal interests blend, even by coincidence.

We postulate six categories of commitment types. They reflect varying degrees of willingness to exert personal effort to support (or hinder) organizational goals.

Partisans (Core +) radiate maximum commitment. They are dedicated and persistent, the backbone of organizations. Unshakable in mind and deed, zealous in fervor and intensity, they are ready to sacrifice self for company good. Wholehearted belief, irrespective of personal benefit, is the key characteristic of a Partisan. Such blind loyalty can, however, hinder the inconoclastic freedom required for revolutionary creativity.

Adherents (Calculative +) are motivated to promote and protect the organization. Their motivation is typically a mix of internal and external elements. They behave proactively to support the system. Positive organizatioanl action is important to them, although the basis is often enlightened self-interest. Building the business for personal reward is the essence of an Adherent. Vibrant creativity is often highest here, since personal benefits are maximized within a clear context of company contribution.

Routiners (Cog +) are a shade more positive than neutral, requiring direct external motivation to fulfill company expectations. Work is done, but passively, and consequences are of little personal value.

Keeping the status quo is all the Routiner wants. Don't look for much creativity here.

Disengageds (Cog -) are psychologically retired, slightly more negative than neutral. Jobs are done and tasks are accomplished, but with no interest and marginal performance. There is no personal involvement. Their passive presence can produce a deleterious effect on other workers, depressing motivation, creativity, and productivity. Weighing a company down is the contribution of the disengaged.

Disaffecteds (Calculative -) may or may not still be associated with the company. Whether from within or without, they work to foil or frustrate the organization, especially when doing so will serve their own interests. Personal profit from obstructing a company is what the Disaffected seeks. Unfortunately, creativity can prosper, if not flourish, under such circumstances.

Adversaries (Core -) are energetic foes of the company, operating actively and perhaps maliciously from either inside or outside. They seek dramatic change in the organization's goals, policies, structure, or leadership, and often nothing less than complete change at the top will suffice. Overthrowing the system, even irrespective of personal benefit, is the mission of the Adversary. Creativity here may be swamped by emotion.

The trick for business? Build towards Core, while respecting Calculative and minimizing Cog—but always stay on the positive side.

THE COMMITMENT MODEL I: INDUCTION AND FORMULATION

We have developed a model of organizational commitment by examining the various factors involved. In *The Firm Bond* (Kuhn and Geis 1984), the Commitment Model is built inductively through organizational theory combined with in-depth personal histories, and then applied deductively to generate the Commitment Builders and Breakers described later in this chapter. Religions are used as the "organizational lens" through which commitment is examined. The key elements of commitment are discerned under the "magnifying glass" of religious fervor and then applied to companies of common kin. Personal, Organizational, and Experiential Factors are inputs to the Model that yield Commitment Strength and Mission contribution as its output. The Model is used in numerous personal studies to improve relationships between individuals and institutions by bringing the benefits of commitment to both sides of the firm bond.

Mission is the heart of group existence just as *meaning* is the soul of group participants. Each is driving energy and directing force. Mission and meaning—the two are related, as groups seek to achieve objectives, and members strive to fulfill purposes, the soundness of the relationship determining the tightness of the bond.

Personal meaning and *organizational mission* are the two poles of our axis. What one does affects the other, intimately, iteratively, consistently. Strong employee commitment, at all corporate levels, correlates highly with long-term company achievement. Personal fulfillment and organizational success are clear and commanding targets, and the cross-organizational methodology uses religion as a guide and business as a goal. The essence is simple. The critical linkage forms between personal meaning and organizatioanl mission, and it is this *firm bond* that becomes our working definition of commitment and the empirical substrate for our cross-organizational methodology.

Input factors for the Commitment Model follow: These are the elements from which Commitment-Creativity Breakers and Builders are derived. The most important relationships are formed between meaning-related variables (Personal Factors), mission-related variables (Organizational Factors), and meaning/mission-related variables (Experimental Factors). (Note that "group" can mean "company.")

Personal Factors are Individual needs as well as other personal variables influencing commitment, independent of any organizational association. The first five are meaning-related variables.

Transcendence: beyond self; interests in ultimates
Autonomy: independence from authority
Achievement: fulfillment in completing tasks
Esteem: sense of personal worth
Power: capacity to influence
Affiliation: sense of belonging and association
Stability: comfort of routine and status quo
Structure: dependency on form and system
Materialism: money, wealth, and associated trappings
Education: amount, level, and kind of schooling
Generalized Loyalty: desire to belong; sense of duty
Locus of control: how life is directed, internally or externally.

Organizational Factors are key factors of the organization affecting member commitment, independent of any personal association. The first four are mission-related variables:

Goal Structure: group mission, purpose, grand design
Permeability: degree of flow between group and society

Leadership: nature and character of the boss
Progressiveness: degree of forward motion; momentum
Cohesiveness: group coherence; internal attachment.
Organizational Esteem: sense of group value and worth
People Valuing: degree to which employees are treated as assets

Experiential factors are elements that emerge from interactions between individual and organization, the experiences that develop from group association. The first five are meaning/mission-related variables.

Importance/Uniqueness: distinguishing the group from others; setting it apart, making it superior
Support: group sustenance and self-help
Reality Congruence: confidence in group pronouncements
Status: personal position in the group
Task Identification: enjoyment of job
Emotional Conditioning: affective, nonrational elements
Rewards: psychic and material benefits
Role Strain: job-related stress
Investment: degree of ego and effort sunk into the group

The interaction between Personal and Organizational Factors helps generate company commitment and therefore enhance individual creativity. Following are some examples of how a company can increase its receptivity for creative expression: creative mechanisms for achieving organizational uniqueness; creative structures for providing support for key people; creative company events that build a sense of emotional identification; and creative strategies getting employees to invest in (bet on) the firm. (Figure 20-1 provides a summary representation of the commitment model.)

THE COMMITMENT MODEL II: DEDUCTION AND IMPLEMENTATION

Selected combinations of personal, organizational and organizational experience inputs are combined to form "compounds" hypothesized to have especially useful explanatory power in analyzing commitment. Sample commitment-building compounds as well as commitment-breaking compounds are shown in Table 20-1.

The rationale for deducing these sample compounds is driven by the overwhelming number of possible combinations of input variables. Selecting useful patterns of inputs is intended to produce commitment principles based upon the model. These principles are tested, amplified, and clarified by use of additional case histories.

Figure 20-1.   Inducing the Commitment Model.

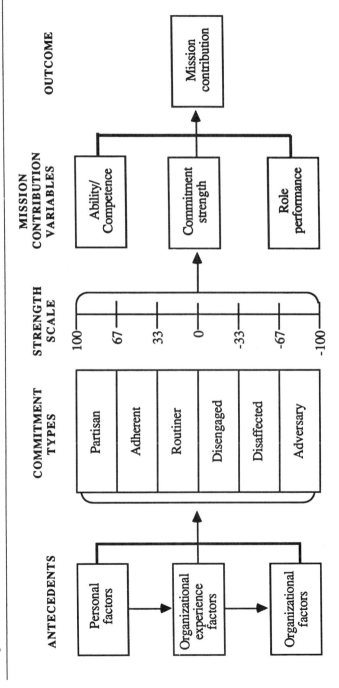

Table 20-1. Deductions from the Commitment Model.

Building Compounds	Elements/Factors (Antecedents)		
	Personal	Organizational	Organizational Experience
Identification	Transcendence Esteem Generalized Loyalty Materialism Education	Goal Structure Leadership Cohesiveness Organizational Esteem Permeability	Importance/Uniqueness Support Task Identification Investment Emotional Conditioning
Confidence	Affiliation Stability Structure Materialism	Leadership People Valuing	Realty Congruence Support Role Strain
Momentum	Achievement Esteem	Progressiveness Leadership	Reality Congruence Importance/Uniqueness
Responsibility	Power Autonomy Achievement Locus of Control Transcendence	Goal Structure Leadership Cohesiveness People Valuing	Support Status Rewards Role Strain
Accomplishment	Achievement Esteem Transcendence	Goal Structure Progressiveness Organizational Esteem	Rewards Importance/Uniqueness Task Identification

Breaking *Compounds*	*Elements/Factors (Antecedents)*		
	Personal	*Organizational*	*Organizational Experience*
Alienation	Transcendence Esteem Generalized Loyalty Affiliation Structure	Goal Structure Leadership Cohesiveness People Valuing Permeability	Support Task Identification Importance/Uniqueness Emotional Conditioning Rewards
Powerlessness	Power Autonomy Achievement Locus of Control	Goal Structure Leadership People Valuing	Status Support Task Identification Rewards
Meaninglessness	Transcendence Achievement Esteem Education Autonomy	Goal Structure Organizational Esteem Progressiveness	Importance/Uniqueness Reality Congruence Investment Task Identification
Worthlessness	Esteem Materialism Education	Progressiveness People Valuing Organizational Esteem	Support Status Emotional Conditioning
Anxiety	Stability Structure Locus of Control Autonomy	Leadership People Valuing Cohesiveness	Role Strain Support Reality Congruence Investment

THE COMMITMENT MODEL III:
APPLICATION AND CASES

Here we take relevant social psychological issues derived from literature largely independent of the model and examine these issues as they affect commitment in case studies of real people and organizations. We have examined the histories of several dozen such people in light of these issues, from both business and religious organizations, in the context of our model. The results evince strong parallels between commitment in commercial and ecclesiastic settings, thereby offering the comfort of qualitative corroboration.

PROBLEMS OF CROSS-ORGANIZATIONAL
METHODOLOGY: MOVING FROM THE
PURE FORM TO MIXED

When one attempts to understand the dynamics of selected organizational characteristics (such as commitment and creativity) by first studying "pure form" groups, what problems emerge in generalizing to each other type of organizations? More specifically, to what extent can (or should) insight concerning organizational commitment derived from studying ideological organizations be applied to business settings?

Some, positively disposed toward ideological activities, might argue that business entities should not presume to ask for the same level of commitment as such groups. God and mammon should keep their rightful places in the hierarchies of the heart. In contrast, others, also having a positive regard toward religion, could cite examples of highly successful commercial enterprises valuing and expecting employee loyalty much in the same manner as a total organization.

Those with more negative feelings about religion, could contend that what they view as manipulative devices pervading religion have absolutely no place in business. They might argue that for employers to condition employees to the organization or to "drug them with the opiates of future promise and hope" mocks the purpose of economic entities.

Our approach avoids such polarization. We simply propose that the dynamics of organizational characteristics such as commitment or creativity are best studied and understood by examining groups having the pure form of that characteristic. We do not argue that other organizational types should employ the techniques, devices, or principles for building or breaking a given characteristic found in the pure form groups. We do not argue they should not. Societal and personal values beyond the scope of our purposes must make these determinations.

DIRECTIONS FOR RESEARCH IN CROSS-ORGANIZATIONAL STUDIES

Studying other organizational characteristics by first exploring the "pure form" organizations for those characteristics has considerable potential value: as in the collegial relationships of professional partnerships such as law and accounting firms, the social relationships of fraternal organizations such as brotherhoods and country clubs, or the bureaucratic process, such as governmental agencies. We would, of course, be particularly interested in studying the pure form of creative relationships, such as entertainment companies, universities, and research institutes.

In such efforts, we believe it vital for some researchers to have worked within such organizations, to have "felt the flow" of thoughts and moods, acts and actions. When understanding organizations, the heart as well as the head must be involved.

NOTES

1. Much of the original ideas, concepts, and models presented in this chapter are derived from *The Firm Bond.* (Kuhn and Geis 1984).
2. The concept of a "special lens" with which to view selectively certain phenomena is derived from Graham Allison's (1971) "conceptual lens," which is his way of describing different frames of reference or models used to explain processes of complex decision making. He writes that "by comparing and contrasting the three frameworks [which he uses to analyze the Cuban Missile Crisis], we see what each magnifies, highlights, and reveals as well as what each blurs or neglects."
3. Erving Goffman (1961) used the term "total organizations" to characterize institutions that place a barrier to social intercourse with the outside world. Our use of the term *total* involves organizations that deal with ultimate or ideal purposes in addition to constructing such barriers.
4. This section is derived from Kuhn and Geis (1984).

REFERENCES

Allison, Graham T. 1971. *Essence of Decision: Explaining the Cuban Missile Crisis.* Boston: Little Brown.

Goffman, Erving. 1961. *Asylums.* Garden City. N.Y.: Anchor/Doubleday.

Kuhn, Robert Lawrence, and George T. Geis. 1984. *The Firm Bond: Linking Meaning and Mission in Business and Religion.* New York: Praeger.

_____ . 1986. "Creative and Commitment: Modeling Meaning and Mission for Individuals and Institutions." In R. Kuhn (Ed.), *Frontiers in Creative and Innovative Management.* Cambridge, Mass.: Ballinger.

_____ . 1988. "Building and Breaking Creativity: What Religion Teaches Business about Commitment." In R. Kuhn (Ed.), *Handbook for Creative and Innovative Managers.* New York: McGraw-Hill.

Discussion

Moderator: Elizabeth E. Bailey

Bailey: Do you get around the phenomenon that I call the "Mrs. Thomas Edison phenomenon"? One night, Thomas woke up and said, "I am so excited. I just had this great idea for a light bulb." He explained how it works to her. Then she turned over to go back to sleep. He said, "How can you turn over and go back to sleep with this wonderful idea?". She said, "To have it work, you would have to wire the world and that is just ridiculous." How do you get around the negative put-down of new ideas when they are suggested?

Miller: One answer is at the microlevel, when ideas are generated. The agreed mode for the group must be to strengthen and build the idea. If that is the agreed mode, it is easier. Problems arise when that is not the agreed mode between the person who is generating the idea and the person who has to live with the consequences.

Gamache: Where we come from, we totally disagree with "The Power of an Idea" (the yellow pencil punched through a brick wall). We say that an idea is an extremely fragile thing. We use words like "giving birth to an idea" or call an idea "somebody's baby" and imply that for an idea ever to come to fruition, it needs much support. Our point is that it is frighteningly easy to kill any idea. We can convince a group of executives that if they don't play the game right, they will kill everything fresh and never get anywhere new. We tell them they have an intrinsic knee-jerk to find the negative, to find the problem, to be judgmental. The medicine that we give them, which is sort of a psychological device, is a baseball cap. Really! On the front it says, "What's good about it?". Anyone who knee-jerks and goes after any negative on the idea gets the privilege of wearing the cap. It sounds hokey, but it reinforces the need to be positive and build on the idea in a playful, positive way. Shortly after the hat is passed two or three times, participants get the idea that to play the game right, they must build on the ideas before going into evaluation. Unless they separate the two phases, they know they are not going to get their money back for their time, effort, and energy. It is the mode in which our creativity-enhancing events are run.

Miller: I find that many managers don't object to the idea as much as the style in which the creativity is happening. Even people who want to improve can feel uncomfortable with visionary (analogy) types of processes. Maps help people feel comfortable with the further reaching. If I do a product attribute by industry application matrix, I can say, "We are over here in cell 3." With that, I can say, "Let's take a guided fantasy to the bottom of the ocean and find a porcupine fish." They at least know where we are. Maps help settle some of that judgmental mind.

Comment: When an organization gets skillful at this process, they can in fact welcome negative concerns. I don't think the issue is one of not having the concerns. People say that ideas are being killed too quickly. When you get skilled at treating ideas not as obstacles to resist but as problems to be solved, then you welcome those concerns.

I am working with a vice-president of an innovation management corporation. In mentoring to the people who work for him, he feels that the single most important thing is to teach them to draw out the concerns regarding their ideas. If you can solve it, great. If you can't, you had better know now rather than later.

Geis: I think the methodologies that respect the privacy of individuals to work on their ideas until they are ready to share with the group are vital. Consider Xerox's advanced work at Palo Alto. This is a computer-based technology where people sit around in a group and work on their ideas—and *at their choice* can send something up to a common screen that is a common work area. Someone else can download it and play with it. I think the whole idea of freedom of privacy, and of technologies that promote it, is very important. It allows one to share an idea only at an appropriate time and only with whom one wishes to share it.

Cooper: I would like to get back to the point that Bob Kuhn was raising. I was struck by the fact that all three of these commercial organizations that are concerned with creativity and innovation use a minimum of research results. I happen to think that relevance as well as truth is a critical scientific criterion. It shows up in the scientific literature. It uses phrases like "not interesting," "trivial," or other insulting terms. You may have complex theorems, but if they're not interesting they're not interesting. What they really mean is *relevant.* It seems to me that we need something more than just studying. This is part of what I was fussing earlier. I mentioned that Paul Lawrence, who is an extremely acute observer, could go through the whole problem of designing a National Institutes of

Health and not notice that one of their outputs should have been creativity and innovation. It is easy to us to see what it is we are looking for and overlook other things that we are not looking for.

I can illustrate this. Somebody introduced me to Archimedes. We are all familiar with the story of how he had to determine the amount of gold in the king's crown. He got in to the bathtub and suddenly saw the principle of specific gravity. He jumped out and ran naked down the street shouting "Eureka!". That is the scientist's version of the story. The advertising agent version of the story is that Archimedes solved the problem of how to advertise a nudist colony without getting arrested.

Comment: Is the objective of creativity and innovative research to come up with a test of some type as we do in psychology with personalities to determine whether an individual is creative?

Harriman: Ours is not. Basically when we work with an organization, they have a goal or business objective that they want to achieve. They are not, at that stage, particularly interested in categorizing who is more or less creative. Our approach is working with them to help increase the odds of getting an innovative solution to the problem, and not the augmentation of creativity per se.

Kuhn: There is much in the literature about tests for creativity, but I haven't seen much relevance in them for business applications. The work that George Geis and I have done has not focused on trying to determine who is creative. I think people are moving away from that. We are trying to define aspects of individuals and, more importantly, aspects of situations to enhance creativity. What can be done in an advertising agency or an R&D laboratory to enhance creativity? That is the question we want to answer, rather than to come up with some IQ test to determine who is the most creative character. Creativity can be stimulated more easily than identified a priori.

Question: Robert Kuhn and George Geis, were you making a correlation between commitment and creativity? In other words, are you saying that the more committed the individuals in an organization, the higher the creativity of the organization?

Geis: I wouldn't make that direct of a connection. I would say that if someone is going to produce a creative act for an organization, the probability is increased to the degree to which that person is committed to the organization. Otherwise what may happen is that the person may take the idea and go someplace else or do it privately on the side. We were arguing that if a creative act is intended to further organizational goals, one of the dimensions to look at is the commitment level of the individuals to the organization or to a subunit within the organization. Often we found that people had relatively low levels of commitment to the organization. Commitment profiles differ substantively among units within an organization and among persons or departments. Yes, we are arguing that, with other things being equal, the extent to which someone is committed to the group will increase the probability that he or she will be creative on behalf of that organization or unit, assuming that there are creative things to be done.

Kuhn: We used the concept of commitment to differentiate between personal creativity and managerial creativity. Early on in our thinking about creativity, we came into conflict between individual creativity and organizational creativity. We are using the concept of commitment to differentiate the two. As well as being a substantive scalpel, it is also an analytical razor.

Question: I wasn't clear on the concept of commitment. How do you handle the literature that says that commitment can be dysfunctional—that people are so committed to a process or an idea within the organization that they are not open to new ideas or new innovations?

Kuhn: We should differentiate between the two connotations of commitment. Your "commitment" is to the thing that needs to be changed; our "commitment" is the psychic identification between individual and organization. We are saying there should be a commitment to organizational goals. We are not saying that there should be a commitment to specific aspects or means or projects. We use the term in a more limited sense, to reflect a personal identification with the overall goals of the whole unit, be it the entire organization or the subunits of it. We are not making any comment about anything else. We are just talking about that internally sensed relationship between the individual and the organization.

Comment: An internal IBM study said that in most of their major successful product introductions, there was a product champion, someone who was extraordinarily committed to the idea. Then comes the distinction between the creativity, meaning the initial spark, and what it takes to make the group produce something new. Commitment may not be the same thing as the creativity, but it may be an essential part of the creative process.

Comment: The commitment may not be to the organization, but to the idea. The two are indeed different. In the kind of organizations that I think Robert Kuhn and George Geis are talking about, there is commitment to an organizational goal, but that may inhibit any willingness to try something new or veer off in a new direction. In the innovations that I have seen develop, there is an intense commitment to an idea and sometimes the idea is very much against the organizational goals.

Comment: Regarding the measurement of creativity in groups, when members work and communicate together, you can decide that certain people seem to come up with these original ideas. You try to build a team of people who have the different requirements. Many people within our company told me that they would rather implement. They don't necessarily want to be the ones who come up with the ideas. If there is any way to measure such aptitudes, it could be useful. If there isn't, then you try to get enough confidence among a group of people to work together and to learn jointly who can play what role on the team.

We must find the people who are willing to be innovators, people who have enough self-confidence to evaluate the new idea and to take the chance on it. Ninety to ninety-five percent of people want to follow. It is important to find out whom they want to follow— whom do they have enough confidence in to follow. Then you can sell your idea to the people that most want to follow. Another problem is identifying roughly 50 percent of the people who act like innovators but don't really want to be innovators and won't proceed on their own until they can follow somebody. There is this difference in creativity. We have not worried about trying to measure it. We have just tried to find out what the people really are and classify them without systematically explaining why they are where they are.

Cooper: I am struck by the fact that in talking about organizations that we haven't heard from Colonel Fox. He spent a great deal of his time describing how people behave differently in different organizations. The same person is usually a member of several different organizations and may behave quite differently in each. I have seen in academic life people who are mildly affiliated with the organization do highly creative and innovative work because they are really part of a profession that is evaluating them. Again, I think it illustrates my point that we tend to see what we want to see. We need some way to make sure that the things that we are not looking at are looked at.

Comment: Some people do identify more with their profession than with their company. That might be the actual strength of Silicon Valley. The fact that people do move around can help cross fertilize ideas—which is necessary to build a technology-driven industry. On the other hand, such rapid movement of talent can destroy a different type of industry because loyalty and commitment to companies is never built. It is a two-edged sword, but it is an important distinction to make: where loyalties are, and how they affect creative management, impacts all organizations.

Comment: I think there is a champion in almost every organization, a person who is committed to an idea. The environment that lets an idea flourish to become a reality is what we are trying to make happen. There is not only the commitment but the pride in the organization.

Comment: Rewriting history is a subtle part of creative and innovative management. I believe that when a new product makes it through a complex organization, history is constantly being rewritten. The original idea may start with an individual, but if that person does it skillfully (in a nonmanipulative way), before long enough people are involved in the process that a small group is formed that feels like they own that idea. The reason is right. Creativity in organizations is not just the idea; it is the process as well. Somebody might have the initial spark, but somebody else might have the creativity to overcome a problem or concern with the idea. A third person may have the creativity that allows moving the idea forward. As that circle expands, it is important both for the initiator and the subsequent participants to be willing and able for the ownership of an idea to extend further out into the organization and not feel that they have to stand up and be the sole owner. Successful ideas are rarely connected to solitary individuals. They are not connected with small groups. New ideas that work are ideas in which the organization takes a great deal of pride. Building such organizational ownership is an important skill.

Gamache: Giving a little bit of our company history, back in the beginning when we were in love with ideas, we felt that if you gave the right idea to a company that it would just automatically work. We then started to concern ourself with the *champion.* We found that if a champion were married to the idea, then it had a better chance of happening. Beyond that, we focused on the concept of the *sponsor,* the individual at a high enough level of authority to protect the champion from management. Management has a tendency to keep pulling up the young plant to see if it is still growing. So the sponsor is needed to protect the company from the champion who is so fixated on his idea that he may do things that are not in the best interest of the company. It comes back again to the personal involvement of the real problem owners, which would be to top management, not only to identify champions, but also to serve in the role of sponsors. We have found that the champion-sponsor team is what makes creative ideas happen.

Chorover: It seems to me that much of this discussion is about what motivates creativity and innovation. Social psychologists talk often about attributions. I think it is rather important for analytical purposes to think about how we use terms like *leadership* and *innovation* and *creativity*. Do we think of these as attributes of persons or as context-dependent functions in an organizational context? I am not sure. Let me express a preference to thinking that innovation and creativity are processes rather than attributes of persons. That may be wrong, but it opens the possibility for ideas and processes to arise from unexpected places. I think we have all had the experience in organizations that so often people who are expected to lead don't do a very good job and get in the way of the leadership process within the organization. One of the tests of creative and innovative management is to make sure that the structure encourages the possibilities for innovation and creativity to arise from unexpected quarters. If you use labels like "the explorer" or "the innovator" or "the manager," then all heads turn in that direction. When there is a need for management, people look to the manager because that is the manager's job. In my experience, I think of these as functions rather than attributes and feel that characterization of them is more conducive to the goals of innovation and creativity.

Comment: From a research perspective, if I listen to what Robert Kuhn was saying, it is possible that there might be some value in the extreme form of extremely creative people. From a practitioner's point of view, my experience is that personality attributes is the wrong question to be focusing on. It should be the operating assumption that creativity is something that a wide range of people can exhibit. Trying to measure who is, who isn't, or how much, is basically the wrong question.

Kuhn: I couldn't agree more. I think the *Business Week* article "Are You Creative?" addresses fundamentally the wrong question. It is even somewhat demeaning. The question should be "How can you become more creative?" "Are you creative?" throws up a block. The question has power.

Lewin: Herb Simons likes the quote "Chance favors the prepared mind." That really says something about the importance of random events in this innovation process and the fact that we have not thought about whether we are getting structures and arrangements that in fact will give us more out of what was earlier called the "garbage can" view of innovation. There is a lot of innovation going on. Some people are more creative at one time than another time. These things are floating around in organization memory—especially what processes, what structures, what mechanisms can increase the likelihood that the prepared mind will respond when chance occurs.

SYNTHESIS

Robert Lawrence Kuhn

A synthesis is not a summary. If you want a summary, read the Overview. If you want a personal sense of things, read on.

What follows are feelings. I have little rationale for these impressions other than that they reflect my personal passions about a vital field and my perspectives for encouraging its continued development. Considering the already weighty tomb, I will be terse. Less, as they say, is more.

Four concepts focus my thoughts. They are the new directions for research in creative and innovative management: 1) conditions of creativity and innovation, 2) continuum of methodologies, 3) elements and techniques, 4) transcendent visions. I will reflect briefly on each direction.

CONDITIONS OF CREATIVITY
AND INNOVATION

The environment is an active participant in the process; stimulating or inhibiting the generation of novelty is determined by the setting and surroundings in which it occurs. You can't force people to be creative or force feed creative ideas into people. You must encourage people to want to be creative, especially if they are the owners of the problem.

Look to new environments of high creativity and innovation in order to understand the process of creativity and innovation—information systems, personal computers, electronic mail. We should consider the reverse as well. It is often possible to study the causation of

331

a thing by examining the conditions and consequences of its absence. What, therefore, can we learn about environments in which creativity and innovation are absent? What causes the void?

Macroscopically, we should consider inflection points—crises, critical incidents, special events wielding major impact, pathbreaking spikes of action, and the pure form of organizational activities. Reflect on the nature of change, how change agents play vital roles. Accountability is also important; it is a powerful control mechanism to distinguish between productive corporate creativity and destructive organizational anarchy.

How to assess creativity? Can we take its measure both before and after the fact? More fundamentally, what are some of the measures that determine whether or not (or to what degree) creativity has occurred? Finally, when dealing with conditions of creativity and innovation, we must continuously ask ourselves if we are even asking the right questions. For example, in working with an organization that wants to conduct a creativity audit, one must ask if creativity is important for that organization. If it is not, why waste the time, money, and effort? Worse still, the impossibility of organizational success will surely be detrimental—frustration, loss of esteem, and discouragement do not a good company make. We always need to be sure that we are asking the right questions.

CONTINUUM OF METHODOLOGIES

Let's construct a spectrum here, from theory to practice. We can start at one end with pure theory, move into controlled laboratory experiments, then to simulations, to tests, to field experiments, to field studies, to case research, to preparing teaching cases, to organizational audits, to assessment programs, to active interventions, to internal use. We can observe a linear progression from one end to the other. No step is sufficient, yet all are necessary.

What about the mechanisms of the methodologies? Real time, large databases, longitudinal studies, and matched-pair analyses are all vital for many of the steps. In a sense, we are building a matrix of metabolies, with the categories of styles on one axis (from pure theory to internal use) arrayed against the kinds of approaches on the other (from real time to matched pairs). We might even think of three-dimensional matrixes that would add the forms of analytical thinking as the third axis (induction, deduction, systematic versus nonsystematic, cross-cultural, and cross-organizational).

I think it is important for some researchers to concentrate all of their efforts in one of the category styles and for other researchers to scoot along the entire spectrum sampling progress regularly at each node. In fact, it is probably valuable for every researcher to experience occasionally each of the other categories, approaches, and forms to expand horizons and view the world wider. This is not an easy prescription, given all of our commitments and responsibilities. Yet I contend that such broadening of perspective is more necessity than luxury, more central than peripheral, especially when the goal is to understand the fogged complexity of organizational creativity and innovation. Considering the diverse methodologies as spectrums or matrixes may help order the wildness and tame the wilderness.

It is a manifestation of this complexity that state-of-the-art research is becoming progressively harder for single individuals to conduct on their own. This is like the situation in particle physics. At the beginning of the century it was possible for a solitary person to advance the field all alone and with perhaps little formal education. Today, if you look at the journals, you often find several *dozen* scientists on one particular project, and they all have advanced degrees and years of postgraduate study. The problems are changing and the field is transforming. So it is with organizational studies.

People are vital. Some would ask the intriguing question of whether people are in fact our problem. These iconoclasts would proffer that perhaps our current methods are sufficient but that our people are deficient.

A similar conundrum we face is the danger of perennial optimism. Perhaps some issues are forever without solution. How would we discern the difference between soluble and insoluble problems in creative and innovative management? Which topics are fit for study and which are not (not now or ever)? Such a differentiation can become one of our most important contributions to research. For the sake of developing fundamental theory, not to mention research efficiency, nothing could be more vital. A corollary issue would seek to define those aspects of creative and innovative management that can be managed, as opposed to those that cannot or should not be so controlled. To attempt to manage inappropriate areas would be counterproductive.

ELEMENTS AND TECHNIQUES

Here we need to consider the stage, styles, theories, practices, and performances—the different kinds of thinking, divergent and convergent, intuitive and analytical. We focus on the importance of knowledge bases, the trade-offs in organizational design, the impact of contingency theory. One recurring theme is the greater relevance of "design" over analysis in sculpting organizations to achieve specified objectives.

Jean-Jacques Servan-Schreiber writes of the power of one simple and clear idea. Accounting, not normally considered a proper substrate for creativity and innovation, was a prime focus. Advances in accounting can stimulate the movement of the entire organization in new directions.

Yuji Ijiri's remarkable incisive concept of impulse and momentum accounting can change the motivational direction of executives, encouraging top managers to become more original and more dynamic—and getting the credit for their successes. Here is one major new development that cries to be implemented by forward-looking organizations. Perhaps companies that are devoid of needed creativity should consider breaking their current mold by implementing Ijiri's innovation.

We also consider breaking traditional standards. Using asynchronous time periods is one example. Who says new product development must adhere to the quarterly reporting cycle? Some other techniques included playfulness, risk containment, quick feedback, freedom from routine, the critical mass necessary in new technologies, and the need for upward communication.

TRANSCENDENT VISIONS

Here we look beyond, if not above. Seeking ultimate issues is especially relevant for creative and innovative management.

Leadership is a vital part of the process, making sense out of complexity and giving direction amidst multiple issues and conflict-objectives.

Survival surfaced as a dominant theme. Survival wore three guises: economic survival in a hypercompetitive environment, with national boundaries providing little security; social survival in a world of inequalities, both intracountry and international; and political survival in a world growing more fragmented, more fierce, and more armed.

Spirituality was a surprise. That spiritual awareness emerged in a conference on management was not expected. Perhaps it should have been. Creativity and innovation, if one thinks about the topic, leads directly to the purpose of human life. What are organizations and their members trying to achieve? What is the ultimate nature of organizations, economic and other? What is human fulfillment? What is human potential? What are human beings? Why are we here?

We traveled from supergalactic clusters to subatomic quarks. We considered personal passion, organizational commitment, world peace, ecological care, and improving the standards of living for all humankind. These all are the domain of creative and innovative management.

NAME INDEX

335

Kirste, K. K., 91
Kirton, M. J., 148, 159, 293
Klein, M. H., 96
Koch, S., 215, 216
Koestler, Arthur, 75
Kohler, Eric, 123
Koontz, Harold, 132
Kozmetsky, George, 1, 3, 15-28, 63,
    118-119, 251
Krasner, L., 215
Krepelka, E. J., 150
Kuhn, Robert Lawrence, 1-7, 20, 62,
    132, 145, 171, 210, 212, 243,
    279-286, 303-321, 306, 310, 311,
    321 n. 1, 321 n. 4, 325, 326, 329,
    331-334

Larntz, K., 91
Lasswitz, K., 214
Laughhunn, Dan J., 137
Lawler, Edward, 287
Lawrence, Paul, 240
Leary, D. E., 215, 216
Lewin, Arie Y., 5, 129-130, 131-142,
    132, 133, 134, 136, 137, 139, 140,
    141, 240-241, 244, 245, 288,
    329-330
Liess, W., 213
Lin, H. T., 149, 150
Lipinski, R. M., 91
Lovelock, J. E., 206
Lubin, S., 92

MacCrimmon, Kenneth R., 138
MacKinnon, D. W., 151, 162
MacLean, P. D., 233
Macy, J. R., 226, 227
Maidique, Modesto A., 136
Mansfield, R. S., 150
March, James G., 89, 131, 137, 138,
    197
Margulis, L., 206
Mark, V. H., 216, 217
Marquis, D. G., 136
Maslow, A., 148
McGuire, Timothy W., 63, 97
McNamara, Robert, 46-47
Meehl, P. E., 101
Mendés-France, Pièrre, 38-44
Merchant, C., 212, 213
Miller, William C., 7, 63, 141,
    287-301, 289, 323, 324

Minton, John W., 132, 133, 134, 136,
    137, 139, 140, 141
Mintzberg, H., 193
Miranti, Paul J., 113 n. 1
Mitchell, Edgar D., 207-208, 227
Mitterand, François, 37, 44, 56
Mohr, L. B., 188
Monge, P. R., 91
Monnet, Jean, 32-36, 37-38, 54, 56
Morgenthaler, D., 119, 120
Morrison, Philip, 235 n. 1
Morrison, Phyliss, 235 n. 1
Myers, 162
Myers, N., 211

Nelson, Richard R., 131
Neville, R., 211
Newcomb, T. R., 91
Newell, Allen, 66
Nisbet, R. A., 187, 188
Noller, R. B., 150, 151, 158
Norman, R. Z., 91
Nystrom, P. C., 140

O'Donnell, Cyril, 132
Oppenheim, Paul, 68
Oppenheimer, J. R., 222
O'Quinn, K., 151
Osborn, A. F., 151, 267

Parnes, S. J., 145, 150, 151, 155, 158
Pavlov, I. P., 223
Payne, John W., 137
Peele, S., 215
Perrow, C., 133
Peters, Thomas, 287, 290
Pettigrew, A., 187, 189
Poincaré, H., 84
Poole, M. S., 187, 191, 192, 193, 195,
    196, 198
Presbury, J., 150

Quinn, James Brian, 287

Raina, M. K., 145
Reason, P., 229
Reese, H. W., 150
Rittle, R. H., 92
Robey, D., 85
Romanelli, E., 196
Rose, L. H., 149, 150
Rothenberg, A., 145

SUBJECT INDEX

ABOUT THE EDITORS

Yuji Ijiri is the Robert M. Trueblood Professor of Accounting and Economics at the Graduate School of Industrial Administration, Carnegie-Mellon University, where he has taught since 1967. Previously he taught at the Stanford Graduate School of Business. He has been a consultant to a number of business and nonprofit organizations. A member of the American Accounting Association since 1963, he has engaged in numerous research and educational activities of the association and was elected as its president for 1982–83. He earned a bachelor's degree and a CPA certificate in Japan, a master's degree from the University of Minnesota, and a Ph.D. from Carnegie-Mellon University. Dr. Ijiri has published over one hundred articles as well as many books and monographs.

Robert Lawrence Kuhn is the Senior Fellow in Creative and Innovative Management at the IC^2 Institute, The University of Texas at Austin, and adjunct professor of management in the Graduate School of Business Administration, New York University. He is an investment banker, corporate strategist, and scholar specializing in mergers and acquisitions, leveraged buyouts, new business formation, venture capital, and innovative financial transactions. He holds an A.B. in human biology from Johns Hopkins, an M.S. (Sloan Fellow) in management from MIT, and a Ph.D. in neurophysiology from UCLA. Dr. Kuhn has written and edited more than twenty books. He is editor in chief of the *Handbook for Creative and Innovative Management* and the *Handbook of Investment Banking*.

ABOUT THE CONTRIBUTORS

Teresa M. Amabile is associate professor of psychology, Brandeis University, Waltham, Massachusetts, and research associate, Center for Creative Leadership, Greensboro, North Carolina.

Elizabeth E. Bailey is dean, Graduate School of Industrial Administration, Carnegie-Mellon University, Pittsburgh, Pennsylvania.

Robert M. Burnside is an associate in the Center for Creative Leadership, Greensboro, North Carolina.

Stephan L. Chorover is professor of psychology in the Brain and Cognitive Sciences Department, Massachusetts Institute of Technology, Cambridge, Massachusetts.

William W. Cooper is acting chairman, Department of Management Science and Information Systems, College and Graduate School of Business, and Nadya Kozmetsky Scott Centennial Fellow, IC^2 Institute, The University of Texas at Austin, Texas.

Richard M. Cyert is president of Carnegie-Mellon University, Pittsburgh, Pennsylvania.

R. Donald Gamache is chairman and chief executive officer, Innotech Corporation, a creativity facilitating company in Trumbull, Connecticut.

353

George Thomas Geis is adjunct associate professor of management science, Anderson Graduate School of Management and Research Coordinator, Center for Human Resource Management, University of California at Los Angeles, California.

Stanley S. Gryskiewicz is director, Creative Development Program, Center for Creative Leadership, Greensboro, North Carolina.

Richard A. Harriman is president of Synectics, Inc., a creativity facilitating company in Cambridge, Massachusetts.

Scott G. Isaksen is director, Center for Studies in Creativity, State University College at Buffalo, New York.

Robert S. Kaplan is the Arthur Lowes Dickinson Professor of Accounting, Graduate School of Business Administration, Harvard University, Cambridge, Massachusetts, and professor of industrial administration, Graduate School of Industrial Administration, Carnegie-Mellon University, Pittsburgh, Pennsylvania.

Sara Kiesler is a professor in the Social and Decision Sciences Department, Graduate School of Industrial Administration, Carnegie-Mellon University, Pittsburgh, Pennsylvania.

George Kozmetsky is executive associate for economic affairs, The University of Texas System, director of the IC^2 Institute, and the J. Marion West Chair Professor at The University of Texas at Austin, Texas.

Arie Y. Lewin is program director of the Decision, Risk and Management Science Program, National Science Foundation, and professor of business administration, Fuqua School of Business, Duke University, Durham, North Carolina.

William C. Miller is principal consultant with S.A.I. Associates, Inc. in Mill Valley, California. He was senior management consultant for managing innovation and change, SRI International.

Jean-Jacques Servan-Schreiber is chairman of the International Committee of Carnegie-Mellon University, Pittsburgh, Pennsylvania. He was a cabinet minister and high official in the French government for many years.

Andrew H. Van de Ven is 3M Professor, Human Systems Management and Director, Strategic Management Research Center, University of Minnesota, Minneapolis, Minnesota.

Karl Weick holds the Harkins and Company Centennial Chair in Management, The University of Texas at Austin, Texas.